PRAISE FOR

GHETTO

A *New York Times Book Review* Editors' Choice

One of the Best Nonfiction Books of 2016 and a Staff Pick,
Publishers Weekly

"[*Ghetto* is] a history of the concept which also serves as an argument
for its continued usefulness. Duneier is a sociologist . . . sensitive to the
sting of 'ghetto' as an insult. But for him that sting shows us just how
much inequality we still tolerate, even as attitudes have changed . . .
Duneier's book makes it easy to see how, through all these changes,
black ghettos in America have remained the central point of reference
for anyone who wants to understand poverty and segregation."
—Kelefa Sanneh, *The New Yorker*

"Mitchell Duneier's powerful book deserves a place in the same lineage
of modern writing that speaks for the cause of human freedom."
—Murray Baumgarten, *Jewish Quarterly*

"A searing and searching examination of the political and cultural history at the root of this powerfully evocative and inflammatory term."
—David M. Shribman, *The Boston Globe*

"As [Duneier's] fine book demonstrates, the meaning of 'ghetto' has
changed over time, responding to political circumstances . . . His rich

intellectual history of the ghetto raises important questions about how we might address the plight of its residents."
—Aram Goudsouzian, *The Washington Post*

"Well-researched, well-written, deeply insightful, and equally illuminating . . . [*Ghetto*] should appeal to anyone interested in the African American urban experience . . . Highly recommended."
—J. F. Bauman, *Choice* (Editors' Pick)

"*Ghetto* is a thoughtful, engaging, and very important book that deftly employs history and sociology . . . Brilliantly argued and examined, it will become a classic in the field and easily withstand the test of time."
—William Helmreich, *Metropolitics*

"Duneier takes readers on a journey full of surprising insights."
—Heath W. Carter, *The Christian Century*

"An arresting, listen-up synthesis of ghetto-living theory and practice over its five-hundred-year history; particular emphasis is paid to the last century, when ghettos shape-shifted with alarming speed. You emerge with an oh-so-better understanding of the forces that fashioned the ghetto."
—Peter Lewis, *The Christian Science Monitor*

"Marvelously rich . . . Duneier's detailed story of ideas, cities, policies and individual scholars offers a politically and historically thick alternative to the type of pseudo-objective, politically blind social science popular with . . . American policy-making elites."
—Raphael Magarik, *Haaretz*

"Provides fascinating insight into the history and the similarities and differences of the now-extinct European-Jewish ghetto and the very much alive African-American ghetto in the United States."
—Ben Fisher, *The Jerusalem Post*

"As we confront our own frustrations with the persistence of racial tension, Duneier's *Ghetto* demands that we review our assumptions and understand how the exercise of our enlightened self-interest contributes to the discrimination we decry. It is essential reading."
—Dennis D. McDaniel, *National Catholic Reporter*

"One of America's preeminent ethnographers, renowned for his exquisite close-focus portraits of the deprived in our cities, now zooms out to wide-angle intellectual history. Tracing the concept of 'the ghetto' from its tangled roots in early modern Italy to its genocidal implementation by the Nazis in Warsaw and its contemporary embodiment in poverty-stricken, subjugated American center cities, Mitchell Duneier offers subtle, unexpected insights into the contours and consequences of race-based residential segregation."

—Robert D. Putnam, author of *Bowling Alone*
and *Our Kids*

"Mitchell Duneier's book on the ghetto explores both the place and the thinking it has inspired. He tells the story of a reality that will not go away. His writing is never superficial, always clear, and sometimes deeply moving. To understand the American city, you need to read this book."   —Richard Sennett, author of *The Craftsman* and
The Fall of Public Man

"Mitchell Duneier's book should be read by anyone who wants to understand the history of the ghetto and how our thinking about race has developed. For many, it will be the equivalent of Robert Heilbroner's *The Worldly Philosophers*, which introduced readers to the history of economic thought—it displays a similar gift for narrative, appraisal, and analysis. In light of recent events in Ferguson, Baltimore, and elsewhere, and the emergence of the Black Lives Matter movement, this book could not be more timely."

—Paul Starr, author of *The Social Transformation
of American Medicine*

"A magisterial recovery of a repudiated concept that brings much-needed historical awareness to the idea and the reality."

—Barbara Kirshenblatt-Gimblett, Chief Curator,
Core Exhibition, POLIN Museum of the
History of Polish Jews, Warsaw

"A wholly new perspective on the ghetto."

—Kenneth Stow, author of *Theater of
Acculturation: The Roman Ghetto in the
Sixteenth Century*

"A major work of original historical research and contextualization that is destined to become a classic."
—Benjamin C. I. Ravid, Jennie and Mayer Weisman Professor Emeritus of Jewish History, Brandeis University

"A careful and wide-ranging intellectual history of the ghetto. We need this book." —Jonathan Holloway, Dean of Yale College

"Taking as its point of departure the character of Europe's Jewish ghettos over the course of centuries, not discounting but contextualizing the Nazis' murderous rejuvenation of the practice, *Ghetto* provides a nuanced and continually illuminating analysis of an idea that long dominated studies of postwar urban African American life. Mitchell Duneier's book is indispensable for understanding the American ghetto as a social and economic reality, an arena of vital culture, and a subject of intellectual inquiry."
—Eric J. Sundquist, author of *Strangers in the Land: Blacks, Jews, Post-Holocaust America*

"In Poland in 1949, W.E.B. Du Bois recognized the 'Negro problem' in the former Warsaw ghetto, drawing a parallel Mitchell Duneier explores with discernment. Focused on particular thinkers in particular times, *Ghetto* reveals how social science actually operates. The result: a brilliant combination of breadth and sharpness, of thought-provoking questions and clear-sighted answers, of Jews and blacks in cities across the Western world."
—Nell Irvin Painter, author of *The History of White People*

"In this ingenious and riveting book, Mitchell Duneier reveals that social scientists were as important as structural racism, urban policy, and economic forces in creating what we've come to know as the modern ghetto. The story of the ghetto's invention is chock-full of misinterpretations, intrigues, and analytical breakthroughs. Revisiting the often elusive relationships between the medieval Jewish ghetto, the Nazi-created ghetto, and the open-air prisons we call the black ghetto, Duneier turns prevailing wisdom on its head, warning us that what we think of as 'ghetto fabulous' may, in fact, be fabulations."
—Robin D. G. Kelley, author of *Freedom Dreams: The Black Radical Imagination*

MITCHELL DUNEIER

GHETTO

Mitchell Duneier is the Maurice P. During Professor and Chair of the Department of Sociology at Princeton University. He is the author of the award-winning urban ethnographies *Slim's Table* and *Sidewalk*.

ALSO BY MITCHELL DUNEIER

Sidewalk

Slim's Table

GHETTO

GHETTO

THE INVENTION OF A PLACE,
THE HISTORY OF AN IDEA

MITCHELL DUNEIER

FARRAR, STRAUS AND GIROUX
NEW YORK

Farrar, Straus and Giroux
18 West 18th Street, New York 10011

The Library of Congress has cataloged the hardcover edition as follows:
Names: Duneier, Mitchell, author.
Title: Ghetto : the invention of a place, the history of an idea / Mitchell Duneier.
Description: First edition. | New York : Farrar, Straus and Giroux, [2015] |
    Includes bibliographical references and index.
Identifiers: LCCN 2015036373 | ISBN 9780374161804 (hardcover) |
    ISBN 9781429942751 (e-book)
Subjects: LCSH: Jewish ghettos—History. | Inner cities—United States—
    History. | Segregation—History.
Classification: LCC HT221 .D86 2015 | DDC 307.3/366—dc23
LC record available at http://lccn.loc.gov/2015036373

Paperback ISBN: 978-0-374-53677-0

Designed by Jonathan D. Lippincott

Our books may be purchased in bulk for promotional, educational,
or business use. Please contact your local bookseller or the Macmillan Corporate
and Premium Sales Department at 1-800-221-7945, extension 5442,
or by e-mail at MacmillanSpecialMarkets@macmillan.com.

www.fsgbooks.com
www.twitter.com/fsgbooks • www.facebook.com/fsgbooks

1   3   5   7   9   10   8   6   4   2

For Howard S. Becker and Ovie Carter,
and to the memory of A. Leon Higginbotham and Edward Shils

CONTENTS

PREFACE

Today, many people understandably dislike the word "ghetto" for its associations with stigmatizing and harmful stereotypes—especially of African Americans. In *Ghettonation: A Journey into the Land of the Bling and the Home of the Shameless,* Cora Daniels writes that "ghetto" today refers to "gold teeth, . . . Pepsi-filled baby bottles, and baby mamas."[1] One New York City councilwoman went so far as to try to ban its "negative usage" in New York City's official government documents.[2] Even a figure as prominent as Mario Luis Small, the first black dean of the Division of Social Sciences at the University of Chicago—the very university where the ghetto was established as a social scientific idea almost a century ago—has written a nuanced essay explaining his reasons for abandoning the idea.[3]

In this book, I hope to show that the ghetto remains a useful concept—provided we recall its rich historical background and stop divorcing it from its past. The word derives from the name of a Venetian island that once housed a copper foundry, or *geto.*[4] Five hundred years ago, in 1516, the Venetian authorities required the city's Jews to live on that island, in an area enclosed by walls. Venice was thus the first place to have a ghetto with today's connotation of restriction in space. In 1555, Pope Paul IV forced Rome's Jews into a similarly enclosed quarter, which, a few years later, came to be called by the Venetian name "ghetto." The term then gradually spread to other European cities where Jews were similarly segregated from the larger population. In all these places, they simultaneously suffered and flourished.

Although the ghettos were demolished in the nineteenth century, in tandem with a gradually swelling wave of Jewish emancipation, the term "ghetto" was increasingly used from the late nineteenth century on, first to refer to dense Jewish quarters in Europe and America and then occasionally in reference to black urban neighborhoods. The word was given even greater prominence when it was reappropriated by the Nazis as they confined the Jews of Eastern Europe behind barbed wire in the late 1930s. A few years later, the idea of the ghetto took on new significance in the United States. During World War II, as black Americans served in the military (usually in arduous roles of logistical support) and witnessed the liberation of the Jews, blacks at home saw parallels between the ghettos established by the Nazis and their own segregated neighborhoods, between the Caucasian purity that whites were seeking to preserve in the United States and the Aryan purity that Hitler was trying to impose on Europe. As they had during World War I, they found themselves asking, in effect, "Have we been fighting once again for everybody else's freedom except our own?"[5]

For many of the undergraduate students who take my seminar on the idea of the ghetto, it comes as news that Jews, not blacks, were the original ghettoized people. This is a first clue to a motivation behind this book: ghettos can get lost. Had my course been offered earlier in Princeton's history, before the mid-1940s, it would have had nothing to do with blacks and no one would have expected it might. Instead, an instructor would have focused exclusively on Jews. The link between blacks and the ghetto has been around for less than 10 percent of the term's five-hundred-year history.

It is not just the Jewish ghettos that have been forgotten by certain younger cohorts. It has become harder and harder to recall the black ghettos of previous generations—ghettos that were quite different from those we know now. And as the word "ghetto" has itself become less meaningful in many quarters, so too have we largely forgotten the way the word was understood in discussions of race, poverty, and place by social scientists,[6] activists, politicians, journalists, and other intellectuals. It's little recognized that the term embodies some of the most brilliant work in the history of the social sciences, much of which was contributed by black scholars such as those presented in these pages.

I have tried to recover that particular history by focusing selectively on a series of figures: Horace Cayton and St. Clair Drake, whose account of the Chicago "ghetto" in the Nazi era underlined the importance of restrictive housing covenants and other coercive measures—and served as an alternative to the famous portrait of the black situation in *An American Dilemma* by the Swedish economist and later Nobel laureate Gunnar Myrdal; Kenneth Clark, who revived the ghetto as an explanatory concept during the civil rights movement to show how segregation was damaging Northern blacks even without Jim Crow; and William Julius Wilson, who showed how the successes of the civil rights movement facilitated the departure of the black middle class from the ghetto, leaving behind a destitute population with a paucity of economic opportunities. In an era when the spotlight was no longer on the problems of poor blacks, he argued that the only way to interest whites in joblessness among black adults or even poverty among black children was to focus on programs that would also help whites. But working around the racism (and classism) of advantaged whites was not in itself enough to build the kind of support he had hoped for.

So we're back to individual ghettos that are left to their own devices, as well as the activists and reformers who desperately try to achieve miracles on the ground. One particular effort garnered recent attention, support, and celebrity for its guiding founder: Geoffrey Canada and his Harlem Children's Zone. He advances the idea that whereas single-focus efforts to improve the lot of the black poor do not succeed, a full-court press will. His initiative also presumes that private philanthropy can sometimes be a substitute for public policy, and at best an integral part of it. Although President Barack Obama tried to make Canada's ideas the centerpiece of a national urban policy, Obama found it impossible to get meaningful support from Congress. Thus far, Canada's success hinges on his own charismatic efforts and on the generosity of a few highly committed white billionaires.

We are left with the remains of an age-old system of exclusion—and no straightforward remedy. Worse yet, we are only now emerging from what has arguably been the largest and most consequential of all recent interventions in the lives of poor blacks: a War on Drugs based, ultimately, on its own misguided fantasy of a solution. The tactic emerged gradually, only after deindustrialization rendered poor urban blacks increasingly superfluous. The black ghetto became a hyperpoliced and monitored zone. Today, most men in the ghetto, subject as they are to paramilitary-style policing such as stop-and-frisk operations, will spend some time in prison. The ghetto can no longer be simply defined as a segregated area in which most blacks live. It is better understood as a space for the intrusive social control of poor blacks. As such, many of the ideas about the ghetto that emerged at the time of World War II may be more relevant than ever.

In this book, I seek a sense of historical awareness that is increasingly missing from our understanding. So much has been lost that needs to be remembered, if only because the ghetto's troubled legacy has not gone away.

GHETTO

1

A NAZI DECEPTION

While W.E.B. Du Bois was studying philosophy at the University of Berlin in the final decade of the nineteenth century, he believed—as do many Americans even today—that racial troubles in the United States were both the most serious in the world and utterly unique.[1] As he later recalled, "Race problems at the time were to me purely problems of color, and principally of slavery in the United States and near-slavery in Africa." Much to his surprise, a fellow student, a Pole from Kraków, scoffed at the narrowness of his view: "You know nothing, really nothing, about real race problems."

Du Bois therefore decided to tour Europe in 1893, to observe social conditions for himself in various countries. From Germany he traveled to Switzerland and Italy, stopping in Venice and Vienna, then making his way from Budapest to a small town in Galicia (currently part of Ukraine). Here a taxi driver asked him whether he would be willing to stop *unter die Juden*. A bit confused by the question, Du Bois agreed, and thus they drove to a small Jewish hotel. There he saw for the first time large numbers of Jews living in a wholly Jewish quarter, as though the early modern ghetto had disappeared in name only. Du Bois continued on to Kraków. Although the idea of a "Jewish problem" gradually grew in his mind, he could not learn much from either Polish students or their professors, all of whom seemed oblivious to it.

Upon returning to Germany, he began to sense the problem

everywhere, but as in Poland, it was rarely discussed. Several minor incidents, however, drew his attention. One time, while visiting a German town with one of his classmates, Du Bois noticed that people were acting strangely toward the two of them. He assumed this was due to his being black until his friend quietly told him, "They think I may be a Jew. It's not you they object to, it's me." Du Bois was shocked. He hadn't realized that his friend's dark hair roused suspicions that he was Jewish.

Du Bois returned to the United States bent on investigating the problem of race. His first great work, *The Philadelphia Negro* (1899)—the book that established his reputation and helped pioneer what was arguably "the first scientific school of American sociology"[2]—was a study of the black sections of the Seventh Ward of that city. In it he never referred to the "ghetto," a term that was used by those who knew it to refer to early modern dense Jewish neighborhoods. Nearly twenty years later, in 1917, on the heels of a summer race riot in East St. Louis, Illinois, Du Bois drew a link between blacks and Jews: "Russia has abolished the ghetto—shall we restore it?"[3] Yet it was only decades later that Du Bois fully graspéd the magnitude of the Jewish problem. After World War II, in 1949, Du Bois made a consequential trip to Poland, this time visiting the zone that during the war had been called the Warsaw ghetto. For this great intellectual of race, who had witnessed race riots in Atlanta and the marching of the Ku Klux Klan through the South, to see total annihilation in the name of racial purity was a transformative experience.

By the time that Adolf Hitler consolidated his power in 1933, the concept of Jewish segregation already had a long and complicated history. In the twelfth and thirteenth centuries, Jews in France and England and the German lands (there was no unified "Germany" until 1870) still lived in semi-voluntary Jewish quarters for reasons of safety as well as communal activity and self-help. They created these neighborhoods near synagogues, and often in the center of towns and near the cathedral, as in Paris. Yet though the synagogue lay at the center of their social existence, the quarters in which Jews lived were hardly cut off from the surrounding city.[4] Medieval Jews had substantial freedom to come and go as they pleased. They were aware of doings in other communities spread throughout the area we call Western and Central Europe. They traveled and had regular contact with Jewish travelers. Some also read local and vernacular literature, and the elite knew Latin and even canon law, the law of the Church.[5]

Nonetheless, Jewish life became increasingly difficult. The First Crusade of 1096 brought great slaughter in the Rhineland, and lay rulers were often exploitative. Thanks too to the Church's growing fears for the purity of the individual Christian, restrictions increased. "Excessive contact" with Jews on the social level—such as sharing a common table or sexual relations—was considered polluting. The severity of Jewish existence under increasingly restrictive rulers and an increasingly hostile populace did not mean Jewish culture was moribund. Jewish life, especially religious and intellectual life, knew periods of true flowering. Moreover, Jewish quarters were almost never obligatory or enclosed until the fifteenth century. The first notable case of obligatory segregation was in Frankfurt am Main. In Barcelona, Jews were also enclosed toward the end of the fifteenth century.

These enclosures were deemed insufficient, however, by those who worried that contact with Jews could lead Christians religiously astray. In 1492, in the now-united Spanish Kingdoms of Castile and Aragon, the joint monarchs Ferdinand and Isabella decreed the expulsion of all Jews who had not yet converted to Christianity. They noted in their decree that enclosed urban quarters had not prevented contact between Jews and Christians, and that the kingdoms' remaining Jews could entice converts back to Judaism—therefore expulsion was the only way to remedy the situation. By that time, Jews had already been expelled from England (in 1290) and from France (in stages between 1306 and 1394). Jews in the German lands suffered great massacres during the fourteenth century, and by the fifteenth were scattered in many small towns. A closed quarter was an impracticality.

Meanwhile, the rulers of Poland welcomed Jewish migrants to help build up the country, despite the objections of the Church. The Jewish population also grew in Italy—mainly due to the entrance of those expelled from north of the Alps into the Italian center and north. For these Jews, the closed residential pattern would be instituted beginning with Venice in 1516.[6]

Although some Jews resided in the city of Venice in the fifteenth century, they possessed no legal status and could not engage in money-lending, which was forbidden. The situation changed in 1509, as Jews living on the adjacent Venetian mainland were among the many refugees who fled across the lagoon to the city of Venice in the face of the invading armies of the League of Cambrai. Although the Venetian government ordered the refugees to go back home after it retook the captured areas, many Jews remained in the city. Eventually, in 1513, the government granted two wealthy Jews, originally from the mainland settlement of Mestre, a five-year charter permitting them to engage in moneylending in the city itself. Presumably the city leaders realized that they could provide the hard-pressed treasury with annual payments while also assisting the needy native poor, whose numbers had been swelled by the war. Some Jews were also authorized to sell *strazzaria*—literally, rags, but, by extension, secondhand clothing and other used items.

Many Venetians, and especially members of the clergy, who prided themselves on having "a most Catholic city," were greatly bothered by the phenomenon of newly arrived Jews living throughout Venice. Consequently, in 1516, the Senate passed legislation requiring all Jews residing throughout the city, as well as any who were to come in the future, to reside together on the island in Cannaregio, which was already known as the Ghetto Nuovo (the New Ghetto) because of its association with the municipal copper foundry previously located across the canal in the Ghetto Vecchio (the Old Ghetto). (*Il ghetto* or *getto* is derived from *gettare*, which means "the pouring or casting of metal.") To prevent Jews from going around the city at night, gates were erected on the side of the Ghetto Nuovo facing the Ghetto Vecchio, where a small wooden footbridge crossed the canal, and also at its other end. Christian guards were to open these two gates at sunrise when the Marangona bell sounded, and close them at sunset—though the closing hour was slightly extended to one hour after dark in summer and two in winter; only Jewish doctors, and later merchants, were routinely allowed outside after curfew. Permission to remain outside the gates was occasionally granted upon special request to other individuals, but almost never—with the exception primarily of a few doctors—was a Jew authorized to stay outside all night.

The Venice ghetto created a completely Jewish space within a much larger Christian polity. The space had little regulation from the outside—the Jews could both govern it and call it their own. It allowed for a certain flourishing. Although the Jews tried to avoid moving to the ghetto, which severely restricted their physical freedom, the institution represented a compromise that legitimized but carefully controlled their presence in the city.

However, the establishment of the ghetto did not ensure the continued residence of the Jews in Venice, for that privilege was based on the five-year charter of 1513. After its expiration, the Senate debated its renewal, with sharp differences of opinion as to what to do with the Jews. Ultimately, socioeconomic *raison d'état* triumphed over traditional religious hostility, and the charter of the Jewish moneylenders was renewed eventually after 1548 for regular five-year periods. Jews thus remained in the city behind ghetto walls and subject to numerous restrictions until the end of the Venetian Republic centuries later.

Within a relatively short time, "ghetto" came to define the enclosed Jewish residential areas in Venice, Rome, and elsewhere. "Isolation in space," writes Richard Sennett, "now became part of the problem defining what it meant to 'be Jewish.'"[7] One informative source on this period is the largely forgotten book *The Ghetto and the Jews of Rome*, written by Ferdinand Gregorovius, a nineteenth-century medieval historian and Polish-born German resident of Italy. His book traces Roman Jews back seventeen centuries to the reign of the emperor Titus, who had conquered and destroyed Jerusalem and brought Jewish prisoners to Rome as slaves. Although Titus despised the Jews, he granted them the right to practice their religion, which they did, on and off, until Christianity became the official state religion in the late fourth century. As Gregorovius put it, to "ancient Roman contempt there was now added the new hatred for the enemies of Christ."[8]

For Jews, things did indeed take a turn for the worse under the Church. Gregorovius describes the various forms of humiliation that they suffered even before being forced to move into the ghetto in the sixteenth century. Pope Paul II (1464–71), for example, began making Jews run Carnival races, which continued as an annual event until 1668. Although Carnival fell in the winter, the team of eight or twelve young Jewish racers were stripped down to their loincloths and force-fed beforehand "so as to make the race more difficult for them and at the same time more amusing for the spectators."[9]

At papal inaugurations and coronations, Jews were required to stand by the side of the road and wait for the procession. Once it reached them, they handed the newly elected pope the scroll of the Law. After reading several words, he would customarily proclaim, "We confirm the Law, but condemn the Jewish people and their interpretation." "Thereupon," Gregorovius writes, "he rode on, and the Jews returned to their homes, either crushed to despair or quickened with hope, according as they fearsomely read the expression in the eyes of the pope."[10]

Such belittlement undergirded and justified the new age of ghettos that would follow. In 1555, Paul IV issued the infamous bull "Cum nimis absurdum," which, among other things, stated that "all Jews should live solely in one and the same place, or if that is not possible, in two or three or as many as are necessary, which are to be contiguous and separated completely from the dwellings of Christians."[11] After centuries of identifying themselves as Romans and enjoying relative freedom of movement, the city's Jews were forcibly relocated from the neighborhood of Trastevere to a small strip of land on the other side of the Tiber, where they were packed into a few dark and narrow streets that were regularly inundated by the flooding river. Two and eventually three gates were built into the ghetto walls, which stretched from the Ponte Fabricio to the Portico d'Ottavia, an ancient structure that had come to be used as a fish market. The walls that once offered Romans protection now became an instrument of imprisonment.

What prompted Paul IV to segregate the Jews in this way? To some extent his decision can be attributed to the chronic and habitual anti-Judaism prevalent across Europe. The official aim of the edict was to press Jews into conversion so that they could be saved from eternal damnation. In his book on the Roman ghetto in the sixteenth century, Kenneth Stow shows that the measure made it clear to Jews that as long as they stuck to their ways and remained different (in faith), they would not be permitted to participate in society at large. The Roman ghetto thus placed its residents in a kind of "social and spatial limbo." Not many Jews converted, so the measure primarily created a mechanism that differentiated "us," those outside the ghetto, from "them," the Jews.[12]

For Jews whose families had lived freely in Rome for as long as anyone could remember, and whose ancestors had arrived before the spread of Christianity, this was a shattering blow. Stow shows that they had always considered themselves integral residents of Rome. Legally, they were citizens, with nearly full rights, though some rights were granted exclusively to Christians, such as permission to hold high office. On a more basic level, the Jews were anything but aliens or foreigners: they shared language and food with others; they spoke and wrote Italian and generally behaved in the manner of other Roman residents.

Stow shows that at first Jews could hardly have imagined that their residential separation would last for centuries. Only after the ghetto was enlarged in 1589 did they begin to grasp that this was their long-term fate and begin referring to the enclosed area as *nostro ghet*—"our ghetto"—punning on the word *get*, Hebrew for "bill of divorce." And about the divorce, they were correct.[13]

The decree also came in the wake of the Protestant Reformation, which had shattered Western Europe's religious unity and placed the pope on the defensive. The Roman ghetto was established as the papacy was anxiously presenting its city as the "New Jerusalem." As the exclusive and divinely sanctioned capital of Christianity, Rome replaced the Jewish metropolis of the Old Testament and served as a preview of the Heavenly Jerusalem and/or Paradise. As pope after pope constructed magnificent churches and ornate fountains and piazzas, and poured money into the construction of the huge, marble-bedecked Basilica of St. Peter's, the enclosure of the city's approximately three thousand to four thousand Jews in a tiny, squalid strip along the Tiber made the city's new constructions that much more spectacular. Indeed, the Jewish residential zone, not far from key ancient ruins such as the Theater of Marcellus, as well as newly constructed churches, was highly visible to tourists and pilgrims. Bereft of new construction, the ghetto offered visual proof of the difference between old and new, Jews and Christians, damned and saved. Its existence enabled ecclesiastical officials to point out the immediate and stark contrast between the physical environment of those who embraced the "true" faith and those who rejected it. The squalor of the ghetto was viewed not as the direct consequence of discrimination and forced overpopulation, but as the natural state and deserved fate of those who had betrayed Christ. If "the perfect symmetry, proportion, and classical order of the new St. Peter's projected an image of Catholic unity, godliness and power," Irina Oryshkevich explains, "... then the patched quality of the [ghetto] ... denoted its users' ... moral crookedness and spiritual myopia."[14]

Although the ghetto removed Jews physically from the rest of the city, daily contact with the outside world continued in Rome, just as it had in Venice. During the day, when the gates were open, Christians were free to enter the ghetto, while Jews could leave to work outside.[15] By the third decade of the ghetto's existence, however, Jews began to experience a strong sense of spatial separation.[16] Some may, in fact, have come to perceive the ghetto as a holy precinct, its barriers recalling the walls of ancient Jerusalem, the Holy City. All the same, culturally speaking, the Jews never stopped being Romans, speaking Italian—if a noticeably Judeo-Romanesco variant—on a daily basis, and writing it in a more formal mode. Moreover, many continued to be knowledgeable, if not always up-to-date, regarding general Italian culture.[17]

The ghetto was always a mixed bag. Separation, while creating disadvantages for the Jews, also created conditions in which their institutional life could continue and even blossom. For Gregorovius, the fascinating thing about the Jews in Rome was that they had survived at all while the great civilization of ancient Rome, which had conquered Jerusalem, had fallen fourteen hundred years earlier.[18]

After centuries of separation, a prime problem for Jewish ghetto residents was that the restrictions imposed on them undercut their livelihoods. By the decree of "Cum nimis absurdum," they were no longer permitted to deal in new merchandise. The fifty or so Jewish banks (really small-scale pawnbroking shops) in Rome were eventually dissolved by papal order. These measures impoverished banking families, who, deprived of funds, sometimes converted to Catholicism. Of the approximately thirty-six hundred Jews who remained in the Roman ghetto by 1843, some nineteen hundred eked out a living by selling or repairing old clothes.[19]

Although there were other ghettos, the Venetian and Roman ghettos are the best-known early examples of compulsory and segregated Jewish quarters established by administrative order from above rather than by social practices that led to voluntary separation. Yet since the ghetto gates were open during the day and Jews could leave while Christians could enter, complete separation was not possible. Jews and Christians in Rome had frequent contact on many levels, despite the enclosing walls. Since ghettoization was based on religion, converts were required to leave and not always permitted to maintain social linkages with those left behind. Although the ghettos were home to many poor, they also contained a fair number of wealthy families. Even in Rome it took several generations behind walls for Jews to become truly indigent. In all of these ghettos, the Jewish community possessed internal autonomy and maintained a wide range of religious, educational, and social institutions, and family life continued much as it had before.

The pernicious circular logic of the ghetto is evident. Isolation from mainstream society, as well as the decrepitude caused by overcrowding, produced notorious conditions, behaviors, and traits that could gradually be invoked to rationalize further negative attitudes and more extreme isolation. The consequences of ghettoization provided an apparent justification for the original condition.

Jews across Europe continued to live in predominantly Jewish quarters, some semi-voluntary, others mandatory, throughout the early modern era. Napoleon was the first to attempt to demolish the ghettos of Italy and free the Jews. Leading his armies through Europe, he spread the idea of liberty and equality as promoted by the French Revolution. In 1797, for example, his troops marched to the ghetto of Ancona on the Adriatic Sea, tore down its gates, and liberated the Jews. Meanwhile in Padua, his troops posted a declaration that read, "First, the Hebrews are at liberty to live in any street they please. Second, the barbarous and senseless name of Ghetto, which designates the street on which they have been inhabiting hitherto, shall be substituted by that of Via della Libertà."[20] The emperor then set his sights on larger targets and soon set free the Jews of Rome and Venice.

Most ghettos in Western Europe fell slowly, but fall they did. Despite Napoleon's efforts, one of the slowest to disappear was Rome's, for the papacy used its power to resist the integration of Jews. Napoleon occupied the city again during his second campaign in 1808–14, but after the French retreat in 1814, Pope Pius VII immediately sent the Jews back into forced segregation in the same dank and overcrowded quarter that they had occupied for centuries.

When Gregorovius visited the ghetto in 1840, about half of its Jews were surviving at mere subsistence levels. Whenever the Tiber inundated the neighborhood, its residents sought refuge on the upper floors of already-overcrowded tenements. "Each year Israel in Rome has to undergo a new Deluge," Gregorovius commented, "and like Noah's Ark the ghetto is tossed on the waves with man and beast."[21]

Seven years later street protests organized by two thousand Roman citizens in solidarity with the Jews forced Pope Pius IX to remove the ghetto's gates. Yet even after these were taken down to the cheers of the Roman population on April 17, 1848, the ghetto remained. The Vatican required that Jews continue to live there, albeit without gates, for another two decades. Not until September 20, 1870, when Italian troops entered Rome to complete the unification of Italy, was the ghetto finally abolished and its residents granted full equality. Thus, the city's Jews, among the first in the world to be ghettoized, became the last Jews in Western Europe to win the rights of citizenship in their own country.

This was the era of Jewish emancipation. According to Jewish scholars, rabbis, and laymen, a new era was at hand; Jewish predictions about the future were almost universally optimistic.[22] The most widely expressed reservation was that integration was too slow. But a prominent dissenter was the Columbia University historian Salo Baron. He argued that the Jews had actually flourished in their separation:

Social exclusion from the Gentile world was hardly a calamity. Indeed, to most Jews it was welcome, and the ghetto found warm champions in every age. There the Jews might live in comparative peace, interrupted less by pogroms than were peasants by wars, engaged in finance and trade at least as profitable as most urban occupations, free to worship, and subject to the Inquisition only in extreme situations (as after the enforced baptisms in Spain and Portugal). They had no political rights, of course, but except for nobles and clergy no one did.[23]

Baron's revisionism was too rosy, but it was true that Jewish traditions were maintained in the ghetto. Some contemporary historians, too, have stressed that the ghetto encouraged Jews to turn inward, concentrating in fruitful ways on their own culture.

By the early twentieth century, the word "ghetto" had acquired an additional new definition. Whereas in the early modern period "ghetto" connoted a place of enforced residence, it now referred to a high-density neighborhood inhabited predominantly but voluntarily by Jews in European cities such as Warsaw, Prague, Vienna, Frankfurt, and Cologne. Such ghettos also existed in urban areas of the United States, such as the Lower East Side of New York or the West Side of Chicago, which attracted poor Eastern European Jews. America's long-established German Jews typically lived elsewhere and felt embarrassed by this recent influx of immigrants. All of them, however, as well as Christians, now largely understood the ghetto as an arrangement not much different from ethnic neighborhoods such as Little Italies, Polonias, or Chinatowns.

Things were not pretty in these communities, as Mike Gold's autobiographical novel *Jews Without Money* (1930)—an international bestseller in a dozen languages—vividly illustrates. No book was more important in bringing the ghetto to the attention of a vast reading public. For Gold, writing about the Lower East Side of Manhattan, the term was synonymous with "slum": a dirty, violent place, full of desperation and poverty, where children stole from pushcarts, threw cats off rooftops, organized gangs against other children from rival blocks, and looked out the window as gamblers shot at each other. There were so many prostitutes that Gold felt compelled to offer a socioeconomic explanation for their presence: "Being a prostitute was easier than being in a sweatshop." If the prostitutes were not making noise, then it was the neighbors, whose every word and movement could be heard through windows or walls. Many families also opened their home to a distant relative or villager straight off the boat who was "sponging" off them. Everyone shared their arguments, lice, and cockroaches.

The Lower East Side ghetto had come about without any legal mandate. Nonetheless, it exacerbated social distance and isolated its residents from the wider society, as Gold's recollection of a sightseeing bus rolling through the neighborhood so graphically reveals: "A gang of kids chased it, and pelted rocks, garbage, dead cats and stale vegetables at the frightened sightseers. 'Liars, Liars,' the kids yelled, 'go back up-town!' . . . What right had these stuck up foreigners to come and look at us? What right had that man with the megaphone to tell them lies about us? Kids always pelted these buses."[24] As Gold explained to his reader, although not without some exaggeration, "I have told in my book a tale of Jewish poverty in one ghetto, that of New York. The same story can be told of a hundred other ghettos scattered over all the world. For centuries the Jew has lived in this universal ghetto."[25]

Enter the Nazis. Contemporary historians, who disagree on many things, now widely agree that the Nazi ghettos were not an inherent part of a premeditated plan for liquidating Jews.[26] No document with instructions on how the Nazi ghettos would be built or run has ever been found, much less a document stating that they should be staging areas for genocide.[27] Yet this consensus should not overshadow the fact that Hitler used the word "ghetto" and articulated what he meant even in his early days in power. Already in 1935, for example, he stated privately to members of the Nazi Party, including his assistant Fritz Wiedemann, whose notes later became public, that Jews would be placed "into a ghetto, enclosed in a territory where they can behave as becomes their nature, while the German people look on as one looks at wild animals."[28]

When discussing ghettos with his Nazi ministers early in his reign, Hitler referred to ghettos as zoolike places in which to display Jews; yet when addressing polite society outside his circle, he preferred to liken them to the Jewish ghettos instituted by the Catholic Church long before. Fewer than six months after he became chancellor, he held a meeting in his Berlin office with Bishop Wilhelm Berning, a delegate from the Conference of Catholic Bishops. Two separate records of this encounter confirm that Hitler presented his case in this light to promi-nent Church officials from the outset. The first consists of a note com-posed by an unknown witness and dated to 1933, now in the files of the embassy of the Holy See: "In his statements Hitler spoke with the highest regard for the Catholic Church. He then brought up the Jewish question. In justification of his hostility to the Jews he referred to the

Catholic Church, which had likewise always regarded the Jews as unde-
sirables and which on account of the moral dangers involved had forbidden the Christians to work for Jews. For these reasons the Church had
banished the Jews into the ghetto."[29]

In the second report, now in the files of the episcopal archives in
Rottenberg, Dr. Joseph Negwer, the canon of Breslau, cited Hitler's precise words: "I have been attacked because of my handling of the Jewish
question. The Catholic Church considered the Jews pestilent for fifteen
hundred years, put them in ghettos, etc. because it recognized the Jews
for what they were. In the epoch of liberalism the danger was no longer
recognized. I am moving back toward the time in which a fifteen-
hundred-year-long tradition was implemented."[30] Negwer also pointed
out that Hitler had requested that the general public be informed only
of the meeting's occurrence but not of the issues discussed.

Boldly stating that the Nazis were drawing on centuries of Catholic
practice, Hitler, in his opportunistic borrowing, framed his ghetto as
a long-established standard operating procedure. The records of this
meeting contain no reply from Berning.[31] Was the bishop left speech-
less because he knew that for centuries Catholics had in fact segregated
Jews in ghettos? Did he remain silent because nobody in 1933, perhaps
not even Hitler, knew that the Nazis would actually implement a full-
scale ghettoization policy? Could Berning simply not have guessed that
the Nazi ghetto logic would so fundamentally deviate from the ghetto
logic invented by the Church centuries earlier?

How Nazis actually thought about the ghetto is evident from a major
meeting of the regime's top party and government leaders that convened
on November 12, 1938. One of the first times the issue came up was in
a discussion of the Aryanization of the German economy. Reinhard
Heydrich, chief of the security service, began by reminding his colleagues that though Jews had been eliminated from the German economy, they still needed to be kicked out of Germany.[32] Getting other
countries to accept them was difficult. A very general eight-to-ten-year
plan to deport as many as ten thousand Jews annually still left a massive
number of unemployed Jews interfering with the everyday life of the
country. Assuming that they would continue to mix with the general

population, Heydrich was against the idea of establishing ghettos. Instead, he proposed that Jews be forced to wear an insignia to make it easier for the police to keep an eye on them. This led to a strong objection from Field Marshal Hermann Göring, who thought the insignia was being proposed as a way of avoiding ghettos. To which Heydrich replied:

> I'd like to make my position clear right away. From the point of view of the police, I don't think a ghetto in the form of completely segregated districts where only Jews would live, can be put up. We could not control a ghetto where the Jews congregate amidst the whole Jewish people. It would remain the permanent hideout for criminals and also for epidemics and the like. We don't want to let the Jew live in the same house with the German population; but today the German population, their blocks or houses, force the Jew to behave himself. The control of the Jew through the watchful eye of the whole population is better than having him by the thousands in a district where I cannot properly establish a control over his daily life through uniformed agents.[33]

A lengthy discussion ensued with no basic agreement until Walther Funk, the minister of economics, made a crucial point: "The Jews will have to move quite close together. What are three million? Everyone will have to stand up for the next fellow. The individual alone will starve."[34] Jews lived spread across different communities in cities and towns throughout Germany. Essentially, Funk's argument was that they would consolidate regardless of where they were: ghettos would arise whether or not the Nazis created them.

Hermann Göring dismissed the potential difficulty of maintaining order in the ghetto. But he could not solve the problem of how to prevent epidemics from spreading from the ghetto's borders to the population at large. Nor could he deal with another major issue: ghettos on German soil would make it virtually impossible to keep Jews out of the Aryan economy. If Jews owned stores in the ghetto, then German wholesalers would rely on their orders. If instead Germans operated those stores, then they would be dependent on Jewish consumers. If no stores were in the ghetto, Jews would have to venture into German zones for daily shopping. A ghetto in German cities thus seemed irreconcilable with the goal of eliminating all economic interdependence between Jews and Germans.

To resolve this dilemma, Heydrich suggested to Göring that Germans no longer provide the Jew with basic necessities. Göring regarded this as unacceptable; "You cannot let him starve," he noted.

Despite their discussions, the high-ranking members of the Nazi Party failed to agree on a concrete plan to build ghettos in German cities. They settled for what was perhaps the next-best thing: a dramatic social marginalization of Jews in German society. The idea was to isolate and demoralize Jews by preventing them from entering the daily routine of German life until a better solution could be found.[35] Among the options was deporting them to Madagascar, a French territory off the southeastern coast of Africa—a particularly appropriate solution, it seemed to the Nazis, as Napoleon had initiated the Jewish problem by emancipating Jews nearly a century and a half before.[36]

In the meantime, Jews were segregated in special "Jew houses" located alongside the Christian population. They were forbidden to enter German theaters, share train cars, or bathe with Germans on beaches and resorts from the fear that touch pollutes. They were also prohibited from purchasing fruit or candy when entering shops: "The Reich Minister for Food and Agriculture has sent a telex on 2 December 1939 forbidding the sale of Chocolate products (chocolate bars, chocolates, and other cocoa products) and cakes of all kinds to Jews with immediate effect. You are requested to instruct the local authorities to inform the retailers of this at once."[37]

Jews' movements around the city were similarly curtailed. They were not allowed to have driver's licenses or own cars. They were barred from governmental districts, public squares, and hospitals. Their children were banned from German schools.

This early meeting makes clear that the main purpose of the Nazi ghetto was not simply segregation, but economic exclusion and control—not as easy to achieve on German soil as some had hoped. Yet less than a year after the Nazis' meeting, the ghetto became a reality—not on German soil, but in Nazi-controlled Poland, and later Czechoslovakia, Greece, Hungary, Romania, Latvia, and Lithuania.

A few weeks after Germany invaded Poland in September 1939, Heydrich sent an order to the chiefs of the *Einsatzgruppen* (paramilitary squads) in Poland telling them that "the first prerequisite for the final aim [is] the concentration of the Jews from the countryside into the larger cities."[38] At a conference in Berlin that same day he explained that this concentration would occur through ghettos, which offered a better way of controlling and eventually deporting this population.[39] What followed in the creation of the Nazi ghettos was an extraordinary exercise of state power.

Hitler's claim that he was reviving the ghetto of the Middle Ages was completely misleading. The Nazi ghetto was something entirely new.

First, the Nazi ghetto illustrated that it was now possible to control a segregated population with absolute efficiency. These ghettos' walls or other boundaries were put in place virtually overnight rather than over several years, as had been the case in Rome or the Frankfurt Judengasse. Such speed was possible thanks to a crucial new technology, barbed wire, which had been invented in the 1860s. Inexpensive and effective, it had first been used by cattlemen in the American West as well as by the British in the Boer Wars and World War I to contain civilian enemies and prisoners of war.[40] It also enabled Nazis to create ghettos at a moment's notice, as evident in a memo by a German official: "[The Lodz ghetto] will be established suddenly on a day to be chosen by me, i.e. at a certain time the boundaries of the ghetto . . . will be blocked off by barbed wire, barricades and other barriers."[41]

The upper echelons of the Nazi regime were thus able to translate their ideas into action with greater speed and efficiency than had ever before been possible.[42] They possessed means of communication and transport that quickly enabled them to trap and hold a massive number of victims within their web.

Second, this efficiency made it possible for the Nazi ghettos to introduce as complete a segregation as the world had ever seen. While the earlier ghettos had allowed relatively easy passage of people and merchandise during the daytime, many of the Nazi ghettos fenced in their inhabitants day and night. Only those who obtained the rare exit permit were allowed to pass through the gates; others who tried to do so were shot. An officer of the Lodz security police in 1941, for example, reported, "I saw a woman climbing onto the ghetto fence, stick her head through it and attempt to steal a turnip from a passing lorry; I used my firearm. The Jewess was killed with two shots."[43] A child might be small enough to sneak out unnoticed to steal bread, but even that was unusual. According to another report from Lodz, Jews remained determined to survive and escape; thirty of them who had tried to flee had been shot in one month.[44] Even in ghettos where Jews were not hermetically sealed and worked elsewhere, they were usually escorted to their jobs in columns.

Barbed wire also enabled the Nazis to make good on Hitler's earlier wish to display Jews as wild animals. A report, dated May 1942, to the Polish government in exile records, "Every day large coaches come to the ghetto; they take soldiers through as though it were a zoo. . . . Often soldiers strike out at passers-by with long whips. . . . They set up genre pictures (old Jew above the corpse of a young girl)."[45]

Third, in earlier centuries religion had justified the segregation of Jews. A defining component of Nazi ghetto logic was, by contrast, race. In *Mein Kampf*, Hitler manipulated German folklore to emphasize the idea of an "Aryan" race, whose purity required protection from "lesser" races, most notably Slavs and Jews.[46] On September 15, 1935, Berlin enacted the Nuremberg Laws, according to which anyone who had three or four Jewish grandparents was considered fully Jewish.[47] The deciding factor was thus strictly racial, based on religious identity two generations removed; for the current generation, actual religious practice or even baptism had no bearing.

Consistent with the focus on race, it was not the German Jew who was thought to pose the greatest threat to Germany's national and racial character, but the *Ostjude*, a name coined after World War I by the Jewish journalist Nathan Birnbaum for the Eastern European Jews, whom he found repugnant.[48] It was this racial type that drove the Nazis to create ghettos as a defensive measure.[49] Although the Nazis saw German Jews as racially inferior to Aryans, the even more dangerous and repulsive character of the *Ostjuden* made it defensible, even correct and necessary, to segregate them. This argument prevailed only after the Nazis came into physical contact with this "peril" after the conquest of

Poland.[50] "Their appearance is the best visual education that our people could receive on the Jewish question," claimed one soldier, while another insisted that only after he and a group of his peers had visited the Jewish quarter in Kraków did they realize the importance and necessity of the racial laws of their führer.[51]

Fourth, as in the earlier enforced ghetto, so too in the Nazi ghetto, problems fed on each other in a vicious cycle. This time the results were qualitatively different. Both qualified German physicians and ideological Nazis claimed that the Jews were carriers of disease who required quarantine.[52] A large poster outside the Warsaw ghetto depicted a man with a louse nestled in his beard and a caption that read, "Jews are crawling with the typhus."[53] In this way the Nazis created the impression that the people relegated to the ghetto had contracted typhus before their arrival there, rather than acknowledging that they had fallen ill because of extreme overcrowding. The purported probability that they would spread the illness was an important reason to have them ghettoized.

Nazi ghettos did not begin as holding pens for subsequent extermination; rather, they were built in anticipation of the Jews' expulsion. The ghettos emerged gradually, with Jews being used initially as slave labor. Only after Jews became superfluous and grotesque due to ill health did the function of ghettos change. Those who initially administered the Nazi ghettos were deeply divided between "productionists" and "attritionists."[54] While the former saw the ghettos as a component of the defense economy, the latter wanted to see the Jews dead. In the beginning, the productionists prevailed. Even in 1941, when the economy of the Warsaw ghetto was described as a "field of ruins," some German officials still argued that the solution lay in integrating the Jews into economic life in Poland as fully as possible. But this argument circulated only for a while. Once the Jews had spent a few years in the ghettos, they became too emaciated, sick, and lethargic to work. Their pathetic condition reinforced the belief that they were subhuman. As Christopher Browning concluded in his authoritative account, "the untenable circumstances within the ghettos and the problems that they posed to frustrated German administrators caused many to long for the day when the Jews would finally disappear."[55] As conditions in the ghetto posed greater and greater problems, the productionists became utterly worn out and were relieved to be alleviated of their burden.[56]

Fifth, the Nazi ghettos were sites of continuous violence and brutality. Residents were forced to watch their fellow citizens die in mass executions, or to participate themselves in stoning fellow Jewish rule-breakers who were later buried in mass graves. To remain alive, to engage in self-preservation, was the only imperative. The ghettos were not places where Jews could live anything approximating a rounded life. Conditions were so at odds with the world's image of a Jewish ghetto that the Nazis were compelled to manufacture a flourishing ghetto at Terezín when the International Red Cross visited in June 1944. Later, this very ghetto would become the basis of a famous propaganda film, one in which few of the apparently happy ghetto dwellers would survive beyond the war.

When Hitler likened his plans for the Jews to Catholic tradition, he expected that the comparison would be taken literally. Five years later, *The New York Times* printed the following statement from a periodical directed by Field Marshal Hermann Göring: "In the Middle Ages . . . Jews in all cities were put into ghettos because it was clear that only complete separation made it possible [for officials] to keep watch on their machinations. . . . A similar development must be brought about again."[57]

Despite their statements to the contrary, Hitler and Göring were nonetheless transmitters of an entirely new ghetto logic. Even their own scholars in the ersatz sociologically oriented fields known as Anti-Jewish Studies and Jewish Studies did not adhere to Hitler's initial claim to the Church. In 1941, a leading Nazi intellectual, Peter-Heinz Seraphim, a sociologist and historian of Eastern European Jewry, wrote:

> Aside from the communal organization of the Jews yet another institution has contributed to the preservation of the unity of the Jews and hence to the strengthening of the Jewry regarding ethnic and economic aspects, the *Jewish ghetto*. . . . Sometimes it is pointed out that this solution [the isolation of the Jews from the non-Jews] is indicated by history . . . [but] the ghetto of the Middle Ages was in essence a voluntary community of dwelling

in addition to which it by no means excluded business contacts between Jews and non-Jews.[58]

Seraphim was writing not to urge the continuation of this kind of relatively open "ghetto." Rather, in his opinion "the ghetto of today, if it makes sense, should be different from the Medieval ghetto, without contact or possibility of contact with non-Jews." The early ghetto, in other words, had been insufficient to do its real job: total segregation.

However harsh and strictly regulated, no previous Jewish quarter, ghetto or otherwise, had ever been established with the express purpose of destroying its inhabitants through violence and brutality. The Nazi ghetto, furthermore, marked the first time in history when a series of oppressive features were brought together in their purest form. Physical space had been organized through the power of the state in fifteenth- and sixteenth-century Frankfurt, Venice, and Rome, for example, but conversion had always been an option. The Nazis' anti-Semitism transformed the ghetto into a means to accomplish economic enslavement, impoverishment, violence, fear, isolation, and overcrowding in the name of racial purity—all with no escape through conversion, and with unprecedented efficiency.

Given the many differences between the earlier European ghettos and those of the Nazis, it is surprising that the same word gained traction for both. It is even more notable that this occurred with so little questioning outside the Reich. After the war, this was attributed to a lack of historical knowledge, and later to the work of historians,[59] but well-educated journalists and even social scientists also played an important role in legitimating the new usage. In a front-page story dated November 12, 1938, *The New York Times* reported that "the ghetto of the Middle Ages was to be reestablished in the modern Nazi Reich."[60] Of course, it might be argued that the reporters of the time had no basis for imagining a ghetto any worse than those of the Middle Ages. But their commentary helped elide the distinctive Nazi twist of using race as a basis for classification, as well as the difference between a ghetto where people can flourish under conditions of relatively tolerant regulation and one where they are doomed to perish.

The first generation of American Holocaust researchers also applied the word "ghetto" to each of these radically different institutions, though not all did so indiscriminately. For example, the pioneering Holocaust scholar Raul Hilberg insisted that Nazism was itself a continuation of a medieval tradition, the ghetto being just one of many medieval institutions that were brought back to subjugate Jews. But even Hilberg emphasized the fundamental difference: "To the Jews the ghetto was a way of life; to the Germans it was an administrative measure."[61] Many others, however, failed to draw the distinction at all. To wit, Oxford's Martin Gilbert, in his bestselling and widely cited *The Holocaust*, states that the Nazis created a ghetto "such as had not existed in Europe since the Middle Ages."[62]

The field of sociology also played its part. Louis Wirth, the distinguished University of Chicago professor who first introduced the concept of the ghetto to modern sociology in 1928, tried desperately to affirm the generalizable quality of the idea by arguing for the continuity between Nazi ghettos and those that had come before. In his 1947 entry on "ghetto" in the *World Book Encyclopedia*, he stated, "The compulsory ghetto died out as a result of the intellectual and social movements of the Renaissance and the industrial revolution. . . . But the ghettos were revived by the Nazis in Germany and by the Fascists in Italy after 1933. In many parts of Europe under Nazi control, ghettos were reintroduced and remained until the end of World War II."[63]

Completely false. However avidly the Catholic Church may have sought to convert Jews, demanding that they be kept in an inferior condition to stress the inferiority of their religion, it basically respected their right to live and observe their own laws. Failing to acknowledge that the Nazi ghetto was an extreme type unlike any other ghetto in history elides the difference between it and the earlier communities, in which Jewish life was able to survive and even sometimes flourish. It also implies that the Nazi ghetto, too, was an epoch unto itself. In fact, whereas the early modern ghetto was established as a permanent institution, the Nazi ghetto lasted but a few years and was simply a link in the larger chain of execution that resulted in the death of 6 million Jews.

The difference between the ghetto as a site of compulsory residence and regulation and the ghetto as a site of slave labor, torture, disease, and death is obviously profound. As Salo Baron would testify at the war-crimes trial of Adolf Eichmann, "Many people, even those who were not Nazis, repeatedly said that the Nazis were actually restoring the conditions which prevailed in the Middle Ages. . . . But [they] brought the world new elements which had no precedent but which were distinct from the whole history of anti-Semitism of two thousand years and more."[64] Many years later, Christopher Browning would write about the Holocaust in general that it "required the invention of a new terminology to denote modes of behavior for which no exact analogy appeared to exist in the earlier historical record."[65]

In failing to contrast places such as Warsaw under the Nazis with the famous ghettos of the early modern era, social scientists missed a golden opportunity to develop a way of thinking about the ghetto that does more than highlight the amount and consequences of segregation. They missed a chance to give due recognition to the variations in both human flourishing and social control that are found wherever people are restricted in space. Just as certain moments in the history of the black ghetto have produced environments where inhabitants have grown personally, developed strong ties of solidarity, and produced a rich cultural life, recently it has been recognized that now there is far less flourishing and more extreme forms of intrusive social control than ever before.[66] Calling Venice and Warsaw by the same name without drawing strong distinctions between them paints over these kinds of crucial differences rather than elucidating them and helping us to understand them.

Today, it is largely forgotten that the Nazi ghetto, not the sixteenth-century ghetto upheld by the Church, was "in the air" when the term came into widespread use to describe black neighborhoods in the 1940s. For many blacks after World War II, the Nazi ghetto provided a powerful metaphor for their own experience. Although in reality the Nazi ghetto was just as different from Harlem and the South Side of Chicago as it was from sixteenth-century Rome and Venice, it nevertheless proved a crucial reference.

"I have seen something of human upheaval in this world," Du Bois said in speaking of the Warsaw ghetto after the war: "The scream and shots of a race riot in Atlanta; the marching of the Ku Klux Klan; the threat of courts and police; the neglect and destruction of human habitation; but nothing in my wildest imagination was equal to what I saw in Warsaw in 1949. I would have said before seeing it that it was impossible for a civilized nation with deep religious convictions and outstanding religious institutions; with literature and art; to treat fellow human beings as Warsaw had been treated. . . . Then, one afternoon, I was taken out to the former ghetto. I knew all too little of its story. . . . Here there was not much to see. There was complete and total waste, and a monument. And the monument brought back again the problem of race and religion, which so long had been my own particular and separate problem."[67]

2

CHICAGO, 1944:
HORACE CAYTON

On October 9, 1944, Virginia Dobbins bought a house on a white block just outside of Chicago's black neighborhoods. A few days later, when she arrived with her belongings, she found the neighbors removing the plumbing.

"We don't want a riot here," the people next door explained. "So we're tearing the house down. We don't want no trouble."

Mrs. Dobbins went to the Eighteenth District police station and pleaded for protection. The officer refused, explaining that while he could send a police car to check the house, he had no special order from the commissioner to guard it. The house was then torched and flooded by neighbors, leaving it in shambles.[1]

A month or so later, a group of black citizens assembled at the AME church in the neighborhood of Woodlawn to consider Virginia Dobbins's case and the larger problem of violence against blacks who tried to move even a few blocks outside Chicago's densely overcrowded black areas.[2] Violence on this scale had not been seen for a generation. Horace Cayton, a black graduate student from the University of Chicago's sociology department, rose before the audience and delivered a set of written remarks that were intended to highlight the social forces that gave rise to this situation.

Cayton was no ordinary graduate student. On his mother's side, he was the grandson of Hiram Revels of Mississippi, the first black man elected to the U.S. Senate. Cayton's parents founded *The Seattle Republican*, a newspaper that was read by whites and blacks alike. When Horace was growing up in the less restrictive racial atmosphere of the Northwest, the family resided in a white suburb and had a full-time Japanese servant. His parents entertained as houseguests some of the most renowned black figures of the time, including Booker T. Washington. By the time Cayton was in high school, Seattle had changed a great deal in response to a large black migration. The newspaper lost many of its white subscribers and went out of business. Before entering college, Cayton had gone to jail for violating Seattle's segregation laws by refusing to leave the white section of a movie theater; he had spent time in a reformatory for juvenile delinquents for participating in a robbery, worked as a runaway seaman, and been a handyman in an Alaskan brothel. During college, he made an about-face and worked his way through school as the first black police officer in Seattle.[3]

By now an accomplished and up-and-coming scholar, Cayton had made a reputation for himself within the black community. He wrote a column for *The Pittsburgh Courier*, an important black newspaper distributed throughout the country. For the past five years he had run Good Shepherd, a large community center on Fifty-First and South Parkway in the middle of Chicago's South Side. He had a good name among liberal whites, who donated generously to Good Shepherd, and also in the black community, where he was viewed as an activist involved in every battle for civil rights. He was regularly invited to speak at white and black churches.[4] In his private life, the strains of his marriage to a white woman exacted a heavy toll on him and deepened his perceptions of the city's racial pathology.

Cayton informed the audience at Woodlawn's AME church that Mrs. Dobbins's son was in the army.[5] This point was probably not lost on the assembled listeners, who were well aware that their sons were combating the Nazis. The labor organizer Charles Collins summarized the view of many blacks at the time: "Negroes know what living in a ghetto is. . . . [They] will gain equality through a United Nations victory only if we open a double second front—against Hitler and against America's worst domestic foe, racial discrimination."[6]

Like Du Bois before him, Cayton had encountered the situation of Jews firsthand on a visit to Europe. Traveling in 1933 with a Swedish student he had met at the University of Chicago, he decided to take some time by himself in Hamburg. Out for a walk, the light-skinned Cayton stopped at a small park and rested on a bench, where he sat in peace until a police officer approached to ask if he was a Jew. Cayton didn't understand, so the officer returned with an English-speaking civilian, who translated.

"No, I'm an American," Cayton replied, though that did not settle the matter.

After the officer and the civilian conferred, the civilian explained, "If you are not a Jew, you don't have to sit on this bench. It is for Jews only."

"I like it here," Cayton replied. "Is there any law that says I can't sit here?"

The officer seemed quite perplexed, and this time he conferred longer with the translator. "The officer says you can sit here if you wish, but it is for Jews. He doesn't understand why you would wish to remain where Jews sit."

Cayton said nothing, and after a few minutes the two men left. Later, he would recall that though he had heard of discrimination against the Jews, this was the first time he had seen it. "It seemed to me even sillier than Mississippi, where discrimination was at least based on color differences. Here they couldn't even be sure what a Jew looked like."[7]

As spatial restriction of blacks increased, the Nazi persecution of Jews became an available analogy for some.[8] One of the first public comparisons appeared in late 1938 in a resolution of the Inter-Racial Committee for the District of Columbia, which stated, "We join with all other people that still adhere to the ethics of our common civilization in protest against the abominable persecution of the Jews. . . . At the same time, we cannot forbear to point out that in many particulars, the sufferings of the innocent minority in Germany [and] Poland . . . are strikingly like the sufferings of a similar minority in our own country. The ghetto now under erection in Germany is segregation of dark complexioned people established in many American cities." The resolution was widely reported, including a story on the front page of *The Chicago Defender* under the headline "Cites Germany's Treatment of Jews Like Race in the U.S."[9]

Speaking in the church basement, Cayton described numerous incidents of bombings and of fires set at the entrances of homes that blacks had recently moved into. He condemned the Chicago police for not making a single arrest. Such terrorist acts had helped create and maintain restricted black neighborhoods throughout the United States since World War I. The most famous incident occurred in 1926 in Detroit. There, a medical doctor purchased a home in a white neighborhood. When he killed a member of a white mob protesting violently outside his house, he was arrested for murder but later acquitted after a high-profile defense by his lawyer, the celebrated Clarence Darrow.[10]

Cayton, however, was not content to speak only of the bombings or police inaction that were uppermost in the minds of his listeners. He was also there to discuss a less visible device that was used to control blacks in urban space: the race restrictive covenant. This innovation, coupled with violence and intimidation, had effectively sealed hundreds of thousands of blacks into tiny sections of the South Side.[11] The restrictive covenant was a highly sophisticated legal device that had been previously used to contain Asians and Jews. In the 1920s and beyond, it was increasingly used to circumvent the Supreme Court's ruling in *Buchanan v. Warley* (1917) that racial zoning by the state was unconstitutional. The ruling intentionally left the door open to white residents who wished to keep blacks out of their neighborhoods by means of private agreements.

These worked simply: whites in a neighborhood would enter into private agreements with one another stipulating that none of their properties would be occupied, leased, sold, or given to blacks (or, in less than 2 percent of the cases, to any non-Caucasians). Thus, a standard agreement might state, "The property owners cannot sell, convey, lease or rent to a Negro or Negroes . . . any of the said parcels," with exceptions for maids, chauffeurs, and janitors, who could live in the garage, barn, or servants' quarters.[12] In Chicago, covenants generally stayed in force for two decades (with automatic renewal) unless owners of 75 percent of the property covered by the covenants voted to eliminate the agreement sooner.[13] The goal was to draw a line that would keep the residents of black neighborhoods from flowing into adjoining communities.[14] Whenever any such "invasion" seemed imminent, property owners did not merely rely upon violence and racial steering; they would also put restrictive covenants into effect,[15] and as a result, decent housing remained inaccessible to blacks.[16]

This, however, was only part of the story. Although restrictive covenants appeared to be the work of individuals collaborating with each other at the neighborhood level, they resulted from the efforts of both local neighborhood institutions and national organizations. At the local level, some of the least visible institutions involved were churches, which played significant roles in the formation of certain restrictive covenant agreements. In Chicago, Detroit, Buffalo, and Philadelphia, they served as meeting places for neighborhood associations, and their ministers, priests, and pastors became personally involved in movements to keep blacks out of their communities.[17]

Even more far-reaching policies of racial exclusion came from national real estate organizations. The National Association of Real Estate Boards, which had over fifteen thousand members, was the most powerful body in the country for the regulation of real estate policy. Article 34 of its Code of Ethics stated that "a realtor should never be instrumental in introducing into a neighborhood a character of property or occupancy, members of any race or nationality, or any individuals whose presence will clearly be detrimental to property values in that neighborhood."[18] In another general statement, the association reminded the realtor that the prospective buyer might be a bootlegger . . . a madam . . . a gangster . . . a colored man of means who [is] giving his children a college education and thought they [are] entitled to live among whites. . . . No matter what the motive or character of the would-be purchaser, if the deal would instigate a form of blight, then certainly the well-meaning broker must work against its consummation."[19] Realtors had no choice but to take such warnings seriously. Failure to adhere to the Code of Ethics could lead to loss of membership and, in practical terms, their firm's inability to function. Thus, while restrictive covenants appeared to be an individual and neighborhood-level practice, they were actually enforced by the work of powerful outside national organizations.[20]

Though the restrictive covenants had a powerful impact, they were hard to track. Since the relevant city records—deeds and tract books—had no cumulative indexes, it was only by plotting one deed after another on a map that a researcher could identify the precise locations of the invisible barriers that sealed blacks in place.[21] Even so, blacks in Chicago and around the nation were aware of the covenants. Since the 1920s, many had been angrily choosing not to risk buying houses because they might later discover a cloud over their title.[22] Black civil rights organizations were increasingly going to courts and legislatures in efforts to bring the covenants to an end. In 1943, a Jewish municipal court judge in Chicago had called them unconstitutional but was overruled by a higher court,[23] and two bills against race restrictive covenants failed to pass the Illinois state legislature in 1944 due to strong opposition from real estate interests.[24]

There was, of course, no comparison between the top-down, state-organized Nazi ghetto and the Chicago ghetto, built from the bottom up by citizens and realtors, but the restrictive covenant brought the technology of barbed wire to the minds of some blacks, including Cayton.[25] Barbed wire, made of sharp points of wire wrapped perpendicularly at regular intervals around two strands of twisted wire, was an unsophisticated and highly visible technique. Its presence announced that the people it enclosed were being incarcerated against their will. By contrast, the restrictive covenant was invisible to the eye and created the illusory impression that the segregation it created was based on happenstance, market forces, or individual preferences. Whereas the construction of a barbed-wire fence or the bombing of a home were public acts, a restrictive covenant could only be detected by its overall results— unless you were a black family that was trying to buy the "wrong" house.

In Chicago, over 80 percent of the deed restrictions applied to individuals with at least one great-grandparent of black stock, while 10 percent restricted anyone with a black great-great-grandparent.[26] These covenants were the means of realizing white aspirations for racial purity in their neighborhoods. For this reason too, the analogy with Nazi aspirations for Caucasian purity came readily to mind for some blacks.

The covenants, violence, and racial steering created territorial restriction and led to overcrowding and misery in black neighborhoods. With the shortage of housing for blacks, buildings began to be used beyond their capacity. When one-family homes were converted into rooming houses and larger apartments into multiple one-, two-, and three-room units, these conversions accelerated property depreciation.[27] Ironically, the decay of housing caused by the restrictive covenants

helped convince whites that blacks were incompetent tenants and
homeowners. The invisibility of the agreements led whites and even
some blacks to believe that this was the natural way of life for blacks,
and that any neighborhood into which they moved would deteriorate.[28]

Cayton's criticism of restrictive covenants touched on an issue affecting
many large cities, including Detroit, Los Angeles, Baltimore, Washington, and Philadelphia. Interestingly, however, in both the North and the
South, some neighborhoods became black despite covenants. In Harlem,
for example, early efforts to use the restrictive covenant had failed
as "the colored invasion [went] merrily along"[29] and blacks settled in
increasingly larger sections of the neighborhood. Only after blacks tried
to move out of Harlem into Washington Heights did restrictive covenants become effective.

During World War II, when new construction came to a virtual
standstill, blacks' migration into Northern cities was rapidly on the rise,
thus intensifying the housing shortages they faced. The restrictive
covenant, along with intimidation and racial steering, hemmed them
in, obstructing their movement into surrounding blocks.[30] Those with
the potential for upward mobility stayed in place, creating districts
where diverse Negro populations typically lived side by side: "the re-
spectable and the disreputable, the moderately well-to-do and the very
poor, the pious and the unsaved, the college graduates and the illiterates, the dusky blacks, the medium browns, the light creams, all thrown
together because all are Negroes."[31]

During this era, the two largest concentrations of urban blacks
could be found on Chicago's South Side and in New York's Harlem. In
part because of their being demographically conspicuous, they attracted
vast numbers of studies. This research examined what happened when
poor blacks moved into census tracts, focusing on the consequent subdivision of property, as well as effects such as white flight, overcrowding,
housing deterioration, and declining home values.[32]

All the same, 75 percent of blacks still resided in the South, and all
the attention to New York and Chicago could disguise certain regional
variations in their living conditions.[33] In the rural South, black tenant
families tended to live apart from white tenant families. In white small

towns, black residential communities could typically be found on the edges, where blacks had usually lived since the Civil War. In a number of Southern cities such as Durham, North Carolina, black neighborhoods were demarked by physical barriers such as railroad tracks or waterways. But more commonly, Southern cities that came into their own after the Civil War, such as Atlanta, Memphis, and Birmingham, featured all-black neighborhoods with additional smaller concentrations of blacks scattered throughout the city. In Atlanta, for example, most blacks resided in two predominantly black wards, with one-third of the city's ninety thousand blacks dispersed in small concentrations among white neighborhoods. As these cities grew at a manageable pace, blacks moved into new construction rather than into older, dilapidated housing that had been vacated by whites. This led to far less overcrowding than existed in either older Southern cities or Northern ones. Meanwhile, in Baltimore and Washington, blacks did not live in their own neighborhoods but were scattered throughout the cities in proximity to whites. This type of "backyard residence pattern," as it was known in these cities, made particular sense in places where blacks were employed in domestic service and other work that required easy access to white neighborhoods. In Washington, whites would frequently reside on one side of the street with blacks on the other.[34]

The South Side of Chicago and Harlem were more than twice as populous as black neighborhoods in Atlanta and Northern cities such as Cleveland and Pittsburgh. In addition to their size, what made New York and Chicago stand out were the unprecedented adjustments they were undergoing in the face of a mass migration of impoverished and uneducated rural blacks.

By the forties, the situations in the Northern cities varied significantly as well. The most segregated populations could be found in Chicago, where 86 percent of the city's blacks lived in majority-black neighborhoods, and in New York, where 70 percent lived in Harlem. Each of these cities also contained other large, less segregated black communities. The cities with the largest black communities tended to be the most segregated, but with clear exceptions. In Philadelphia, for example, only 55 percent of blacks lived in primarily black neighborhoods, while in Boston, with the country's twelfth-largest black population, only 37 percent did. Yet despite such variations among cities, a state-of-the-art demographic study concluded, "A high degree of residential segregation typified every city with a sizable Negro population."[35] It took some time before all of them moved in the direction of Chicago's and New York's segregation, but they did.

Ten blocks away from the basement of the AME church where Cayton condemned the racial covenants lay the University of Chicago campus. Cayton was one of the many graduate students drawn to the school by Robert E. Park, the leading figure of its renowned Department of Sociology. Park had originally been a newspaper reporter for the *Minneapolis Star*, but left journalism to obtain a doctorate at the University of Heidelberg. Upon his return to the United States, he worked for seven years as assistant to Booker T. Washington at the Tuskegee Institute, where he grew skeptical of the potential of social activism.[36]

Park questioned the validity of abstractions about society made at a distance from the everyday activities of people and communities. For this reason, he sent his students out into neighborhoods such as Chicago's Chinatown, Little Italy, Germantown, and Polonia (the city's Polish community) to observe everyday life firsthand. Unlike Jacob Riis, who had studied the lower classes through the lens of his working-class intermediaries (particularly the police), Park encouraged his students to get to know these communities on their own terms. Under Park's supervision, these class exercises became dissertations, then monographs, published chiefly by the University of Chicago Press. His students wrote nearly two dozen books, often with introductions by him, on life in Chicago in the 1920s and 1930s.[37] Among these works are the early classics of the sociological fieldwork tradition, including *The Gold Coast and the Slum*, *The Taxi Dance Hall*, and *The Gang*.

Park employed Darwin's model of evolutionary change occurring in ecological niches to illuminate the immigrant groups' struggle for survival in the city.[38] His theory of human ecology came close to dominating sociology in the United States. Trying to elevate sociology to a science by introducing generalizable concepts and metaphors derived from plant ecology, Park believed he could better explain how populations distributed themselves in the physical spaces of a city and how those spaces interacted with others in the urban system.[39]

Human ecologists of the time regarded the city as a kind of organism that was neither designed nor controlled by man. Hills and rivers, transportation lines, highways, and economic necessity significantly determined how populations initially arranged themselves in neighborhoods and communities. Within each city, neighborhoods would then develop through processes of selection, in a way that corresponded not to official administrative units, but to the functions necessary to sustain the life of any large group. According to the Chicago School, every large city had its central business district, vice zone, "hoboemia," the equivalent of a Chinatown, and a Jewish ghetto, none of which, however, normally corresponded to city wards, school districts, or census tracts. Birds of a feather flocked together in what were referred to as "natural areas"; this was thought to be the result of competition, domination, invasion, and succession, much as Darwinian evolution specified for natural systems. The great power of natural forces, as opposed to man-made intentions, was a major theme of Park's writing, leading him to believe that social activism had severe limits in bringing about significant change, at least in the short term.[40]

Park's colleague Ernest Burgess divided up the city into well-known concentric zones. As he saw it, land values were highest in the central business district, where the largest number of people came together from different locations to shop and work. Land speculators usually bought up the buildings adjacent to the central business district with the expectation that businesses would expand outward. These speculators, concerned mainly with future value, left the buildings to deteriorate and to be occupied by immigrants and black migrants from the South. This "zone in transition" became the site of slums and ghettos, which provided cheap housing for migrants, who wanted to be close to expanding industry. But the invasion of neighborhoods by factories meant that traditional community institutions disintegrated, and with them social control. This was exacerbated because migrant groups, whether immigrants from Europe or blacks from the South, arrived with old-world cultural and social backgrounds, which were very different from those found in the city. Social controls also broke down in the face of the very different expectations that greeted them.[41] The zones of the city, including these ghettos, evolved as part of a dynamic adaptive system. As each group improved its situation, it moved to a new zone, farther from the center, opening up space in the transitional zone for new arrivals.

Stressing the importance of one particular ecological niche or another, sociologists in this tradition emphasized the impact of a neighborhood's characteristics on the people who lived there. Those characteristics were thought to exert effects independent of the characteristics of the people who moved into them. This approach was adopted by the Chicago School's most prominent criminologist, Clifford Shaw, whose 1929 book *Delinquency Areas* demonstrated that neighborhoods near Chicago's Loop, the stockyards, and the steel mills had had high rates of delinquency for many generations, despite the constant succession of different races and nationalities.[42] Shaw further discovered that when delinquents were found in neighborhoods with low crime rates, they tended to have originally become delinquent while living in neighborhoods with high rates.[43] Thus, the impact of living in a disorganized neighborhood as a child had long-term consequences. The case for what sociologists now call "neighborhood effects" seemed strong.

Even as the Chicago School became well-known for highlighting the community as a unit of social control or disorganization, its followers also pioneered a new way of understanding the formation of neighborhoods by distinguishing between areas of "first" and "second" settlement. In the beginning, all migrants (regardless of education or occupation or ability) might end up in the same neighborhood. But that was only the start of the story. The Chicago School sociologists spent much time thinking about how migrant populations differentiated themselves when moving into areas of second settlement. As Park wrote, "The keener, the more energetic and the more ambitious . . . move into an area of second immigrant settlement, or perhaps into a cosmopolitan area in which the members of several immigrant or racial groups meet and live side by side."[44]

The first generation of the Chicago School saw little difference between the experiences of blacks and other migrants when they first settled in a city, and even when they tried to move out of the areas of initial settlement.[45] But by the late 1920s it was becoming increasingly clear that the situation for blacks was different, due to strong anti-black racism and the violence that accompanied it. Even then, the early

Chicago School did not fully take into account the restrictions blacks faced on account of their race. These early sociologists paid more attention to how blacks, like others, differentiated themselves into particular zones on the basis of occupation or ability than they did to the external pressures that kept them in one contiguous area, or the impact of particular community conditions upon them.

This emphasis was also adopted by the school's first prominent black student, who had preceded Cayton at the university, E. Franklin Frazier. His dissertation, *The Negro Family in Chicago* (1932), focused on segregation *within* the black community. While aware of distinctive disadvantages faced by black urbanites, Frazier believed that the fundamental sociological problem was urbanism itself. Reflecting a common thread of sociological thinking of the time, both in the United States and abroad, Frazier thought that the city led to a loss of social control and an increase in social deviance ranging from family desertion to criminality. He saw wide variation in deviant activity within the different zones of the black community as well as between the black districts and the rest of the city. He could have attributed the variation to the neighborhoods in which different populations of blacks lived, as well as to the general tendency for their neighborhoods to be excluded from many patterns of urban life. Instead, his explanation hinged almost entirely on what he considered the preexisting cultural and economic characteristics of migrants themselves. What mattered most was not the contrasting features of neighborhoods, but the characteristics of the people who chose to live in one versus another. Providing an alternative to this view became increasingly important to subsequent generations of sociologists.

As an undergraduate at the University of Washington, Cayton had aspired to become one of Park's protégés in Chicago. When Park visited Seattle in 1930, the chair of the UW sociology department, Roderick McKenzie, who himself had studied with Park, introduced Cayton to the great scholar. When Cayton told Park that he was interested in Negro history, Park replied that Negroes didn't have any history. Incensed, Cayton retorted, "Everything has a history, even the chair I am sitting in," and walked out of the room.

Despite his resolve never to meet with Park again, Cayton applied and enrolled in the doctoral program at the University of Chicago in the fall of 1931. Not long after his arrival, he ventured into Park's office and was greeted with open arms. According to Cayton's later account, Park had simply been testing Cayton in Seattle. In Chicago, the two embarked on a lifelong friendship.[46]

Cayton, described by one sociologist of the time as "jovial, charming, and clever,"[47] inserted himself at the center of the intellectual life of the sociology department. During his first few years in the department, he coauthored a book on blacks and labor unions with an economist at Columbia University. He also worked as an assistant for the political scientist Harold Gosnell and did much of the research for what would become Gosnell's minor classic, *Negro Politicians*, though he received no credit for his contribution.[48] Afterward, he sought the tutelage of two other key figures, W. Lloyd Warner and Louis Wirth. Warner, a social anthropologist, had moved from Harvard to Chicago after conducting important community studies on social inequality in the United States. In the late thirties, he invited Cayton to direct a new study sponsored by the federal Works Project Administration on black neighborhoods in Chicago. Realizing that a study of the entire black community would seem unreasonably large, Warner had limited his request to the WPA to a study of juvenile delinquency. However, once he had the money, he and Cayton guided the project toward studying the social structure of the entire black community as well as its relationship to the city.[49] Cayton led a team of between 150 and 200 interviewers supervised by twenty graduate students who ran the project out of a church basement on the South Side.[50]

The researchers were not, in the main, professionals, but residents who were interested in studying their own black communities.[51] They did such things as hang around public spaces to document lower-class life and attend fraternity and sorority dances to learn about the upper classes.[52] They conducted nearly ten thousand interviews and collected huge amounts of historical and statistical data.[53] The project exemplified the unique fieldwork-based approach to the study of black life in the United States that Park had envisioned.

Louis Wirth, Cayton's other mentor, had been an early protégé of Park's. In 1928, as a young German Jewish emigrant doctoral student at the University of Chicago, Wirth wrote *The Ghetto,* one of the first dissertations in the discipline of sociology as it was emerging in the United States. Wirth argued that while the ghetto was an instrument of control and isolation, it could also be viewed as a form of toleration in which a minority group subordinates itself to the majority.[54] Although the ghetto was thereby unequal, its inhabitants always found life more interesting inside its walls than on the outside.[55] Wirth appreciated the ghetto for its religious and cultural vigor. He emphasized how geographic and social isolation offered a refuge for the Jew in an anti-Semitic world.[56] "Without the backing of his group, without the security that he enjoyed in his inner circle of friends and countrymen, life would have been intolerable."[57] All of it was ultimately nurtured by the strong family life to be found in the ghetto. Wirth urged his readers not to place so much emphasis on the confinement of ghetto life and dismiss the "ideals, aspirations, and passions" that could also be found there.[58] In ghettos from Frankfurt to Prague to Vienna to Rome to Venice, one could find a population flourishing in commerce and banking, literature, music, and philosophy.

Yet Wirth was deeply ambivalent about the ghetto. He feared that it "aroused the worst passions of non-Jewish demagogues" and caused Jews to be discriminated against as a separate body.[59] As a self-described "assimilationist," Wirth saw in the ghetto's history a cautionary tale about the dangers of remaining isolated from the rest of society. At the same time, he recognized that overly hasty integration could also trigger racial hostility, and he went so far as to refer to the high intermarriage rates he saw in both Berlin and Chicago as alarming.[60] But he wished above all to show the European and American Jews of his time what could happen if they did not assimilate, quoting the prominent Cincinnati rabbi David Philipson: "How to break these up and disperse their denizens over the surface of this broad, fair land, and make them self supporting, self respecting citizens, is the great problem now pressing for solution."[61]

For Wirth, the ghetto's problematic feature was its power to isolate and concentrate. The earlier European ghettos, he believed, had forged Jews into a physical and social type with even a distinct physiognomy. Confined for life in restricted physical spaces, they had inbred and developed common mannerisms. Such physical marks, which Wirth believed had both social and biological roots, became a "racial uniform" that led to the further singling out of the group. By forcing Jews to live apart, their enemies had unintentionally "helped to develop and preserve a distinct population in their midst."[62]

This was the lasting dangerous effect of dense concentration and isolation. Although Wirth realized that the ghetto had formed partly through imposed constraints, he believed that the long-standing Jewish tendency to self-segregate contributed significantly to the group's isolation. Reiterating a common belief among his fellow sociologists at the University of Chicago, he claimed that regardless of their past, ghettos were now communities that arose from a combination of market forces and the proclivity of "birds of a feather to flock together." In sum, though fully aware of the ghetto's history, he pictured the ghettos of Chicago and New York as sites of cultural self-preservation at least for the first generation.[63]

Yet a countervailing theme of Wirth's writing on the Chicago Jews was the desire of some for mobility upward *and* outward. Unlike immigrant groups who would be depicted in later sociological works, many Jews were not held back by a sense of loyalty to their community. As soon as they got a chance, some significant number uprooted themselves from their fellow Jews. Unlike the blacks, who would later keep trying to break through restrictive covenants to the borders of existing neighborhoods, Jews moved far away from the ghetto and their fellow Jews. They, or at least their children, moved to better neighborhoods such as Rogers Park or South Shore, or surrounding suburbs, with each generation moving farther from where it started out. Nobody stayed put. Nevertheless, economic success and assimilation led to other problems. Prejudice and discrimination were rampant and, according to Wirth, the Jew's "self is divided between the world that he has deserted and the world that will have none of him."[64] Thus, although each generation was in a different position with respect to its immigrant origins, all of these generations stood in a similar relationship to the mainstream society. This realization reactivated the very consciousness that caused Jews to participate in a collective life, including often moving back to the ghetto.[65]

Wirth's book was influential on sociologists from the outset. Among historians, however, a very different discussion was emerging. In the same year that Wirth published *The Ghetto*, Salo Baron, the eminent

Columbia University historian, published his article "Ghetto and Emancipation: Shall We Revise the Traditional View?"[66] Although Baron did not refer to Wirth's book, he made a full-scale assault on all those whose "belief in the efficacy of a process of complete assimilation has been proved untenable."[67] Since he believed that Jews had, in many respects, been better off with "a full, rounded life" in the ghetto, he concluded that assimilation was not in their interest.[68]

Wirth saw the ghetto as a concept that could apply to other isolated ethnic and racial groups in the contemporary city. Until this point, the term "slum" had been used to describe impoverished neighborhoods with run-down tenement housing. But in the lexicon of the Chicago sociologists, the slum was always associated with individualism and communal social disorganization. For at least a generation prior to World War II, the general view was that the social life of slums had disintegrated, with "community institutions ceasing to function."[69] While Wirth used the words "ghetto" and "slum" interchangeably at times, he was clear that the ghetto had not disintegrated. "Life was well organized, and custom and ritual played an organizing and institutionalizing role, which still accounts for the high degree of organization of Jewish communities, often verging on overorganization, and the persistence of old, outworn institutions long after their *raison d'être* has ceased to operate."[70] He left it an open question whether other ethnic neighborhoods were also well organized, though he claimed that the Italians, Poles, Chinese, and even blacks moved into their neighborhoods for the same reasons as the Jews did.[71]

Indeed, the very generality of the concept of the ghetto was what interested Wirth, in addition to the substantive fascination offered by the Chicago of his time. Aspiring to help make sociology a social science on a par with natural science, Wirth introduced the ghetto as a concept that could be applied to cases from the Middle Ages to his own day. "Chicago's ghetto is younger than that of New York," he wrote, "just as the New York ghetto is a mere upstart compared with that of Frankfort; but the characteristics of the ghetto are not to be measured by the years that a given area has been inhabited by Jews. The ghetto, no matter where it is located, has a long history, and is based upon old traditions of which the American ghetto is a mere continuation—a last scene of the final act."[72] For scholars of the 1920s, those acts began with the Middle Ages, including the most famous instance, the Jewish quarter of Frankfurt. Wirth devoted an entire chapter of *The Ghetto* to it on the grounds that what had happened there could be said to typify the history of all Western European ghettos.[73] He used the history of the Frankfurt Jews to illustrate his larger sociological conclusion, one with clear implications for the situation of Jews in America during the 1920s: their district, known as the Judengasse, originally came into being to meet the needs of the Jews for a communal life. Over time the Jews had built "invisible walls" around themselves; they only came to resent their insular life when it became compulsory.[74]

Wirth's account emphasizes and takes for granted the ghetto's voluntary origins. It focuses on how Jews separated themselves from the rest of society, and how residual social contact with Gentiles in Frankfurt led to frictions that brought about more stringent and compulsory forms of segregation. This image of the ghetto served as a convenient historical example for Wirth because he believed that Chicago's Polish and Russian Jewish ghetto was in similar danger of separating itself from the city's general population by building invisible walls around itself.

Yet Wirth's characterization of the Frankfurt Judengasse is highly questionable. In the Middle Ages, a small but significant number of laws governing daily life were passed by Church councils and major assemblies constituted of bishops and prelates. One of the most important of these was the Council of Basel, beginning in 1431, which issued the directive that Jews "should be made to live in designated communities or cities, which are divided from the residences, and which are located as far away as possible from churches."[75]

In the preceding century, Jews had been encouraged by the city council to move back to Frankfurt. Although they could not hold office or join the military and were forced to pay an annual "Jew tax" for living in the city, they had been permitted to conduct business, associate with Christians, and live among them. Most Jews chose to live in a particular neighborhood, but many Christians lived there as well, including, from 1364 to 1374, the mayor. A considerable number of Jews lived outside the Jewish neighborhood, in other zones of the city.

One would not know from Wirth's account of the Judengasse's history that it was brought about by much larger social institutional forces that transcended the city of Frankfurt, rather than any particular social interactions within Frankfurt itself. For the Council of Basel had called for the segregation of Jews everywhere, and the city of Frankfurt had essentially ignored the edict for nearly a decade. Only in 1442, when King Frederick IV visited the city and discovered that the separation had not taken place, did he demand that Jews be isolated. So clear evidence exists that separation was indeed imposed on the Jews, but not a trace of real evidence—in the histories used by Wirth or in the Frankfurt archives I have consulted—indicates a self-imposed isolation.[76]

Why, then, did sociologists so readily believe Wirth and allow his account to become the received wisdom of the field? Political motivations to read the past through the lens of the present may have been in play. Many American sociologists supported the assimilationist project. As with other German Jews, Wirth sought to emphasize that throughout history Jews had suffered most when they failed to integrate. He was bent on showing that American Jewish ghettos shared a predicament with the principal ghettos of Europe. They too, he believed, began as voluntary and were at risk of becoming involuntary.[77] Wirth was a member of a generation of Jewish intellectuals who worried that impoverished and culturally isolated but voluntary ghettos in cities from Warsaw to Chicago might threaten Jewish security and acceptance. The ghetto grouped poor and unassimilated Russian, Polish, and Romanian Jews together in dilapidated quarters. It also created and preserved opinions and forms of behavior and dress that differentiated Jews from their Christian neighbors. Jews everywhere were associated with these peculiar traits and poor conditions, and were also judged by them. In short, the ghetto deepened differences and incited animosity. In Wirth's opinion, ghettos were a problem Jews had brought on themselves; they were a menace that had to be eradicated.

Wirth was wrong to argue for a causal connection between the existence of "voluntary" Jewish quarters or local frictions and the later emergence of involuntary ghettos. Some cases may have fit his argument. But he barely mentioned anti-Semitism and missed the real story: a society that thought it could live with Jews by imposing regulations on them became a society whose fear of Jews was so great that it deemed such regulations insufficient and segregation the only means to avoid danger.

The idea most relevant to the black ghetto was thus not that when a people enact their own separation, it creates enforced exclusion, but instead that separation—and stigma—arise from outsider hatred and organized forces. Those forces typically transcend the local, whether Frankfurt in the case of Jews or Chicago in the case of blacks. Besides the heritage of official slavery and Jim Crow in the South, modern Chicago was formed through the racist exclusionary policies of neighborhood improvement associations, anti-black federal housing programs, court rulings, and national real estate organizations. The facts of Frankfurt's history would have been more useful than the Wirthian fictions for scholars who, like Cayton, were trying to understand the U.S. racial situation. And even within the United States, Jews themselves experienced the kind of denigration that helped keep their neighborhoods at least somewhat segregated. It was well-known at Cayton's time that when a Jewish family moved into a neighborhood, the houses next door and across the street would immediately go on sale and get purchased by other Jewish families.[78]

The experiences of other immigrant groups, first and foremost the Chinese, would also have been of interest to blacks trying to understand their midcentury ghettos. Residents of Chinatowns found themselves in oversupply after the completion of the transcontinental railroad in 1869. Yet, as had been the case with black migrants from the South to the North, the flow of immigrants from China continued. Cries on all sides led to the Exclusion Act of 1882. As early as 1892, a federal court in California recognized the legality of a San Francisco agreement not to rent to a "Chinaman or Chinamen."[79] The need to seek safety within the boundaries of the community was impressed on the few new immigrants by frequent stonings of Chinese as they walked up Washington or Clay Street from the piers.[80] White toughs in nearby North Beach or downtown Union Square also amused themselves by assaulting the Chinese who wandered into their neighborhoods by chance.[81] The Chinese could not buy houses outside of Chinatown until 1947, when some wealthier members of the community escaped their dense and overcrowded precinct and established a suburb in the nearby districts of Sunset and Richmond.[82] The 1920 census reveals that 41 percent of the total Chinese population in America at the time was wedged into tightly defined neighborhoods in San Francisco, New York, Oakland, Chicago, Los Angeles, Portland, Seattle, and Boston, the remainder living in small towns and rural areas. Although the Chinese were the first racial group to be forcibly segregated by restrictive covenants, early social scientists essentially ignored the group when searching for a conceptual apparatus to understand the black experience.

Along with the Jews and the Chinese, the most studied American immigrant slum dwellers were the Italians, particularly the southern Italians, whose dark skins elicited treatment resembling that doled out to blacks. They were regarded by many whites, including some sociologists, as an inferior race. In the 1940s, Italians were on the minds of many of Cayton's colleagues and professors in the University of Chicago sociology department because they were the subject of a remarkable doctoral dissertation written by one of Cayton's classmates, William Foote Whyte. Whyte had endeavored to show that even where family life did not conform to the middle-class norm, poor immigrant communities were highly organized. His dissertation, *Street Corner Society: The Social Structure of an Italian Slum* (1943), would become a sociological classic when it was published, but it perturbed Louis Wirth, who was one of the professors on Whyte's dissertation committee. Perhaps Wirth saw in Whyte's manuscript, in the title itself, a problem for his own theory of slum neighborhoods. Wirth saw slums such as the Italian North End of Boston as very different from the highly organized Jewish ghettos. The idea that they had any "social structure" at all ran counter to an emphasis on the slum as beset by internal social dysfunctions that, reasonably enough, the majority culture needed to restrict and keep under control. Whyte would later recall that Wirth began his questioning at the final dissertation hearing by asking him to define a slum. The goal was to show that Whyte could not actually do so without referring to social disorganization. But Whyte refused to fall into that trap and insisted that a slum "was simply an urban area where there was a high concentration of low income people living in dilapidated housing and under poor sanitary and health conditions."[83] How organized or disorganized it was could only be determined case by case, Whyte argued.

Whyte's point was that not all impoverished and congested areas with substandard housing were alike. In Cornerville, the pseudonymously named Boston neighborhood that he studied, the southern Italians were packed together in tiny apartments that could only contain them when they slept. Among themselves, the residents and shopkeepers kept up a vital system of material and psychological mutual support. Their vibrant street life was linked to the integrative functions of an active political machine and, as was well noted both internally and by outsiders, the world of organized crime. However disreputable, such linkages were crucial to the group's upward mobility, and also functional for sustaining internal social order.

This was the main story that generations of readers would take from Whyte's account of an organized slum. Yet buried within his book was an account of Italian slum life that received little note. Whyte showed that by the 1940s, Cornerville had also taken on the characteristics of a colony. The teachers, social workers, and settlement workers who came there every day were neighborhood outsiders who looked down on the great masses of Italians. As Doc, his leading subject, tells Whyte at the end of *Street Corner Society*:

You don't know how it feels to grow up in a district like this. You go to the first grade—Miss O'Rourke. Second grade—Miss Casey. Third grade—Miss Chalmers. Fourth grade—Miss Mooney. And so on. At the fire station it is the same. None of them are Italians. The police lieutenant is an Italian, and there are a couple of Italian sergeants, but they have never made an Italian captain in Cornerville. In the settlement houses, none of the people with authority are Italians.

Now you must know that old-timers here have a great respect for schoolteachers and anybody like that. When the Italian boy sees that none of his own people have the good jobs, why should he think he is as good as the Irish or the Yankees? It makes him feel inferior.

If I had my way, I would have half the schoolteachers Italians and three quarters of the people in the settlement. Let the other quarter be there just to show that we're in America.

Bill, those settlement houses were necessary at first. When

our parents landed here, they didn't know where to go or what to do. They needed the social workers for intermediaries. They did a fine job then, but now the second generation is growing up, and we're beginning to sprout wings. They should take that net off and let us fly.[84]

Cornerville's inhabitants experienced their neighborhood as an outpost of the wider society, one in which they were rendered dependent on the WASPs and the Irish and denied the opportunity to be in charge of their own destiny.[85] So continuities existed between the black ghetto to come and the Italian quarters as depicted by scholars such as Whyte. But there were also sharp differences. Whyte's main story focused on the struggles of individuals who were forced to choose between loyalty to the group and upward mobility as a generational transition lured them away from the slum. Thinking in terms of the more limited opportunities for blacks, this problem is a luxury. If an Italian made it out, he or she received recognition in the wider society but became an alien in the local community. This dilemma and therefore the category of "slum" itself was of limited conceptual value to blacks in that era, since, no matter how successful, they could not move out of their restricted neighborhoods. The Chicago School model, in which immigrants assimilated freely if they wanted to—that for each group, their time would come— had no meaningful conception of racism.[86]

By the time Cayton spoke to local black citizens at the Woodlawn church, he had been questioning whether black communities resembled any of the immigrant neighborhoods that had been described by Park, Wirth, and their students. His challenge to the Chicago School also asked whether black communities, like the immigrant slums, occurred naturally through voluntary or quasi-voluntary forces. Cayton's challenge soon grew even more pointed—and became more explicitly political—as an inconvenient fact dawned on him: the University of Chicago was backing restrictive covenants, and its researchers were consequently indirectly complicit in the misery that they themselves were documenting.

The small strip of land known as Chicago's Black Belt was bound by Sixty-Seventh Street on the south and Twelfth Street on the north. Restrictive covenants financially backed by the university encircled the area on three sides, with State Street on the west and Cottage Grove Avenue on the east marking the beginning of white neighborhoods. Just east of the Black Belt, and enclosed on the opposite side by Lake Michigan, stood the University of Chicago and its properties.[87]

Many South Side residents assumed the university's role in race restrictive covenants enjoyed general white support. For them, that role came as no surprise, and the university's actions have been documented by later historical research.[88] Through his interactions with the area's blacks, Cayton discovered that they already viewed the university as antagonistic and unfair in its attitudes and actions. Among the well-known reasons that South Side residents resented the university were that its medical school had accepted only one black student in the recent past and that black medical graduates had been forced to do their internships in secondary hospitals outside the university's system. The school's open and flagrant refusal to admit black patients to its medical center (save the emergency room) was also a point of contention.[89] To make matters worse, the university's hospital was routinely accused of overcharging blacks for its medical services in the emergency room.

A more important issue for Cayton, however, was that the university seemed to feel that its mission was inextricably linked to preserving white demographic dominance in its local neighborhood, Hyde Park, from blacks wishing to escape the densely packed and degraded Black Belt nearby. Cayton believed that the overcrowding caused by the restrictive covenants led not only to the juvenile delinquency that his and Warner's WPA study was documenting, but also to the impoverishment of local residents caused by higher rents and limits on their access to good medical care.

Cayton's discussions with Wirth focused on the university's role, and for that he had chosen the right person. After publishing his study of ghettos in history, Wirth had gone on to become a liberal activist in Chicago. He helped run the American Council on Race Relations, which was dedicated to alleviating both racial tensions and black poverty.[90] Unbeknownst to Cayton, Wirth had been privately struggling over black housing with the university's administration since the mid-thirties, when its real estate department had consulted its urban sociologists on what to do about the growing black neighborhood gradually encroaching on the campus. After meeting with staff from this office in the winter of 1936, Wirth composed a private memorandum that questioned whether an "enlightened" university could legitimately be part of any effort to stop blacks from living wherever they wanted. Not only was it wrong, but it was destined to fail. "One unit of effort invested in aiding the Negro to obtain decent living quarters and adequate community facilities, is, it seems to me, worth ten units of effort invested in the organization of the whites in whatever subtle measures they might contrive to keep the Negro out," Wirth wrote.[91]

At the time Virginia Dobbins's house was destroyed in 1944, Robert Maynard Hutchins, the university's illustrious president, renowned for his defense of civil liberties, had long resolved to ignore Wirth. Hutchins had taken a strong dislike to him after many polemical battles over the value of the social sciences.[92] Hutchins had gone on public record in support of restrictive covenants, and he had even been forced to acknowledge that university funds were being used to maintain them.[93] The school had discreetly given financial backing to the Woodlawn Property Owners Association in particular. The secretary of the association boasted that 100 percent of the university district of Woodlawn was covered by restrictive covenants. The organization had no objections to Chinese or Japanese residents, but it had successfully excluded blacks by means of a block-by-block plan from 1941 to 1945. "We must refuse to sell to colored people, regardless of whether covenants are valid or invalid," said T. L. Lusk, president of the association. "If the colored people are convinced that life in Woodlawn would be unbearable, they would not want to move in. . . . We are going to save Woodlawn for ourselves and for our children."[94]

A pamphlet sponsored by the association and published in July 1944 rallied support for restrictive covenants on behalf of the 350,000 white Chicagoans in the armed forces. It warned of the possibility of having to greet returning white soldiers with the apologetic statement "You have won a good fight. . . . But, at the request of a very limited number of people hereabouts, we have altered your home and neighborhood conditions while you were away fighting for America. So sorry."[95]

Some of the more educated blacks whom Cayton met appeared to believe that the University of Chicago's interests and actions were so fundamentally opposed to the welfare of black citizens that its sociology department had no business overseeing a study of a local black community funded by the WPA. A letter written by the Big Brothers Association of Chicago to the federal Works Project Administration argued that the university's researchers could not "conduct any survey or render any report in such matters that would be anything other than a fraud in public information, designed to ridicule, and hold the colored citizenry up to public scorn."[96] In the eyes of these blacks, an inherent conflict of interest rendered researchers incapable of properly recognizing the University of Chicago's role in sustaining black poverty and delinquency.[97] Cayton and Wirth discussed this issue in a series of letters, and agreed that the university held that it was in its interest to maintain covenants so that it could "continue its work for mankind, unhampered by close Negro residence."[98]

Whatever validity there was to the idea that Jewish ghettos and other ethnic neighborhoods in Chicago may have been created through natural economic and social forces[99]—itself a highly contested notion[100]—the Chicago black communities we know today were not. At the time that Wirth and Park first promulgated their theories about "natural areas," the black ghetto, as it came to be known around the time of World War II, barely existed. Black neighborhoods up until then were less overwhelmingly black and were typically kept confined through acts of intimidation and violence by whites. The restrictive covenants that eventually helped create the ghetto made their first appearance in Chicago only in 1927 and 1928.[101] Wirth's 1928 book was most likely already in press, and it would take time before the impact of the covenants would be both felt and apparent. While mechanisms of intimidation were always present in some way, it was now clear to anyone, including the researchers at the university, that black settlement patterns were unnatural and based on white aspirations to racial purity. They did not resemble those of other ethnic and racial groups.

In the 1920s, these Chicago-based founders of American urban sociology may reasonably have believed that their ideas on the Jewish communities of Europe and America would help make other migrant communities, including those of blacks, intelligible, and that these ideas might encourage more humane policies at both the local and the national levels. They could scarcely have foreseen that one day the entire world would associate the ghetto first and foremost with compulsory holding pens for execution in Europe, and later with black neighborhoods that were neither natural nor voluntary. Furthermore, they could not have known that the scholars most responsible for the term's new meaning in the social sciences would be their black protégé, Horace Cayton, and his future coauthor, another of their black students, St. Clair Drake. As an undergraduate at Dillard University in New Orleans, Drake had worked as an assistant on another comprehensive study, *Deep South*. In the late 1930s, he came to the University of Chicago with Allison Davis, a black Chicago professor and coauthor of *Deep South*, for what was supposed to be a one-year visit but soon turned into full-time doctoral training in anthropology.[102]

The 1930s were exciting years for Cayton and Drake to be graduate students in Chicago. The South Side was home to a wide-ranging intellectual life within the black community. There, they might one day make the acquaintance of a struggling young black man on the cusp of becoming an internationally famous author and, on the next, meet a gangster who was a hero to the ghetto's masses for turning illegally earned profits into legitimate businesses. The links between the University of Chicago and the surrounding ghetto were often surprising.

Take the case of Richard Wright. In 1936, when the aspiring novelist sought to cope with the Great Depression by registering for poor relief, the social worker assigned to his case was Mary Wirth, the wife of Louis Wirth. Mrs. Wirth came home to her husband one evening with a glowing report about the young writer and arranged for them to meet. Wirth was out the day that Wright came knocking, but he was welcomed by Horace Cayton, who was working in the office and cordially invited him inside.[103]

Wright had no publications or credentials to recommend him. He had been unemployed for months and was struggling to support himself and his mother on meager public assistance. Though Cayton was technically a graduate student, he had been running the large WPA-sponsored study of the Black Belt for several years. According to Wright, Cayton enthusiastically showed him some of the maps, tables, and statistical information that Cayton's team was compiling on life in black Chicago, and Wright left intrigued by the study and impressed by its scope and depth. The meeting would lead to an important friendship that shaped Cayton's greatest successes and failures in the years to come.

Or take the day in 1937 when thousands of people crowded the streets on the South Side of Chicago for the opening of Jones Boys' Store, one of the first black department stores in the United States. This was significant not merely because it turned a black who'd opened a successful store into something of a hero, but also because the Jones brothers had made their money in the so-called policy rackets. Now, after decades of being known for running the largest gambling operations in the United States, they were attempting to achieve respectability in the formal economy.

Outside the store that day, Cayton observed crowds of ordinary citizens and celebrities, including the boxer Joe Louis and the dancer Bill (Bojangles) Robinson. He had reason to feel more than mere sociological interest in what he observed. Over the past several years, he had developed a personal relationship with the Jones brothers. Although it is well-known to this day that his study of the South Side was funded by the grant Warner received from the federal government's Works Project Administration, as little as 25 percent of the money may actually have come from that source. Cayton was constantly desperate for more income for a project that had become much larger than anyone had anticipated, and the racketeer Jones brothers became important sponsors. Indeed, had it not been for the mob money (including additional funds from J. Livert [St. Louis] Kelly, president of the waiters and bartenders union, who was known to prey on union people and legitimate businesses), Cayton's project might have come to a very different end.[104] He could possibly have lost control of his research materials to the Swedish economist Gunnar Myrdal and never written the book that established his reputation.

Gunnar Myrdal's name does not come up very much in social science courses today. Yet from the end of World War II through the 1970s, no scholar was more influential in the field. Myrdal's massive study of racial inequality, *An American Dilemma*, was sponsored by the Carnegie

Corporation, a foundation created by the industrialist Andrew Carnegie with a long history of supporting important studies on pressing social issues. Its grant to Myrdal was one of the largest ever given by any foundation to a single social scientific study. The book he produced would for decades be considered the definitive statement on racial problems in the United States.[105] Even his most relentless critic, Oliver Cox, a black Marxist sociologist who believed that Myrdal had only skimmed the surface of the race problem's causes, acknowledged, "As a source of information and brilliant interpretation of information on race relations in the United States, it is probably unsurpassed."[106]

Published as American blacks were fighting with the Allies against the Nazis, *An American Dilemma* appeared at a time when many believed the world was looking closely at how the United States was dealing with its own racial problems. In the Cold War years that followed, racial tensions in the North increased after soldiers came home to compete for jobs. The existing system of Jim Crow in the South further damaged the country's reputation. Communist propaganda made effective use of this situation, particularly since the United States had depended on the loyalty of black servicemen and factory workers during the war.

As an economist, Myrdal seemed well suited to analyze what appeared to be one of the most pressing issues facing American blacks: unemployment and discrimination in the workplace. The Carnegie Corporation endeavored to legitimize the project by appointing a foreigner to achieve a detachment that could not be assumed from a U.S. citizen, black or white. It sought a modern-day Tocqueville who would show that Americans could only learn certain truths from foreigners.[107]

The Carnegie Corporation had a long-standing policy of asking outsiders to write reports. Accordingly, in this instance too they sought a person from a country with high scholarly standards but no history of imperialism that might make blacks suspect that the study was not impartial.[108] Myrdal began *An American Dilemma* with a statement on his status as an outsider who had never lived in a black-white society, and who "being a stranger to the problem . . . had perhaps a greater awareness of the extent to which human valuations everywhere enter into our scientific discussion of the Negro problem."[109]

By choosing a Swedish economist, the Carnegie Corporation explicitly overlooked more knowledgeable black and white American scholars such as, for example, E. Franklin Frazier, the black chair of Howard University's sociology department, who had devoted themselves to studying racial problems in both the South and the North.[110]

Myrdal was uneasy. Although he believed that he could bring critical distance to the problem, he also realized that insiders' highly privileged access to knowledge was crucial to the realization of the project. He therefore proposed to the foundation that it form a committee consisting of "a Southern White, a Northern White, and a Negro" so that different viewpoints would be represented.[111]

The Carnegie Corporation officers did not see the advantages of insider knowledge; indeed, they felt that any involvement of insiders would result in "side glances as to what was politically desirable and expedient."[112] Thus instead of agreeing to the committee, they promised Myrdal that he would be able to recruit academic assistants representing different perspectives. With massive resources at his disposal and not a little hubris, Myrdal hired some of the most accomplished black and white scholars in the country to assist him.

Horace Cayton was among the few social scientists asked to join the project who did not have a doctorate or professorial appointment. Cayton's involvement in the project has not been systematically addressed in the historical literature. In his magisterial biography, *Gunnar Myrdal and America's Conscience*, the historian Walter A. Jackson mentions Cayton briefly, noting that he had "failed to turn in [to Myrdal] a promised memorandum on the social structure of the Negro group."[113] Jackson does not discuss the matter further, although he suggests that Cayton's failure to hand in the draft deprived Myrdal of key insights into the black lower classes.

Why did Myrdal, who had the nation's leading social scientists at his disposal, care about the contribution of this particular graduate student? And why did Cayton fail to complete the contribution he had allegedly promised to this prestigious study?

At the time Myrdal began his collaborative work, many thought that his chances of succeeding would be much improved if he could recruit some of the Chicago sociologists. He could have gone directly to

Robert Park, then the leading scholar on race in the United States. But Park's view, as one of his students summarized it, was that "the city is curiously resistant to the fiats of man. Like the robot, created by man, it goes its own way, indifferent to the will of its creator."[114] This idea that social life was a function of gradual, natural processes was not well suited to Myrdal's endeavor. Anticipating a new era, the Carnegie project was based on the idea that institutions could use systematic knowledge to effect social transformation. The Chicago sociologists were invested in creating a science, but not an applied science that would intervene in the world.

Myrdal wanted access to the Chicago School, with all its accumulated knowledge about black Americans in their local environment, without having to buy into its founder's laissez-faire framework of social change. During the early years of the study, Myrdal did not feel entirely comfortable with Chicago's other senior scholars. He asked Wirth for a report, but also expressed his distrust of him in confidential memos.[115] Among the blacks whom Myrdal invited to join his staff were some of Park's best students, such as Charles Johnson, a distinguished sociologist at Fisk University who had written the report on the 1919 Chicago race riot for the Chicago Commission on Race Relations.[116] Both Johnson and Cayton had by now shown signs of discomfort with Park's view of social change as a natural process, as attested by Cayton's activism and Johnson's comment that "it is not enough merely to wait watchfully for time's slow solution of social ills. . . . There are steps that can be taken immediately to correct the old ills."[117]

By extending an invitation to Cayton, Myrdal sought access to an additional aspect of Park's intellectual legacy, namely, his and the Chicago School's focus on the impact of community life and physical space on social interaction and social outcomes. Myrdal was determined to get hold of the fourteen monographs that formed part of the Warner-Cayton research project on the South Side and asked in his letter that Cayton bring as much of the Chicago material as possible.[118] Since massive WPA funding and research time had gone into preparing the material, Myrdal knew that it was an exceptional treasure trove, not least because it was unpublished. If he could obtain it, particularly before it was published elsewhere, he could document the culture of daily life and interactions in a Northern city within his broader examination of American race relations and thus add immeasurable depth to his book.

Myrdal should have had a leg up in hiring Cayton, and not only because Cayton was always broke and trying to hustle money to keep the WPA-sponsored project alive. Cayton and Myrdal had already developed a friendly if fleeting rapport in 1933 when Cayton paid a visit to Stockholm. They were introduced by a Swedish classmate of Cayton's from the University of Chicago who had been traveling with him. During that visit, the student arranged for them to have dinner at Myrdal's home. Later, in the United States, Myrdal learned from the Carnegie Corporation that Cayton had done credible research and had completed all requirements for his Ph.D. at Chicago save his dissertation.[119] Myrdal was also told that while Cayton had effectively run the Good Shepherd Community Center, where he had office space and secretarial assistance, he had no research money to turn his voluminous materials on the South Side into a book.[120] Myrdal therefore expected that Cayton would be interested in working as a member of the prestigious research team and receiving funding. This assumption, however, turned out to be fraught with problems.

In 1939, Myrdal offered Cayton a six-month position in the project's New York office.[121] Cayton raised a concern immediately. Myrdal's team had two types of positions: staff devoted full-time to the project, and experts enlisted to write reports on specific fields. Cayton said he was puzzled because he was assigned to neither of these categories and wouldn't have any clear responsibilities. Obviously, he told Myrdal, they just wanted him for his mass of documents, interview transcripts, and field notes.[122] He could not practically give up his apartment in Chicago, as well as his own project, to come to New York for six months. He would, however, be willing to come for a full year, provided that Myrdal paid him to write his own book while he was preparing memos for the project. Myrdal had entered into this arrangement with other, more senior white and black scholars, including Charles Johnson.

Evident from the letter exchange between the two is how badly Cayton needed the money and how well Myrdal understood this. All the same, Cayton had deep reservations about working on Myrdal's team. During the negotiations, he made clear that his own priority was to turn the materials he had collected through the WPA project into a publication that would fulfill his intellectual vision and allow him to receive full credit. Shortly after Myrdal's offer, he received a three-page letter from the New York office requesting various types of data from his WPA study. Reluctant to turn the material over, he wrote to Myrdal repeating that he would have to receive money to write a book of his own based on the materials, and that if any materials from the study were used, full credit should go to him as the program director and to the Works Project Administration as its sponsor.[123]

Between the summer of 1939 and the winter of 1940, Myrdal made several trips to Chicago, during which he tried to talk Cayton into an arrangement. Myrdal even got his wife, Alva, who later won the Nobel Peace Prize, to socialize with Cayton's wife, Bonnie. But Myrdal could not talk Cayton into budging on his demand that he also be given money to write his own book.

On February 16, 1940, Cayton went to the New York offices of the Carnegie Corporation to make a special case for the funding he would need, speaking about how broke he was. (He told Carnegie officials that he had even put most of the sixty dollars they had given him for this trip into paying the project's bills.) Emphasizing how expensive it was to run the project, he explained that he had only been able to make do by having many people only nominally on the payroll. Louis Wirth, who acted as scientific supervisor, never received a penny. Cayton spoke openly about his relations with a variety of corrupt individuals on the South Side, including the editor of *The Chicago Defender*, whom he described as a journalistic prostitute because he had demanded remuneration for publicizing the WPA study. Such publicity was necessary for interviewers to gain access to various establishments, but the publisher had stated that the *Defender* "was a business and not an educational enterprise."

All this, despite the fact that the WPA project had the publisher's wife on the research payroll. Cayton was quite open with the Carnegie Corporation about his financial straits: only 25 percent of the money for his project came from the WPA and other foundation support. The rest was donated by the community, which he acknowledged included the racketeer Jones brothers and the labor racketeer St. Louis Kelly.[124]

None of this was enough to convince Myrdal or the Carnegie officials. On February 27, 1940, an impatient Myrdal wrote Cayton to tell him that time was running short but that it was still possible to integrate the Chicago materials. He wanted Cayton to make all of the materials available as soon as possible and ended with his own inconclusive promise: "I still hope that at the end of such a shorter period of working just for our study, an arrangement could then be made making it possible for you to write the book on Chicago which would give you the full academic credit for the results of the long study you have been directing."[125]

Over and over, Cayton claimed that he would participate only if Myrdal agreed to pay him a stipend that would enable him to live comfortably, draft memos for the project, but also write his own book. Each time, Myrdal replied that as much as he would have liked to, he could not obtain such funds from the Carnegie Corporation, yet nonetheless asked Cayton for his materials.

By March 2, 1940, things reached a boiling point as Cayton became furious, standing up in no uncertain terms to the senior scholar, to whom he wrote, "The latest proposal, which would put both myself and my material at your disposal . . . for a sum of money which I could not even live on comfortably and which would give me absolutely no academic recognition, seems grossly unfair."[126]

Myrdal's frustration with Cayton was only one of his many concerns in the winter and spring of 1940. In April, as the Nazis marched into Denmark and Norway, Myrdal knew that Sweden might be next. He thus made the difficult decision to go back home with his wife and children to be there for the national crisis. His decision delayed the composition of An American Dilemma by a year.

When Myrdal returned to the States to write the book in 1941, Cayton was far from his mind. With no access to the Chicago materials, he gave up trying to focus on any of the big cities of the North. This may explain why, though framed as a study of the "American" race problem, An American Dilemma notably concentrates on the South. While this was seemingly justified because three-quarters of the black population resided there, the book's coverage of the North was perfunctory by any standard.[127]

Although the Carnegie Corporation had charged Myrdal as an outsider to look at America in "a wholly objective and dispassionate manner," he rejected from the outset any notion of disinterested social science. The first task of the social scientist, he claimed, was to make his biases explicit through a statement of his value premises. For Myrdal, these premises derived from the "American Creed," the set of ideals based on "the dignity of the individual, fundamental equality, and certain inalienable rights to freedom, justice and fair opportunity" that derived from the founding documents of the United States. Myrdal was thus not exactly what the Carnegie Corporation had claimed. He was neither objective nor much of an outsider—since his value premises were ultimately those that had been officially nurtured for centuries on American soil. He argued that his main task as a social scientist was to help America to realize its own ideals and thus be part of its social transformation. In another sense, though, Myrdal was the ultimate outsider. He took on the establishment of U.S. social science in the manner of someone who owed no allegiances. Taking aim at the Chicago School and its key architect, who died the year *An American Dilemma* was published, he argued that Robert E. Park's fatalistic emphasis on "natural" forces had led the social science of race in America down the road of "a systematic tendency to ignore practically all possibilities of modifying— by conscious effort—the social effects of natural forces."[128]

Unlike most authors of books on the race problem, Myrdal told his readers, he would not spend all of his time writing about blacks themselves. He would not focus exclusively on their peculiarities, and why they live as they do. While he viewed black culture as a *"distorted development, or a pathological condition, of the general American culture"* (Myrdal's italics), he argued that apart from the influence of white prejudice, nothing about blacks was inherently peculiar.[129] The "Negro problem" lay in the minds of white Americans, who controlled American society. Their treatment of blacks was to blame for the sad circumstances in which most blacks lived. He would present as much data as possible to document this social reality, but he argued that what made the situation of blacks a "social problem" was the complicated relationship between objective conditions and beliefs. Through a process of mutual causation, the perception of black inferiority gives rise to the condition and the condition gives rise to the perception. Though he called this "the theory of the vicious circle," Myrdal actually imagined that things need not spiral downward. "If, for example, we assume that for some reason white prejudice could be decreased and discrimination mitigated, this is likely to cause a rise in Negro standards, which might decrease white prejudice still a little more, which would again allow Negro standards to rise, and so on through mutual interaction."[130]

Myrdal's key task as a social analyst was not to focus on blacks in and of themselves, but to understand "the Negro problem" as a particular moral situation in which conflicting values were held, not only within white communities, but by individual whites themselves. The Negro was a "problem" not only to be summarized by statistics about his or her objective condition. In meeting with people from all walks of life, Myrdal inferred that they themselves experienced the situation of blacks as a moral issue. "They brood over it in their thoughtful moments," he concluded. "Even a poor and uneducated white person in some isolated and backward rural region in the Deep South who is violently prejudiced against the Negro and intent upon depriving him of civic rights and human independence has also a whole compartment in his valuation sphere housing the entire American Creed of liberty, equality, justice and fair opportunity for everybody."[131]

Prior to World War I, Myrdal argued, most whites believed that blacks were an inferior species of mankind, but this view had lost respectability and gradually been destroyed, especially among those with a college education. White people had lost faith in the theories of white supremacy that had ordered their lives for generations, yet they had not actually changed their lives to any considerable extent.[132] They subscribed to a creed that emphasized the broad ideals of democracy and equality, yet their actions toward blacks remained prejudiced, ungenerous, and motivated by hatred. Myrdal's main hope for the future was that sophisticated people didn't actually believe in black inferiority anymore. They were deeply troubled by the contradiction between their egalitarian principles and their attitude toward black citizens. This was the "American dilemma."

Myrdal was so much of an optimist that even in the Nazi era he made the astounding claim that "we have today in social science a greater trust in the improvability of man and society than we have ever had since the Enlightenment."[133] In that spirit, perhaps, he argued that whites would resolve the dilemma by carrying out their ideals. The greatest barrier to their doing so was ignorance of what was going on. The Northerner "succeeds in forgetting about it most of the time," so much so that many people in big cities who are well educated about world affairs have virtually no idea what conditions are like for blacks in their own city. Myrdal believed the answer lay in publicity. "A great many Northerners, perhaps the majority, get shocked and shaken in their conscience when they learn the facts. The average Northerner does not understand the reality and the effects of discrimination as those in which he himself is taking part in his routine of life."[134]

Myrdal's optimism about social change also drew on improvements in the administration of justice to blacks in the South—the decline of lynching, the rise of equality before the law—as well as upon improvements in education that would make it more difficult to keep blacks disenfranchised. The words of the white writer John Andrew Rice had made an indelible impression on him: "The Southerner's attitude toward the Negro is incredibly more humane than it was in the South I knew as a child."[135] Myrdal also believed that while such changes in American ideals were naturally occurring, work such as his could also pave the way.[136] As we've seen, this optimism differed quite a bit from the view of social change embodied in the theories of the century's leading social scientists, most notably the late William Graham Sumner of Yale, as well as Robert Park, who believed that social science and legislation were ineffective in changing people's values—social change occurred both slowly and naturally and could not be hastened.

Myrdal's book would become most famous for its optimism about white America's living up to its ideals, but other of its key ideas would be ignored. Among these was Myrdal's claim that analysts of the black condition should not focus on single causes such as employment, housing, education, stability in family relations, orderliness, and crime rates. Instead, he argued, "Everything is cause to everything else," an idea that he called "the principle of cumulation."[137] Because there was no principal cause, there was no magic bullet; he did not believe in panaceas. When circumstances made it necessary to emphasize just one or a few factors, it was important to concentrate on those that could raise the black standard of living as quickly as possible.[138] For example, higher rates of employment might immediately improve education and health care, while efforts to reform education or health care could take much longer to affect other parts of the system. Myrdal thought that as black living standards approached white living standards, white prejudice would decrease. "The Negroes' poverty, ignorance, superstition, slum dwellings, health deficiencies, dirty appearance, disorderly conduct, bad odor, and criminality stimulate and feed the antipathy of the whites for them," he wrote.[139] The black way of life was brought about by white race prejudice, but white prejudice was, in turn, built on the objective conditions inherent in that way of life. The goal should be to focus on raising the black living standard as quickly as possible.

In all of this, Myrdal did not spend much time on the residential context in which blacks were living, whether in the North or the South. In the first of only two appearances of the word "ghetto" in his fourteen hundred pages, he referred to the Jewish ghetto.[140] In the second, he made an offhand reference to "the crowded lower class Negro ghetto."[141] From that point on, he dropped the word altogether. Yet even though his focus on the urban North was minimal, he was not oblivious to the processes that led to segregation in the North. Segregation was enforced by white people. Restrictive covenants and residential segregation were also at the root of other kinds of segregation; they made it possible for public officials to discriminate against blacks without doing harm to whites.[142] When blacks *could* break through into white neighborhoods, the law of the vicious cycle took effect. Myrdal explained it in this classic statement:

> When a few Negro families do come into a white neighbor-hood, some more white families move away. Other Negroes hasten to take their places, because the existing Negro neigh-borhoods are overcrowded due to segregation. This constant movement of Negroes into white neighborhoods makes the bulk of the white residents feel that their neighborhood is doomed to be predominantly Negro, and they move out—with their attitudes against the Negro reinforced. Yet if there were no segregation, this wholesale invasion would not have occurred. But because it does occur, segregational attitudes are increased, and the vigilant pressure to stall the Negroes at the borderline is kept up.[143]

Myrdal thus saw the Northern form of urban residential segregation as a substitute for the etiquette and Jim Crow laws that had brought about institutional segregation in the South. He made a point of emphasizing that Southern whites had never particularly wanted blacks to live separately from them, because they derived too many benefits from their proximity.[144] Under conditions of Jim Crow, it had not been particularly difficult for whites to keep blacks "in their place" through ceremonial distance. Now the only way to achieve institutional segregation was through residential segregation.[145] Having lower-quality schools, police protection, or hospitals was much easier if the only people affected were blacks. This was a very different understanding of segregation from anything that could be found in the earlier Chicago School. Myrdal viewed Northern segregation not as something naturally occurring in social life itself, but as a phenomenon of the majority's power over a minority population.

But though Myrdal knew that the white majority had the power to enforce black inferiority in many different ways—via proximity or distance—he did not assume that the new Northern residential segregation would maintain the kind of white supremacy that had prevailed in the South. To the contrary, he argued that in the North whites would ultimately accept blacks as equals: they were preparing "for a fundamental redefinition of the Negro's status in America."[146] Myrdal predicted continued riots in the South and racial progress in the North without riots. Because the large black Northern migration seemed to have abated, whites and blacks no longer felt as much tension in conflicts over jobs. In addition, the North was developing a new awareness of the discrepancy between black living conditions and the American Creed.[147] "The average white Northerner," he maintained, "will probably agree with a policy which holds open employment opportunities for Negroes, because, as we said, he is against economic discrimination as a general proposition."[148]

Though Myrdal ended his book on a note of optimism that change would proceed on its own, he offered *An American Dilemma* as an intervention into the realm of values that could propel further action. To appeal to the conscience of whites, in which he had so much faith, Myrdal massively documented the damage that racial prejudice was doing to blacks. He believed that if he presented America with the realities of the situation—the discrimination that blacks faced in the labor market, in housing, and in education—whites would be forced to act.

What would happen if whites did not act as he expected? On this point, he said contradictory things. First he argued that Southern blacks were apathetic and uneducated, characterized by a defeatist mentality, and afraid to express an opinion. Then, hundreds of pages later, he predicted rising protest: "America can never more regard its Negroes as a patient, submissive minority. Negroes will continually become less well 'accommodated.' They will organize for defense and offense. They will be more and more vociferous. . . . The Negroes . . . have the advantage that they can fight wholeheartedly."[149]

Many years later, Myrdal would claim to have predicted the emergence of the civil rights movement in the South. Yet even if one takes his second prediction at face value while dismissing the first one, he certainly did not imagine a successful mass movement.[150] When speaking about blacks' capacity for protest, he came up with the Back to Africa movement as his example.

An American Dilemma was published to rave reviews as a two-volume set in 1944. Over the next decade, Myrdal's ideas were adopted by a presidential commission appointed to recommend a future course of action. His ideas resonated in the speeches of President Truman and Martin Luther King.[151] His book was cited by the U.S. Supreme Court in *Brown v. Board of Education* as evidence of the damage caused by segregation and was widely read.[152] Myrdal's belief in "the possibility of rapid, even induced, social change" appealed to the more progressive social scientists who wanted to break with the prevailing model that change must be slow and gradual and natural.[153] They also appreciated his suggestion that whites and not blacks were responsible for America's racial troubles.

In 1941, a full two years after Cayton's first discussions with Myrdal, he and his collaborator, Drake, and their professor, Warner, submitted a book proposal of their own to Harper and Brothers, the company that was to publish *An American Dilemma*. In those days, as now, doctoral students in sociology at Chicago and across the country sought to publish their dissertations with the elite University of Chicago Press, which, in the previous two decades, had published most of the outstanding studies in the field. But Cayton's friendship with Wright and other young writers fueled his literary ambitions.[154]

Although known as the Cayton-Warner Project, two-thirds of the writing was by St. Clair Drake. While Drake focused on the lower and middle classes, and the church as subculture, Cayton dealt with the upper classes and gangsters. Together, they made a natural team as co-authors. The work was to tell the story of Chicago's black community in the century preceding World War II with a focus on Chicago's Black Belt between 1938 and 1943.[155] Making no allusion to the forthcoming *An American Dilemma*, the Chicago researchers proposed to do what Myrdal and other social scientists of the time were not doing. That is, they set out to link the circumstances of everyday black urban life with the mechanisms that restricted the space of black neighborhoods—and to do so within the context of an increasing interest in race on American soil. In their book proposal, Warner, Cayton, and Drake noted that the end of the war provided the right moment for their work, that the American public would be ready to discuss "the Negro problem" in the context of what had just taken place around the world.[156]

Harper and Brothers rejected the proposal. Whether this had anything to do with the publisher's commitment to Myrdal is conjectural, but the three coauthors were undaunted. Cayton aspired to release a trade book, and Richard Wright, who had become the most distinguished black novelist in America with the publication of *Native Son* (1940), came to his aid by shepherding the book to Harcourt. The company's editor, John Woodburn, told them that his house would be interested if they could secure an introduction from Wright and enliven the book's style.[157] The completed manuscript was submitted approximately one year later without Warner's name. Just as Cayton had once stood up to Myrdal, so he now boldly asked his own mentor to withdraw his name from the book since he had contributed none of the writing: "I feel that just two signatures, [Drake's] and mine, should appear on the book and your assistance in the whole project should be acknowledged."[158]

Warner immediately accepted this arrangement and graciously provided an introduction outlining the history of the project. Yet once Wright submitted his introduction, Warner's contribution was relegated to an appendix, another demotion to which he did not object. Thus,

American social science saw its first book on "the black ghetto," written by two black graduate students with no affiliated white author. With *Black Metropolis*, Cayton fulfilled his goal of producing a book that was at once a work of literature and a serious contribution to social science.

In addition to reading *Black Metropolis* as a dialogue with both Myrdal and the historical moment, we can also see in this book the beginning of an underlying conceptual apparatus that gave new meaning to the ghetto concept in social science. In particular, Drake and Cayton used the ghetto idea to (1) highlight the difference between black neighborhoods and other neighborhoods; (2) ascribe ghetto conditions to a vicious cycle of outside repression and inside decay; (3) argue that the separate institutions brought about by the ghetto were inherently inferior to those outside while still serving as a source of pride and a rounded life; (4) show that the life trajectories of ghetto residents were mainly due to the community context in which they lived, rather than the characteristics of the people who moved there; and (5) emphasize that while the ghetto was crucial to understanding the life chances of Northern blacks, it was not a magic bullet that explained all problems of black people.

At various points in their book, Drake and Cayton refer admiringly to Myrdal, which perhaps helps account for the fact that *Black Metropolis* was not interpreted as a debate with *An American Dilemma*. Yet with the benefit of the correspondence between Cayton and Myrdal as background, it is only natural to ask how the two books compare. The answer sheds light on future efforts to understand the ghetto and can also help us see how it mattered that Myrdal was unable to strike a deal with Cayton.

Black Metropolis was published in 1945, when any study of race in America was unlikely to have gained the kind of immediate recognition that greeted Myrdal's book of the previous year. But the study did receive two major reviews in *The New York Times*. The paper's principal daily book critic, Orville Prescott, an influential figure in the literary world, called it "one of the important documents of our time." He wrote that "never before have so many hundreds of black and brown individuals been directly quoted as to how they feel about the matters closest to their hearts."[159] What neither he nor anybody else appeared to have noticed was that the book is not merely a study of black Chicago, but of white Chicagoans as well. Few books before or since have done such an effective job of getting inside the hearts and minds of whites on race.

In filling in the details on race in the North that Myrdal did not have at his disposal, Drake and Cayton opened with the first black settler in Chicago, tracing the history of the city's black community through World War I and the race riots of the 1920s, to the period of World War II in which they were living. One of their pivotal agendas was to explain the particularities of racial discrimination in the North, where the color line was not so rigid: signs were not posted pointing COLORED here and WHITE there, there were no lynchings, blacks were not denied an education, and they were treated with respect at the ballot box. Surely, Drake and Cayton acknowledged, this was "evidence of democracy at work," but their focus on the racial attitudes of the white population refuted Myrdal at every turn.[160]

"With nearly everyone in [Chicago] verbally committed to a belief in democracy, freedom, equality, fair play, and similar civic ideals, why does a color-line persist?" they asked. "The answer lies partly in the fact that these are not the ideals men live by, however much they may believe in them."[161] Whether or not the two black authors took on Myrdal in an explicit way, their argument could not have been more different from his. Simply stated, they claimed that change is driven by economic necessity and political expediency, *not* by any obligations that Americans feel to their Christian-democratic ideals—unless those ideals intersect with political and economic imperatives such as those dictated by a war or a depression.[162] The "beliefs men live by" are different from their verbal commitments.[163]

They argued that while the high ideals of American democracy are prominent in Northerners' talk, their folk beliefs in black inferiority have a much more profound impact on everyday life. These beliefs are a "watered down" version of Southern ideologies of black inferiority, which in the North are not taught in schools or propagated in any formal way, as they are in the South. Instead, the schools and formal institutions of the North transmit the ideals, while the folk beliefs constitute a powerful alternative system of racial doctrines transmitted in conversations between adults and children and in play groups. They are verified by the objectively low position children see blacks occupying in the society at large. White adults in the North place great pressure upon one another not to incorporate blacks into friendship circles and, especially, into their families. They seek to avoid any and all risks of blacks tainting their blood.

The ultimate goal of segregation is to ensure Caucasian purity, but the economic competition posed by black workers provides another incentive to keep blacks in their "place." Drake and Cayton show that blacks had not been permitted to compete freely in the labor market, in part due to the unions and in part due to the corporations themselves. Throughout much of the book, on these and other issues, they give voice to Chicago's whites, who spoke freely to their white investigators.

"Employers don't want to deal with Negroes," one worker told them. "We've made a rule that no colored person can hold office in our organization," a union man said. "The trouble with colored men is that they want to run things. . . . Now you've got to have white people running things if you want to get anywhere."[164]

What is striking is the lack of subtlety and the virulence of the anti-black sentiment that comes across on page after page: "I'm not prejudiced, but I'd burn this building down before I'd sell it to any damned nigger," said one man who was making plans to move. Another man who owned a tavern on the edge of a black neighborhood was asked if he had any black customers. "No, and I don't want any of the black bastards hanging around here. All they can do is cheapen the tavern's name."[165]

Drake and Cayton argued that the white population was committed to protecting its "privileged position," whether through maintaining a black "job ceiling," a "black ghetto," or social inequality in everyday relations between the races. Indeed, it might have been difficult for Myrdal to be so optimistic about whites acting on the ideals of the American Creed if he had been privy to all of these materials.

Life for blacks in Chicago was not all doom and gloom. When blacks attended movie theaters, baseball games, boxing matches, and race-tracks, they sat wherever they wanted and enjoyed these events the same way their fellow white citizens did. Blacks were permitted to shop wherever they wanted and to try on shoes, garments, and hats. Proprietors were not motivated by ideals, but by the "almighty dollar." To be sure, in all places where recreation demanded active participation, Drake and Cayton reported that segregation was still the norm. Thus, in public dance halls, skating rinks, and bowling alleys, the color line remained fully intact.

A third of *Black Metropolis* focused on the "world within a world," which the authors called Bronzeville, to signify the more pleasant aspects of black life that were symbolic of an authentic black identity. Drake and Cayton explained that many community members avoid referring to themselves as black and see "bronze" as more accurate because most of them are closer to brown anyway.[166] Only when community members referred to the exploitative and nonvoluntary dimensions of the segregated black community did they tend to refer to "the Black ghetto."[167] Bronzeville and the black ghetto were therefore two sides of the same coin. Racism had created the covenant, which brought about particular environmental conditions, which in turn gave rise to *both* pathological conditions *and* a rich manifestation of black life and culture. "Throughout the remainder of this book we shall use the term 'Bronzeville' for Black Metropolis because it seems to express the feeling that the people have about their own community. They live in the Black Belt and to them it is more than the 'ghetto' revealed by statistical analysis."[168]

Echoing their mentor Wirth's take on the Jewish ghetto, the authors argued that separation created a refuge for blacks in a racist world. Emphasizing Bronzeville's cultural vigor, they argued that blacks therefore had no particular interest in mingling with white people, having accommodated themselves over time to a dense and separate institutional life—"an intricate web of families, cliques, churches, and voluntary associations, ordered by a system of social classes"—in their own black communities.[169] This life so absorbed them as to make participation in interracial activities feel superfluous. Like Myrdal, the authors believed this world had come into existence in response to white rejection, but they argued that for blacks it no longer had a completely unhappy meaning. On the contrary, the average black person living on the South Side of Chicago did not think of this institutional life as subpar, but as a source of pride.[170] Drake and Cayton devote a full chapter to those dominant interests of Bronzeville that fully absorbed the population, including "staying alive," "enjoying life," "praising the Lord," "getting ahead," and "advancing the race."

To understand how blacks actually felt about segregation, the authors distinguished the color line at work from the color line in the neighborhood and in social life, such as in churches and family life. Blacks, they argued, were adamant about not being kept out of workplaces on the basis of their color, but when it came to where they lived, the story was different. They wanted their neighborhoods to be able to expand into contiguous white areas as they became too crowded, but they did not actually care to live among whites. When it came to socializing for its own sake, blacks were not especially interested in equality. Meanwhile, whites were more tolerant of transgressions when they occurred in the realm of social life, taking a "live and let live" attitude toward the occasional black who joined a white church or intermarried. This was because most whites perceived quite accurately that blacks were not trying to cross the color line en masse.[171]

Of course, even most blacks who had no desire to associate with whites nevertheless resented being rejected. Thus, Drake and Cayton quoted the editor of a black newspaper who wrote, "Anybody who says he doesn't believe in social equality is an advocate of the Hitler theory of superior and inferior races."[172] The authors sided with him. They viewed the subjective acceptance of segregation as a confused state of accommodation that needed to be corrected. Echoing An American Dilemma, they argued that institutions that were segregated were inherently unequal and had less economic and social power. While segregation had some benefits, such as significant achievements in the arts and literature and profits for black businessmen who held a virtual monopoly, none of this could ever compensate for the overall costs in terms of poverty and ignorance and inequality, including in the workplace.

Drake and Cayton never intended "the ghetto" to be the kind of concept that could clarify all problems that related to human subjugation in general or to Northern blacks in particular. Black Metropolis viewed the population of the ghetto, first and foremost, as an industrial working class. The book devotes significant attention to their experience as a people restricted by racial discrimination to the lower rungs of the industrial hierarchy, including the steel mills and slaughterhouses. Their sense of exploitation stemmed as much from their position in a racist economy as from their restriction in physical space. Drake and Cayton acknowledged that if forced segregation were to be eliminated, many of the ghetto's problems would go away. But not all of them. Black inferiority was mainly maintained by *both* the ghetto *and* the "job ceiling" (including high unemployment), with no clear connection between living in the ghetto and being unemployed. Eliminating the restrictive covenant and loosening the ghetto ring would relieve many problems, but blacks would remain inferior and exploited unless they could attain much higher employment and better jobs. This was a tall order, and given the anti-black racism in the North, Drake and Cayton were never optimistic that such conditions would prevail.

Consistent with their modest view of the concept's explanatory power, they dispensed with the ghetto as a historical concept. Rather than tracing it systematically across time, the authors were content to find the idea of the ghetto useful for understanding their own city and society. As they wrote, "Understand Chicago's Black Belt and you will understand the Black Belts of a dozen large American cities."[173]

The term "ghetto" first appeared in *Black Metropolis* when Drake and Cayton reported that black newspapers and civic leaders held that race restrictive covenants had produced a "Black ghetto" on Chicago's South Side and argued that "new areas should be opened to break the iron ring which now restricts most Negro families to intolerable, unsanitary conditions."[174] Quoting the local *Hyde Park Herald*'s report on a speech proclaiming the efficiency of restrictive covenants in maintaining "Caucasian" purity, the authors argued that this device is "like a marvelous delicately woven chain of armor" surrounding all the neighborhoods in which they live. . . . This "fine network of contracts" is always mainly aimed at blacks.[175] The authors stated that even the chairman of the mayor's committee had characterized the black community as a "ghetto," and that participants in the mayor's 1944 conference had generally agreed that most social problems within the Black Belt were fundamentally related to restrictive covenants.[176]

Drake and Cayton regarded the ghetto as a metaphor for both

segregation and Caucasian purity in the Nazi era, and it was in this sense that the use of the word was particular to the historical moment. Referring to those middle-class blacks who try to move out, Drake and Cayton wrote, "They have slowly filtered southward within the Black Belt. Always, however, they hit the invisible *barbed-wire* fence of restrictive covenants" (emphasis mine).[177] Barbed wire was a symbol of Nazi ghettos rather than something invented in sixteenth-century Venice. Beyond barbed wire and racial purity, we see, not surprisingly, little other direct reference to the Nazis in Drake and Cayton's book. They could assume that by now most scholars—and, increasingly, most blacks and whites—were familiar with what had just taken place in Europe. They could treat "ghetto" as a word in common use, but one that could nevertheless be deployed for their own political purposes.

Drake and Cayton were not attempting to make a literal comparison to or draw actively upon the Jewish experience under the Nazis. In no respect, moreover, did they claim similarities between any aspects of Jewish and black life. Their ghetto concept was built on a framework that had little to do with how Jews had actually lived. The nonliteral, metaphorical quality of this link is significant because in the 1940s, while some blacks wanted to be seen as "America's Jews" and even identified strongly with Jews, any identification was full of ambivalence.[178] Drake and Cayton emphasized that 75 percent of the merchants in the ghetto were Jewish, and "suggestions were made that all Jews should be expelled from Bronzeville."[179] Furthermore, the amount of oppression experienced by the two groups in the United States was completely different, as one Jewish commentator remarked at the time: "Where the Negro is on the whole barred from any but the most menial services in American society, the Jew has far greater freedom and can attain high positions in professional or public life."[180] Blacks therefore identified far less ambivalently with brown- and black-skinned people the world over, including the Japanese Americans interned during World War II.

Although Drake and Cayton's conception of the ghetto drew on Nazi imagery relating to racial purity, it does not appear to have been inspired, even metaphorically, by an image of the Nazi ghetto as a vehicle of control. To live in the ghetto was to be without police protection, so absent were the police from everyday life. The authors used the word "toleration" to describe the attitude of law enforcement toward a number of illegal community institutions, including those associated with drugs and gambling. White society seemed to take a "live and let live" attitude to whatever went on in the black communities.[181] The "reefer dens," call houses, and gambling operations known as policy stations—all illegal community institutions—were taken for granted.[182] An entire class of racketeers known as the upper shadies formed an influential segment of the ghetto's upper class. Illegal businesses could easily thrive as long as the appropriate police officers had been paid off.

Rather than control, the authors' use of "ghetto" was inspired by the metaphor of segregation, which is why on a few other occasions they and their subjects also referred to the ghettos of the Middle Ages. Beyond their reference to the concrete conditions caused by the covenant, Drake and Cayton did not invoke the ghetto to refer to any of the ways in which the ghettoized were controlled by external institutions, as Whyte did in his use of the colonial metaphor in the analysis of Italian Cornerville. Although they certainly recognized that the fate of Black Metropolis was tied to the national and even the global political and economic situation, they also mostly wrote as if once a residential area was enclosed, its problems stemmed from local neighborhood conditions such as overcrowding or an abundance of liquor stores. As in Wirth's analysis of the Frankfurt ghetto, Drake and Cayton saw most of the tensions in Chicago as local phenomena. External forces such as the University of Chicago or the state or federal government played little role in their analysis. Most important, the role of real estate agencies in Chicago received less than half a page, and the significance of national real estate and financial institutions was not discussed. Though the authors had fundamental differences with their predecessors, in this sense their work was continuous with that of their Chicago School mentors.

Drake and Cayton's use of the term "ghetto" is meant to highlight the differences with other neighborhoods throughout the city. On the one hand, the area in which all ghetto dwellers lived had the characteristics

one might find in any slum: run-down streets, overcrowded and dilapidated buildings, proximity to factories, subpar transportation services.
Whether they be Italians, Chinese, or blacks, the residents of all slum
neighborhoods are blamed for the conditions of the neighborhoods
they inherit. On the other hand, in the ghetto, "the 'undesirable' racial
factor is . . . merged with other unattractive features . . . [so] that the
separate effect of race cannot be disentangled."[183] The distribution of
other ethnic or racial groups into their slums might occur according to
natural laws of a free market, but nothing was natural in the distribution of over half the blacks in Chicago in the most "blighted" areas of
the city. This was an absolute condition, not one that varied across
neighborhoods.

Restrictive covenants had artificially brought about the black ghetto.
Drake and Cayton thus broke with the major assumption of the Chicago
School, the understanding of the distribution of racial and ethnic groups
as a natural phenomenon. They argued that the ghetto was primarily
the result of white people's preference not to have black neighbors,
though they also viewed it as partly a consequence of the vested interest
of black business owners, politicians, and preachers in maintaining a
black community.[184] While many blacks understood they had more
political clout and group solidarity because they lived in the ghetto, they
were still annoyed at being forced to live there. Here they seemed to be
borrowing from Wirth's idea that whereas the Jews had made a deliberate choice to live separately, they resented their isolation when it was
made compulsory.[185]

The ghetto marked blacks as "fundamentally different" in that its
residents did not enjoy the same trajectory as immigrants.[186] Immigrants other than Italians were thought to move to an area of secondary
settlement as soon as possible, whereas for blacks the ghetto was a permanent residence. The authors concluded that "Negroes, regardless of
their affluence or respectability, wear the badge of color. They are expected to stay in the Black Belt."[187] When the original sociologists of the
Chicago School distinguished between areas of immigrant first settlement and immigrant second settlement, they argued that people with
greater ambition, energy, intelligence, and diligence moved out of their
initial neighborhoods. For Drake and Cayton, blacks who migrated to
Chicago had no choice but to select into the community and could not

select out. They did not deny that a few problems had less to do with the consequences of overcrowding than with the kinds of people that migrated into the community. These included high illness and death rates, which were sometimes caused by the health problems of migrants before they arrived in the Northern cities. More crucially, however, the trajectories of ghetto residents had much to do with the characteristics of the community per se.[188] The fundamental difference between the black and white communities was represented by this simple statistic: blacks were living ninety thousand per square mile while whites were twenty thousand to the square mile.[189] Extreme overcrowding led to run-down buildings and schools that ran on shifts, leaving many children "on the streets" for the remainder of the school day.[190] Drake and Cayton believed that such aspects of black life, which contributed to pathological behavior such as juvenile delinquency and teenage pregnancy, were attributable directly to the restrictive covenant.

In arguing that the ghetto was a fundamentally different kind of neighborhood, Drake and Cayton looked carefully at the physical and social environment that exerted an influence on the day-to-day lives of the people living there. Referring to local influences such as cheap movie houses, dance halls, and taverns, all of which had proliferated on the South Side by World War II, middle-class residents and church people reported, "It's hard to keep girls straight over here."[191] Prostitutes, pimps, professional gamblers, and even murderers made it difficult for any "decent" person to walk the streets without experiencing deleterious and demoralizing cues. The Ida B. Wells housing project, constructed between 1939 and 1941, placed sixteen hundred lower-class families in the midst of this all.[192]

Whereas Myrdal saw the black condition generally as a vicious circle, Drake and Cayton applied that logic more specifically to the ghetto and its related conditions. In the ghetto, the black way of life was rendered visible in a form that could justify further white discrimination. Once in place, the ghetto led to a perception that an area was "blighted," that blacks gravitated there, and that it was the natural home to the city's inferior outcasts. Actually, it was a place where rents were low, where blacks had no choice but to live, and where nobody else wanted to settle.[193] "There is a tendency to blame the group for the condition of the area," Drake and Cayton point out,[194] and "the existence of these conditions has become a convenient rationalization for keeping Negroes segregated."[195] Blacks, who are "unfit" to be a part of society, must therefore be "quarantined behind the color line." But segregation exacerbated the differences and reduced the chances that blacks could ever participate as equals. Thus, they became "the victims of circular reinforcement," and the ghetto made the problems of blacks run on their own.[196] The ghetto also had an intangible result. Its very existence—dangerous, disease-ridden, congested, and run-down—reinforced the stigma that all blacks everywhere in the country already bore. All blacks were associated with the ghetto and judged by it, including the upper classes and those who resided beyond its perimeters.

As black scholars endeavoring to study the black community, Drake and Cayton had an enormous advantage. As men, however, they might have been at a severe disadvantage when it came to presenting a balanced portrait of the lives of black women in the ghetto. Yet in retrospect, one of the most surprising aspects of *Black Metropolis* was its complex portrait of women's experiences, especially as compared to those of Myrdal and most other scholars of local life. This might have been impossible without the team-based style of fieldwork facilitated by the massive grant from the federal Works Project Administration.

With this money the investigators hired female interviewers, who both observed and questioned people in a wide variety of settings. Drake and Cayton focused particularly on family life, domestic work, and religion, domains where women were heavily represented. The church received a significant amount of attention, and women were seen as constituting the "faithful few" within the ghetto. Drake and Cayton believed that the emotional needs of women were frequently satisfied by their active participation in churches.[197] They also focused on women who owned small businesses, sat on hospital boards, and belonged to elite social clubs. This helped them see modes of ghetto organization that might have been missed had men been the only focus.

Whether they looked at the top or the bottom of the class structure, their analyses frequently got to the heart of relations between the sexes. They discerned, for example, that women were not emotionally satisfied with their intimate lives at home. In one typical look at lower-class gender relations, the authors refused to accept the simple and stereo-typical notion that high rates of male unemployment during the De-pression had caused women to become the dominant figures in black families. Taking the female perspective, they concluded that although black women might hold the purse strings, men were still in a strategic position to compel women to "take love on male terms."[198] Even if a man was no longer attracted to a woman, he was still inclined to exploit her need for sexual gratification and "trade love for a living," Drake and Cayton argued.[199] The female, feeling devalued because she was not loved for her own sake, thus developed various strategies of resistance such as "I'll let him love me (and I'll love him) until he doesn't act right. Then I'll kick him out."[200] In their discussion of male desertion, Drake and Cayton mainly adopted the perspective of the abandoned black woman. Though this might be seen simply as a phenomenon of missing data—the males were no longer present to be interviewed—it neverthe-less stands in stark contrast to later work that explained male desertion exclusively from the male point of view.

Long in advance of feminist approaches to labor markets, Drake and Cayton showed a specific interest in the gendered character of the job search during the Depression. They sent investigators to the "slave mar-kets," those street corners where black women assembled to wait for white housewives to hire them for the day after bidding their wages down.[201] Comparing the work some women ended up doing against their actual training, the authors illustrated how a lack of social networks made it difficult for many of them to find work in the fields for which they had trained. "Having no references, it was hard for me to get a good job," one woman told them.[202] In this analysis, the authors not only displayed remarkable skill in describing the situation in which these women found themselves, but also successfully elicited their inner feelings about it. "Colored girls are often bitter in their comments about a society which condemns them to 'the white folks' kitchen,'"[203] they write.

In their discussion of how black women got typed and channeled into specific kinds of jobs, Drake and Cayton showed that race and class played an important role. White women with high school diplomas had no trouble landing jobs as clerical workers in downtown firms, whereas blacks with the same education could mainly work at such jobs only if they became available in the Black Belt.

The authors showed that upper-class black women in their study had more in common with their husbands than they did with other black women in the ghetto: upper-class women, like men, might be regarded as community leaders. Both engaged in civic activities, such as sitting on boards of community organizations or raising funds for organizations such as the NAACP.[204] When they prioritized the interests of the black race above all others, they were referred to as "Race Men" and "Race Women": "She derives prestige as well as personal satisfactions from 'advancing The Race,' and she is the keeper of the upper-class conscience."[205] Drake and Cayton's focus on the class backgrounds of women living in the ghetto thus led them to see that black women could hardly be described as a homogenous group.

For a book that was written by two male authors during an era when feminist consciousness was not yet prevalent among scholars, *Black Metropolis* contains a remarkable number of female voices from the ghetto and a serious analysis of gender. This is particularly notable when the book is compared against other works of social science at mid-century, including *An American Dilemma*.

What came of Cayton's opposition to the University of Chicago's role in designing and maintaining the restrictive covenants? In *Black Metropolis*, the authors only once mention the university's view of the covenants as a "permanent *cordon sanitaire*." They offer no analysis of what both Cayton and Wirth had acknowledged in their unpublished correspondence, namely, that the university had been complicit in creating the covenants and thus the very ghetto that they were now studying.

We can merely speculate on why they chose not to address the issue. Perhaps Drake and Cayton did not feel sufficiently empowered to embarrass the liberal university that had nurtured them and their professors. They may have needed to ensure that the administration would not begin hounding the sociology department. As noted, Robert Maynard Hutchins, the powerful university president responsible for the restrictive covenants, harbored a general disdain for sociology and many of its practitioners, including Wirth.[206] It would not have done much good for these scholars to alienate Hutchins further. Drake and Cayton were as compromised as any other American sociologists, and perhaps more so because their future careers depended on the good-will of white scholars who themselves relied on the favor of university administrators.

As black participants in the life of the South Side, Drake and Cayton were classic insiders, which has certain advantages in sociological work on marginalized groups. The Carnegie Corporation, seeking a detached observer who was not embedded in local power relations, perceived Mydral as the ideal outsider. Had Myrdal had access to all of Cayton's materials, he might not have felt constrained in exposing the University of Chicago. Cayton might even have led Myrdal to think about the concept of the ghetto and the racism that was essential to understanding black life in the North. However, precisely because Cayton and Drake's ideas on the nature and mechanisms of racial discrimination differed from Myrdal's and were based on their own research, it became essential for them to claim full credit. Today, *Black Metropolis* remains a major inspiration for efforts to understand racial inequality, due to its focus on Northern racism, physical space, and the consequences of residential segregation. Although it is a weaker book for its failure to explicitly highlight the university's role in maintaining the Chicago ghetto, the focus on the general phenomenon of restrictive covenants is sufficient to make clear that an administrative device was being used to restrict space in the service of racial purity. That, as well as the authors' new understanding of ghettos as compulsory rather than voluntary, befit the Nazi era.

Drake and Cayton's social position as blacks helped them gain access to cultural truths within the black community that might have been inaccessible to Myrdal on his own. But they might also have been compromised by that insider status, which included close ties to gambling and labor racketeers. One of the Jones brothers, who helped support their research, went to prison while they were preparing their study. Their chapter on the gambling network, which they dubbed "poor man's roulette," painted the Jones brothers as race heroes.[207] The brothers' financial support was never acknowledged in *Black Metropolis*. The policy racket was quite controversial even within the black community, but Drake and Cayton ended up giving short shrift to those ministers, teachers, social workers, and businessmen who deplored the moral decay it bred. This omission may have been influenced by the financial support, but without such funding, *Black Metropolis* might have never come to be.

Despite the extraordinary accomplishment of Drake and Cayton's book, their later careers did not reflect its success. Neither author received a doctorate for his work on *Black Metropolis*, most likely because it was coauthored. Each of them had written enough of the text to submit what would nowadays be considered a brilliant thesis. By the mid-1960s, senior sociologists at the University of Chicago were asking in disbelief how the department could have failed to award them degrees.[208]

That their careers did not reflect the importance of their contribution can be attributed only in part to intellectual currents of the time or the second-class citizenship granted even to leading black scholars in this period. Nor can it be pinned fully on the policies of the University of Chicago sociology department, which produced the greatest black social scientists of that generation but never invited any of them to join its faculty. Even when compared to other black academics, Drake and Cayton received little recognition. Was this the result of their unwillingness to subordinate themselves to Myrdal? Black scholars who had been affiliated with Myrdal enjoyed significant careers. The Swedish economist made tireless efforts to activate his networks on their behalf.

This explanation can only take us so far. Cayton had been exceedingly loyal to Robert Park and Louis Wirth, and he had access to all of their social networks. The fact is, Cayton never completed his doctorate, perhaps for multiple reasons. He himself acknowledged that his excitement about getting into public life was one problem. His relationship with Richard Wright might also have stymied him. He idolized the great writer and his ability to express indignation about white racism. As Robert Washington observed in a brief and poignant article on Cayton, "Wright functioned outside constraints that confronted professional Black sociologists. . . . Cayton felt but was unable to articulate [such emotion] within the mainstream sociological perspective on race relations."[209] Sociology, which was establishing itself as a systematic social science, had no space for writing of this sort, and, as Washington emphasizes, no critical theoretical perspective focusing on white racism.[210]

Cayton did secure a position at Fisk University in Nashville, where he worked briefly in an office next to Robert Park, who had by then retired to Fisk from the University of Chicago. But Cayton wanted to remain in the North, where academic standards were stricter. Ultimately, he hated his job running the Good Shepherd Community Center: "I had come to feel that the community center was a sop thrown to the Negro community by wealthy and middle class whites. . . . I wanted to quit and find a job where I was not controlled by white philanthropy."[211] Moving to New York City, he became a columnist reporting on the United Nations for *The Pittsburgh Courier* and ended his career in staff positions at the American Jewish Committee and the National Council of Churches.

Drake, on the other hand, began teaching at Roosevelt University in downtown Chicago. From there he fought as an activist against the University of Chicago's involvement in restrictive covenants and its emerging programs of black-targeted urban renewal. Later, he completed a dissertation on black immigrants in England, became an adviser to the independence movement in Ghana, and wrote a widely praised two-volume study on the black diaspora, *Black Folk Here and There*. Toward the end of his career, he became founding professor of African and African American Studies at Stanford, where he spent the last seven years of his working life.

Largely as a result of the work of the National Association for the Advancement of Colored People (NAACP), five cases challenging the judicial enforcement of restrictive covenants were brought to the Supreme Court between 1948 and 1953. These cases were crucial in eliminating a barrier against access to housing.[212] The court ruling was complex. Because the covenants had been drawn up by private citizens, they were legal under the Fourteenth Amendment, which protected the rights of individuals to engage in private conduct, regardless of its discriminatory nature. However, once these contracts were challenged in court, they were now seen as gaining their binding power from state enforcement, and the Fourteenth Amendment forbade the enforcement of discriminatory action by the courts. Effectively, the contracts were illegal, or at least unenforceable. With the rulings in the restrictive covenant cases, one of the specific mechanisms that created the Chicago ghetto and drew the attention of Drake and Cayton went away.

The ghetto that Drake and Cayton studied from the later years of the Depression into the 1940s was a social space about which people felt deep ambivalence. Founded on white aspirations for racial purity, the community was felt by many blacks to be flourishing even while its parallel institutions were largely inferior to those found in white society. Not surprisingly, many of the residents saw things in more positive terms, as they were migrants whose point of comparison was the Jim Crow South. Perhaps because the racial covenants that were partially responsible for shaping the ghetto were eliminated, Bronzeville—the more positive side of the coin—would dominate perceptions of ghetto life for at least a little while. Not until the subsequent decades would analysts of black life begin to see the ghetto more clearly as a phenomenon of control, one in which human flourishing increasingly took a backseat to pathology and to domination by external powers.

Black Metropolis played a key role in introducing the concept of the ghetto into the discussion of racial inequality at midcentury. But had Hitler not resurrected the term "ghetto" for his newly restricted Jewish quarters, would the term still have been adopted by blacks on the basis of some imagined connection between the older ghetto in Venice and the American variant?

We cannot say no, but neither can we take it for granted that blacks and others would have called their restricted neighborhoods "ghettos" in the absence of the Nazi reference. One way of finding out whether the Nazi ghetto had a direct influence on the American use of "ghetto" to denote black urban neighborhoods would be to look at a vast number of books in which the term "ghetto" appears. If the connection between the Nazi and the black ghetto is correct, one would expect to find a rise in references to black ghettos only *after* the rise of Nazi ghettos in popular consciousness. We would not expect to see a spike in the term *before* Nazis began implementing them, or even before the Nazis rose to power. When I did such a survey, which would until recently have been impossible, this is precisely how it turned out.

Graph 1 shows the number of sources in a sample consisting of just

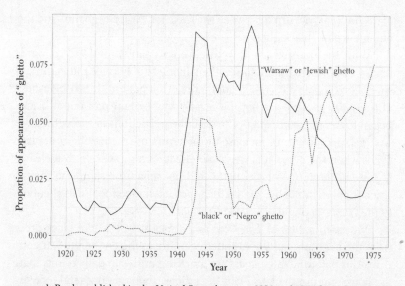

GRAPH 1: Books published in the United States between 1920 and 1975 from the Google Ngrams corpus. The figure shows two time-series, one depicting the frequency of the phrase "Warsaw ghetto" or "Jewish ghetto" and a second series depicting the frequency of the phrase "black ghetto" or "Negro ghetto." Both series are plotted as a proportion of the total number of appearances of the word "ghetto" in each time period.

over 800,000 books cataloged by Google Books and published in the United States between 1920 and 1975 that contain either the phrase "Warsaw ghetto" or "Jewish ghetto," or the phrase "black ghetto" or "Negro ghetto." (I chose "Warsaw ghetto" because it was much more common than "Nazi ghetto," though a search of that term brings up an identical pattern.) In addition to counting the number of sources, I reviewed nearly all the sources I could track down in order to assess the quality of my method and the context of term usage.[213]

My reading revealed that prior to the Nazi era, the term "black ghetto" or "Negro ghetto" had only been deployed occasionally to describe entire neighborhoods or efforts to restrict blacks to certain run-down neighborhoods. In these discussions, an allusion or implicit reference was sometimes made to early modern Jewish ghettos. But in this period the concept of the black ghetto had never taken root. References to the Warsaw ghetto began to rise in the 1940s; directly afterward, a massive jump occurred in the number of references to the "black ghetto." A lag of several years occurred between the spike for "Warsaw ghetto" and the emergence of "black ghetto."[214]

With the massive rise in restrictive covenants from 1927 onward, blacks came increasingly to see their living situation as a forced measure. The Google data reveal another relevant pattern. If consciousness of the Nazi ghettos was not the reason why certain prominent blacks began to use the word "ghetto" to describe restrictions in space, then we would expect to see an increase in the term's use sometime in the late 1920s when the covenants went into effect on a mass scale. But clearly the use of the term "black ghetto" did not spike in response to the restrictive covenants of the late 1920s; rather, it followed the rise in attention to the Nazi treatment of Jews in Europe.[215]

My examination of *The New York Times* as well as the black press from the beginning of the twentieth century to the end of the war confirms this pattern. Newspapers are more responsive to daily events than are books, and in the late 1930s the articles about ghettos tend increasingly to discuss the Warsaw ghetto, while the ones from the early 1930s are mostly about Jews in their pre-Nazi living places. Around 1941 and 1942, we see the onset of significant discussions that compare the situation of blacks with that of Jews and refer to the black ghetto as a forced measure created by the restrictive covenant.[216] An article from the time reporting on meetings of the City-Wide Citizens Committee on Harlem has the subheading " 'Black Ghetto' Charged."[217] The placement of "Black Ghetto" in quotation marks underscores the strangeness of its use here. After the Warsaw ghetto uprising, which brought more coverage to the Jewish ghettos in the mass media, references to black ghettos continue to increase. Then, as the Google data show, in the 1960s, in yet another bump, "ghetto" became inextricably associated with blacks, finally overtaking the "Jewish/Warsaw ghetto" usage in 1965. It is to that era that we now turn.

3

HARLEM, 1965:
KENNETH CLARK

During the civil rights era, the black ghetto came into greater prominence within social science. The civil rights movement likewise set the
stage for the emergence of another significant black scholar, Kenneth
Clark, a crucial figure for the study of black life, including ghettos, for
decades to come. In the fifties, early in Clark's career, after the Supreme
Court had put an end to restrictive covenants, attention had moved
away from the ghetto. By the 1960s, as it became clear that the urban
North would be the setting for the next crucial phase of a civil rights
strategy, attention shifted back. Clark was integrally involved at every
point.

Born to Jamaican parents in the Panama Canal Zone, Clark moved
to Harlem with his mother at age five. Upon graduating from an almost-
all-white high school in New York City, he attended the nation's preeminent black college, Howard University, where he studied with some
of the nation's leading black intellectuals, including the sociologist
E. Franklin Frazier, the philosopher Alain Locke, and the psychologist
Francis Cecil Sumner. At Howard racial justice became an intellectual
pursuit for Clark, as these scholars encouraged the idea that systematic
study could be an instrument of social change.[1] The faculty-student relationships at Howard were informal, and Clark received much of his
education outside the classroom in the professors' homes or local bars,
sometimes drinking beer with them. In 1934, as editor of the school

newspaper during his senior year, he wrote an editorial that launched his career as a civil rights activist decades before the students of the 1960s had joined in the cause. His editorial condemned segregation in restaurants in the U.S. Capitol and argued that none should be off-limits to blacks. Clark and fellow militant Howard students, inspired by the article, decided to protest.

In Washington, D.C., which was not unlike many Deep South Jim Crow cities, the Howard students were expected to keep quiet. Heading for the Capitol, Clark and his fellow students marched with picket signs that proclaimed it intolerable that blacks were not permitted to eat in the building's restaurants. The students were arrested, taken to the station, and booked. As cells were being readied, a six-foot police captain with an Irish brogue came out of the back room of the precinct. When he heard that they had been arrested for picketing against segregation in the Capitol, he shouted, "Let these young men go. Take their names off the books. They should be praised, not arrested."[2]

The story of the protest appeared the next day on the front page of the Sunday edition of *The Washington Post* as well as inside *The New York Times* under the headline "Negro Students Rush Congress Restaurant in Vain Effort to Test the Rule Barring Race."[3] When the students returned to campus, the university president, Mordecai Johnson, was considerably less sympathetic than the white precinct captain had been. He was upset because he believed that by picketing the students had jeopardized the college's appropriation from Congress. Howard University was a unique institution in being the only private university to receive almost its whole subsidy from federal funds. In effect, the institution was dependent on the goodwill of the congressmen from the Jim Crow South who dominated Congress. The Howard president had the student protesters brought before the school's faculty-run disciplinary committee. Addressing its members, he made it clear that Clark should not get his diploma later that spring. The students should be suspended.

After testifying before the committee, they were told to leave the room. A number of committee members wanted the students expelled, but the chairman, the political scientist Ralph Bunche, would hear nothing of it. Still in his early thirties, Bunche was one of the rising stars of the Howard faculty and would decades later win the Nobel Peace

Prize. He announced that if the committee voted to expel the students, he would leave along with them, a threat that did the trick: no discipline occurred. The incident marked the beginning of a lifelong friendship between Bunche and Clark.

While he was at Howard, Clark met his future wife, Mamie Phipps, a student from a well-to-do family in Hot Springs, Arkansas. Together, Kenneth and Mamie became the first blacks to enroll in the doctoral program in psychology at Columbia University. During the preceding summer, Mamie had gotten a job in the Washington, D.C., office of Charles Hamilton Houston, the black lawyer who would argue some major civil rights cases in the era leading up to *Brown v. Board of Education*. In Washington, she also met Thurgood Marshall and just about every other leading civil rights lawyer. She left for graduate school with a sense of urgency to advance the elimination of segregation.

At Columbia, Kenneth Clark became interested in neurophysiological psychology, which he believed would be the future of the discipline. But he also felt that specializing in that area would be a cop-out, given the need for social psychologists to deal with issues of race and the problems of blacks. When he learned from his adviser Otto Klineberg, a scholar of racial differences in intelligence, that Gunnar Myrdal had been regularly working in a cubicle in the rafters of the Columbia library, he immediately sought him out and requested to be made part of Myrdal's staff. Myrdal responded by asking to see some of Clark's papers. According to Clark, the senior scholar was not impressed, finding them sloppy, but Clark's persistence and Klineberg's intervention ultimately paved the way to a staff job that paid a generous salary of $175 per month. Mainly, Clark worked as an assistant to Klineberg, an adviser to Myrdal, contributing to the research on race and intelligence. This was the period right after psychologists began discrediting the theories of intelligence that had served as a basis of the Southern caste system. The environmentalism that Clark and his mentors pursued demonstrated that whereas the social and cultural context in which blacks and whites lived was crucial, there were no innate intellectual differences between the two groups. Myrdal drew heavily on Clark's summary of the accepted scientific literature and became increasingly impressed with the young doctoral student, sometimes inviting him to lunch.

Kenneth Clark wrote a dissertation on memory, but was much more inspired by Mamie's work than his own. Her doctoral research, completed in 1943, had focused on how children in segregated communities become aware of their blackness. Upon their graduation, Kenneth took a job at City College, but Mamie was blocked from most interesting jobs as both a black and a woman. In 1946, she and Kenneth decided they both wanted to use their psychological training to help their community of Harlem, and they saw Mamie's difficulties as an opportunity. They would cofound a social service organization for troubled Harlem youth, which she would run. With a small loan from Mamie's father, they purchased furniture and rented a space, then pursued a series of donors to help them fund the center long-term. After they were turned down for funding by every government and social service agency they approached, they finally received crucial support from the fortune of Marion Rosenwald Ascoli, a wealthy Jewish philanthropist from Chicago.[4]

Northside was to be a community-based mental health facility that would focus on youth in Harlem. The goal was not simply to try to get children to behave better, or to conform to white middle-class norms, as is typically the case for institutions of this kind. Mamie and Kenneth believed that such an approach was flawed because it asked young people to adapt to abnormal circumstances: run-down housing, poor schools, and a larger community that was not oriented to "respecting their humanity."[5] They would focus on their clients and the community of Harlem at the same time. Most significantly, this entailed working closely with the local schools and the housing authorities, to improve situations that the children were responding to.

When *An American Dilemma* came out, Clark had already spent two years as the first black full professor at City College of New York, where he was independently researching the impact of prejudice on young children, an outgrowth of Mamie's earlier dissertation work. At the college, he was absorbed by heavy teaching loads, but the atmosphere was intellectually stimulating, due to the extraordinary students who enrolled at CCNY in that era. The cafeteria was a hangout for such future luminaries of the New York intellectual world as Irving Kristol, Irving Howe, and Daniel Bell. Two of Clark's pupils, Daniel Patrick Moynihan and Nathan Glazer, would go on to play major roles in the debate over the ghetto.

Outside CCNY, Clark belonged to a small group of black activists, scholars, and lawyers who were using the courts to press their case for racial justice in the belief that the race problem in the United States could only be solved through litigation. The Southern idea of separate but equal, which Myrdal viewed as a crucial conundrum for whites of that era, was now being taken on in the courts. When Clark's research on young children and prejudice was presented in a paper at a White House conference organized by Harry Truman in 1950, Clark was catapulted into the center of the litigation strategy on the impact of school segregation.

In 1954, when the U.S. Supreme Court decided to hear desegregation cases, Clark's research was adopted by the lawyers who were preparing a brief that summarized the emerging consensus on separate but equal in the scholarly community. His studies had demonstrated that when black children were shown dolls of different skin colors, they tended to favor the white ones. Clark argued that this indicated that blacks in segregated schools were internalizing feelings of inferiority. When the Supreme Court ruled on the segregation cases in *Brown v. Board of Education,* it cited Clark's research as evidence for the claim that segregation between blacks and whites in public schools had a detrimental effect on black children. The court ended with the words "And, see generally, Gunnar Myrdal, *An American Dilemma* (1944)."[6] No doubt the Carnegie Corporation had much to be happy about. Not only had they invested so heavily in Myrdal's project, but their project had helped train Clark as an activist scholar as he watched Myrdal work at close range.

The Supreme Court's reliance on Clark's work turned him into a larger-than-life folk hero both inside and outside academia. Interviewed on numerous television and radio programs, profiled in newspapers and magazines, he soon found himself in the milieu of New York City's social elite, where he hobnobbed with the rich and famous. Intellectuals, politicians, and activists took his opinion seriously. He became friendly with both Martin Luther King and Malcolm X. Malcolm visited Clark's largely white classes at City College as a guest lecturer and even welcomed Clark's son, Hilton, when he came around to the mosque.

As a nearly lifelong resident of New York City and its suburbs and a child of Harlem, Clark was among the first to perceive that the

problems addressed by the civil rights movement and those confronted
by blacks in the Northern cities were very different. Desegregating
lunch counters and achieving voting rights were all fine and good in the
South, but they did nothing to address the privately sanctioned housing
segregation, slumlords, run-down neighborhoods, and police abuse pervasive in the North.[7]

Clark had continued helping Mamie with her work at Northside,
but he was becoming impatient with a clinical approach that could only
change a small number of lives, one at a time. He wanted to keep his
focus on the youth of Harlem, but he felt that for every child that could
be helped at Northside, thousands of others were ignored.

The funders had also been a problem. In 1960, Marion Rosenwald
Ascoli threatened to leave the board of Northside and remove her
annual subsidy if the Clarks did not adopt a more traditional psychiatric
approach to dealing with the children of Harlem. This was the beginning of an era that saw increasing tension between blacks and Jews over
control of black organizations and even the civil rights movement. After
thinking about it for a few days, the Clarks decided that no matter how
much money Ascoli had, she would not turn Northside into what would
feel like a colonial outpost to them. They would not accept the paternalism of a donor who insisted she knew better than they did what the
children of Harlem needed. "We'll take our chances and seek funds
elsewhere," they told her.[8] Ultimately, after a stressful time for the Clarks,
they replaced Ascoli's money with funds from a number of other sources,
including the City of New York.

In 1961, the Clarks learned that the Jewish Board of Guardians had
received a grant of hundreds of thousands of dollars to set up a youth
program in the Harlem community, and Northside was getting none of
it. Why, they wondered, were they not called upon to administer this
money? Kenneth Clark was beginning to articulate a perspective on
the powerlessness of ghetto blacks, who were dominated by whites. The
whites thought they knew better and expected the natives to be grateful
to their benefactors. This condescension was characteristic of a colonial
relationship, and he coined the phrase "social work colonialism" to drive
home his point.[9]

Later that year, Clark read that President John F. Kennedy's Committee on Juvenile Delinquency was gearing up to give a significant grant to

Mobilization for Youth (MFY), an organization on the Lower East Side of New York City. Founded by Richard Cloward and Lloyd Ohlin, distinguished white social work and criminology scholars at Columbia, the organization was set up to provide delinquent youths with better opportunities and to directly involve the residents in efforts to change the community. Noting that Harlem had a delinquency problem of its own, Clark set up an organization, Harlem Youth Opportunities Unlimited (HARYOU), to apply to bring similar funds to Harlem. HARYOU engaged in what was known as "action research" to improve employment and educational opportunities for the youth of central Harlem while systematically researching their needs. Due to infighting between Clark and Harlem's congressman, Adam Clayton Powell, Jr., over who would control the millions of federal dollars that would come into Harlem through the organization, Clark quit after just two years. He was no more willing to work under the thumb of a black politician he did not respect than that of a Jewish donor.

Before he left HARYOU, however, Clark directed a massive research project about central Harlem, a study that put him in contact with a community that was completely different from the one he had grown up in. That had been a Harlem with caring teachers, responsible parents, and hope. Now he confronted what he called a Harlem of neglect and despair. Self-published by HARYOU as *Youth in the Ghetto: A Study of the Consequences of Powerlessness and a Blueprint for Change*, the 620-page document was the first statement by Clark of his emerging perspective on the ghetto. He believed that the pathologies of the Harlem community were tied directly to the residents' powerlessness, to their inability to control their own lives and destinies.[10] In a chapter that would inspire more militant black activists in what became known as the Black Power movement, Clark argued that the Harlem community

> can best be described in terms of the analogy of a powerless colony. . . . Its social agencies are financially precarious and dependent upon sources of support outside the community. . . . Its economy is dominated by small businesses which are largely owned by absentee owners, and its tenements and other real property are also owned by absentee landlords. . . . Harlem's schools are controlled by forces outside of the community. . . .

In short, the Harlem ghetto is the institutionalization of power-lessness. Harlem is made up of the socially engendered ferment, resentment, stagnation, and potentially explosive reactions to powerlessness and continued abuses.[11]

Youth in the Ghetto argued that the powerlessness of Harlem's youth could not be overcome by a "saturation of social services" or any methods that failed to yield independence.[12]

None of this could be successful, Clark argued, without also improving the educational system in Harlem. He argued for compre-hensive programs, including the construction of preschool academies to educate all the children between three and five years old in the com-munity. The emphasis of these preschools would be on language facility and other means of developing the use of concepts. On top of that, fam-ily counseling would be provided to educate teachers and parents alike in the special problems of early childhood. These programs would be regularly evaluated for effectiveness by systematic and objective criteria.

By 1963, as many Northern blacks came to look more closely at their own situations, some realized that the coalition with white liberals could be an obstacle to reform in the North. Many blacks in Northern ghettos believed that the "turn the other cheek" strategy of the civil rights movement had to be replaced by militancy and upheaval. Al-though Clark publicly stated that King's "love the oppressor" philoso-phy was psychologically unhealthy, he also opposed the militants of the Black Power movement, comparing them to Southern racists in their ethnocentrism.

Thus, Clark was a safe bet for the liberal establishment. In 1963, Boston's public television channel invited him to conduct a series of wide-ranging interviews with James Baldwin, Malcolm X, and Martin Luther King. Face-to-face in front of the camera, Clark and Malcolm X appeared socially distant and even tense. One would not have known that Malcolm X had been regularly visiting Kenneth Clark's classes at City College as a guest lecturer, or that Clark's son had been spending time with him. Clark asked him what he thought might happen not only in the South, but also in cities such as Philadelphia, Boston, and

Los Angeles. The minister predicted riots, but also made it clear how little the goal of integration meant to blacks such as himself less than a decade after *Brown*.

> "Well, Dr. Clark, as you know, these Negro leaders have been telling the white man that everything is under control. . . . And now the Negro leaders are standing up and saying that we are about to have a racial explosion. . . . And a racial explosion is more dangerous than an atomic explosion. . . ."
>
> "What will be the consequence of this explosion?" Clark asked.
>
> "Anytime you put too many sparks around a powder keg, the thing is going to explode. And if the thing that explodes is still inside the house, then the house will be destroyed. . . . If the black man is able to separate and go onto some land of his own, where he can solve his own problems, then there won't be any explosion. The Negroes who want to stay with the white man, let them stay with the white man. But those that want to leave, let them go. . . ."
>
> "As I understand your position, Mr. Malcolm," Clark continued, "the only thing that can save us from a catastrophic explosion is complete separation."
>
> "Complete separation! Complete separation is the only solution to the black and white problem in this country."[13]

Next summer, the explosions that Malcolm X predicted came to pass. A charge of police brutality—a fifteen-year-old boy shot by a white officer—led to the first major outburst in the era, the Harlem riot of 1964. Later that summer, riots occurred in Brooklyn, Rochester, and Jersey City, demonstrating that the alienation felt in Northern ghettos was unlike anything the country had seen in the early years of the civil rights movement. The white establishment was running scared.

In 1964, Malcolm X announced, "The Black man has seen the white man's underbelly of guilty fear," and correctly predicted the eruption of even more severe riots.[14] In the summer of 1965, the Watts ghetto in Los Angeles exploded. It took twelve thousand National Guard troops to restore order, by which time thirty-five people were dead, nine hundred injured, and thirty-five hundred arrested.[15] The riots, which did not end at Watts, highlighted what Clark had already perceived, namely, that the focus on black rights had moved North. The problems that now needed to be confronted were of a completely different order as black separatists such as Malcolm X, Stokely Carmichael, and H. Rap Brown came to epitomize a relevant alternative to Martin Luther King. Black leadership was now divided over whether segregation was better or worse than the integration that might result from eliminating ghettos.

While all hell was breaking loose in the American city, Columbia University might have seen fit to try to hire its prominent alumnus Kenneth Clark to teach in its school of education or psychology department. After all, he was right around the corner at the resource-strapped City College, and his research was based in the nearby community of Harlem.

In 1964 the Institute of Urban Studies of Teachers College at Columbia hired Herbert Gans, an expert on poverty and urban life. Gans was a refugee from Nazi Germany who had come to the United States in 1940 at age thirteen and later enrolled at the University of Chicago. There he had studied for his bachelor's and master's degrees with one of Park's protégés, Everett Hughes. Later, Gans received a doctorate in urban planning from the University of Pennsylvania. Two years before taking the Teachers College position, he had published *The Urban Villagers*, an acclaimed ethnography of working-class Italians in Boston during the era of urban renewal. Like Whyte in his *Street Corner Society* of the 1940s, Gans saw working-class Italian culture as dominated by strong family ties. Poor Italian Americans were depicted as lacking the interest or willingness to leave their subsociety, which increased their anxiety about being displaced by the urban renewal program, which was indeed about to force their relocation.

Gans used the term "urban village" to describe an area "in which European immigrants—and more recently Negro and Puerto Rican ones—try to adapt their non-urban institutions and cultures to the urban milieu," usually "at the mercy of the housing market."[16] He pointed out that often the urban village is described in ethnic terms—"Little

Italy, The Ghetto, or Black Belt," but they were all ultimately "first or second settlement(s) for urban migrants."[17] Whether those migrants were black or white was not the main concern. Race and ethnicity were reducible to class both in these communities and in American society more generally. He argued that neighborhoods known as Little Italy or the Black Belt merely gave ethnic names to a common experience: life in an overcrowded, low-rent neighborhood. Looked at in retrospect, the book illustrates that despite the publication of *Black Metropolis* two decades earlier, no conceptual apparatus for distinguishing between the situation of blacks in the ghetto and the residential situation of white immigrants had entered into sophisticated sociological thought.

When social scientists did conceptualize the distinction, it was usually framed in terms of value differences. The following year, for example, Nathan Glazer and Daniel Patrick Moynihan published *Beyond the Melting Pot: The Negroes, Puerto Ricans, Jews, Italians, and Irish of New York City.* Unlike the Italians depicted in Gans's study (upon which Glazer and Moynihan relied for their information about Italians), blacks were seen as different because they were accused of having little family life. In an argument that prefigured the later Moynihan report, they wrote, "Migration, uprooting, urbanization always create problems. . . . But when the fundamental core of organization, the family, is already weak, the magnitude of those problems may be staggering."[18] Recognizing the "crude, brute fact of discrimination," they argued:

The same facts can be responded to in different ways. The Japanese in California before the war found it impossible to get good jobs outside of the Japanese community; Jews until the Second World War took it for granted that they would find few jobs in engineering or with large corporations. But at the same time, Japanese attended college in phenomenal numbers; they became the best educated racial group in California. Jews did the same. . . . This overtraining also meant that when the barriers came down these groups were ready and waiting. The Negro today is not. It is true his experience has been more frustrating, prejudice more severe, personality damage more extensive. And yet in some ways the situation is better; never has there been more opportunity for education and training at government expense, never has there been a more favorable environment for minority students in colleges, never have there been so many opportunities making the struggle of education light in contrast to the rewards held out.[19]

Ultimately, Glazer and Moynihan—reflecting their own version of the classic Chicago School model—did not believe any differences between the ghetto and white neighborhoods mattered much because in the end they would disappear: "New York will very likely in the end be an integrated city—or rather something even better, a city where people find homes and neighborhoods according to income and taste."[20]

While Glazer and Moynihan were optimistic about the future, the trends of the time should have led at best to nothing more than a mixed prognosis. The ghetto of the civil rights era was wholly different from the ghetto that existed at the time of World War II, when only one-quarter of the U.S. black population lived in urban areas. By the 1960s, roughly three-quarters of blacks resided in cities, mainly in the North. In Philadelphia and New York, the overall percentage of blacks doubled in that period. In Los Angeles, Detroit, and Chicago, the percentage tripled.[21]

Over these two decades, much that was known about the situation of blacks in the North became outdated. Take the social status of the migrants. At the end of the war, the average migrant was uneducated, possibly illiterate, having grown up in a rural farming community or small town. By the mid-1960s, by contrast, most migrants were moving to Northern cities from Southern cities. They arrived there with more education than the whites who remained to greet them. Inequality within black residential areas increased as educated blacks took on more middle-class jobs than ever.[22]

With suburban development after World War II, whites with higher incomes finally had housing alternatives that had been unavailable to them previously. By the 1960s, with much of the housing vacated by whites now available to blacks, the demand for urban housing no longer so exceeded the supply. The meaning of racial separation also became different. With schools no longer legally segregated, thanks to *Brown v. Board of Education*, whites now had an impetus to leave the cities, and especially the city schools, behind. Getting into a separate jurisdiction made de facto segregation easier to obtain—as well as other suburban amenities such as open space and bigger homes.

Although the economic and educational attainment of Northern blacks improved significantly over these twenty years, high levels of racial segregation did not decline in the North. No matter how well some blacks did economically, they still ended up living in black neighborhoods. Even when higher-income blacks were the first to move into white neighborhoods, those areas quickly became predominantly black. The black neighborhoods kept expanding in size, though compared to the 1940s, middle-class, working-class, and poor blacks resided ever more apart from one another within those neighborhoods.

No ethnic or racial group had ever been so isolated from mainstream American society. Thus, by the mid-1960s, as blacks grew increasingly resigned to the belief that the ghetto was here to stay—at least for the foreseeable future—they had no choice but to speculate that the ghetto would only grow bigger and bigger.[23] While the civil rights movement focused on their right to rent and buy anywhere in the city (so-called open occupancy) as well as on de facto segregation in public schools, many more militant blacks in the Black Power movement saw control of the ghetto's educational, political, and economic institutions as the far more relevant goal.[24] In seeing Black Power as a fundamental aspect of change, new leaders saw the idealism of whites as myth and called for a different kind of commitment to end repression. The call for Black Power renewed Clark's observations from the HARYOU report that ghetto dwellers were subject peoples living in a "powerless colony."[25] In its comprehensiveness, Black Power paralleled an important aspect of Myrdal's thinking, one that had unfortunately been largely ignored by the social scientists who were to follow. He had argued that the situation of blacks was caused by "a great number of interdependent factors, mutually cumulative in their effects," rather than by any single factor.[26] Unfortunately, the era that was to follow took the opposite tack as liberal social scientists turned to one-shot approaches. Among the most significant of these lines of thinking were those focusing on geography, family, and culture.

GEOGRAPHY

When Drake and Cayton wrote about the economic situation of blacks in the forties, they viewed the ghetto as a dwelling space for massive numbers of poor who were subject to separate discrimination in the labor market. In their work, nothing about the ghetto per se caused this economic disadvantage. Indeed, poverty inside the ghetto was a partial result of labor market discrimination that took place outside the ghetto. Following the 1965 Watts riot and those soon to follow in other U.S. cities, this way of thinking about the ghetto underwent a major transformation. The California Governor's Commission charged with studying the riot's causes drew national attention to a hitherto-barely-recognized problem: the link between high black unemployment and the geography of jobs.

Anyone driving on an urban expressway during morning rush hours in the mid-1960s—one lane crowded with white-collar workers driving to a central business district from the suburbs, and another crowded with poorer inner-city residents heading to blue-collar jobs in suburban office or industrial parks—would have observed the budding trend noted by the commission: a mismatch between where the jobs were and where poor people lived.[27] Distance in miles was exacerbated by low ownership of cars among poor people. Only 14 percent of Watts households owned cars, as compared to 50 percent of Los Angeles residents. The commission recognized the handicap this posed to job seekers in the ghetto and concluded that the situation had "had a major influence in creating a sense of isolation, with its resultant frustrations, among the residents of south central Los Angeles."[28]

Prior to the 1960s, the sociological literature did not take into account the spatial components of unemployment, despite its acknowledgment that blacks were—as Drake and Cayton observed— "disproportionately represented in the ranks of the unemployed" and lower-paid jobs.[29] Even those who wrote about ghettos did not see the ghetto spatiality itself as a reason for black poverty. Rather, blacks tended to work in occupations that were the first to be affected by economic crises; blacks were the last hired and first fired; there were not enough jobs for all the migrants from the South; many unions discriminated in their hiring practices. As a physical space in which blacks were confined, some analysts saw the ghetto as benign and even, in some ways, positive. Many blacks working within it could depend on the community's "wage-earning masses" to support their white-collar jobs, while those engaged in service-related and manual labor could travel by public transit to white-owned factories and homes.[30] The pre-civil-rights-era literature on ghettos did not take up the idea that the earnings and employment opportunities of blacks were bound by their restriction to a particular space of the city.

After the Watts riot, the Governor's Commission publicized what was essentially a new idea. Until that moment, it had been circulating only in a mimeographed paper by John F. Kain, a Harvard economist. Kain had noticed that something important was taking place wherever poor urban blacks were living. His unpublished paper from 1964—"The Effects of the Ghetto on the Distribution and Level of Nonwhite Employment in Urban Areas"—was the first to recognize that workplaces employing low-wage employees were no longer located in urban centers.[31] With the spread of suburbanization and the completion of a national highway system since World War II, the distribution of jobs had changed.

By the mid-1960s, fifteen years of expansion had altered not only the distribution of the metropolitan area's population, but also that of its workplaces. A study of forty large metropolitan areas revealed that whereas barely 10 percent of jobs in wholesale had been located on the outskirts of these cities in the immediate postwar period, by the mid-1960s that figure had risen to nearly 33 percent, with a similar shift—15 percent to 31 percent—occurring in service jobs. While in 1948 less than one-quarter of retail jobs in these metropolitan areas had been in the suburbs, by 1963 that number had risen to nearly 50 percent. As for industry, by 1963, 50 percent of manufacturing jobs in these cities lay on the periphery.[32] Restriction to the ghetto now meant something quite different from what it had at the close of World War II. Geographic and spatial factors (the location of work and residence) were now possibly as important as nonspatial factors (discrimination, lack of skills) to the understanding of the labor market for ghetto dwellers.

Kain argued that developments in transportation and communication had facilitated a more flexible use of land, allowing manufacturing, retail, wholesaling, or housing to spring up in new areas. Companies, factories, and other sources of employment that had once found it advantageous to be located in urban centers now discovered that it was unnecessary to pay the additional price for such centrality. Proximity to ports, rail lines, and freight terminals became increasingly irrelevant as more and more goods were transported by truck. Firms—especially those engaged in manufacturing or wholesaling and thus dependent on trucks—could enjoy lower transport costs if they relocated near major highway intersections in the suburbs. Similarly, the sharp rise in automobile ownership diminished the need for public transportation, allowing companies to move farther from mass transit hubs. Many firms found it easier to attract employees to locations that, though farther from the center, offered free parking and a healthier environment. In sum, the advantages of a central location diminished or vanished altogether.

All this took place, Kain observed, while blacks remained confined to housing in ghettos. This led to fewer job opportunities for a significant percentage of the poor.[33] The problem of the ghetto thus assumed an entirely new character. Kain argued that the failure of mass transit to keep up with the relocation of workplaces was highly disadvantageous to poor blacks restricted to particular areas by racial discrimination. For those so confined, the availability and cost of public transportation were especially critical.[34]

Kain asked how commuting costs affected poor blacks in particular. Since whites could choose where they lived based on where they worked, housing was not as critical a question for them. Even if they could not move closer to their jobs, they could move near transportation lines that might get them to work. Constrained in their housing choices by discriminatory practices, blacks suffered more acutely from the effects of suburbanization. Since few mass transit lines traveled from the ghetto to the outer suburbs, many workers had to travel to the central business district and then transfer to a bus that took them to work outside the city. Even worse, most jobs that moved away from the central city required a car, and poor blacks were not likely to own one.

In the early sixties, little empirical data existed on how individuals and families responded to commuting.[35] Kain and his research team spent the decade leading up to the civil rights movement laying the groundwork for such a study by analyzing the data collected by transportation authorities in various regions. Crucially for Kain and his team, the data revealed where surveyed households lived and worked. By thinking of the ghetto as a transportation issue, Kain came up with new hypotheses on how to decrease unemployment among poor blacks.

As Kain pointed out, even when regular mass transit lines did provide service between the central city and its suburbs, they tended to operate only during peak hours, since an efficient transit system depended on large numbers of riders traveling at the same time. As workplaces moved away from the central city, however, such transit schedules became problematic. Workers who depended on "rush hour" public transportation had to leave at the end of their shift, thus missing out on possible overtime pay. This involved costs not only for them, but also for their employers, who were unable to schedule staggered shifts. Thus, Kain wrote, "as jobs, and particularly blue collar jobs . . . shifted from areas that [were] relatively well served by public transit to areas that [were] poorly served, employment opportunities for low income households dependent on public transit service [were] reduced."[36]

The California Governor's Commission report built on Kain's ideas, which became known in academic circles as the spatial mismatch hypothesis. It concluded that the local bus service in Watts and greater Los Angeles, which was run by one private and three different public entities, was inadequate for workers who lived in Watts. Since the transport system's services were not synchronized with one another, no free transfers existed between different lines. Travel from one part of the city, such as Watts, to nearly any other neighborhood thus required more than one fare. The commission called for public subsidies that would reduce fares and grant free transfers.

Although Kain stated quite clearly that better transportation was only one way to increase the employment rate of poor blacks, "spatial mismatch" began to circulate beyond the academy and to be perceived as a problem to be solved in isolation. Two diametrically opposed solutions were offered. First, the government could create incentives to encourage corporations to locate closer to ghetto neighborhoods. Kain argued, however, that this would be expensive, entail a high subsidy per job, reduce pressure to integrate housing, and perpetuate the pattern of racial segregation. He also worried that the creation of jobs in ghettos would cause huge numbers of blacks from the South to move to

Northern cities and thus aggravate the already-serious problems in those ghettos, while having no positive effect on their income or employment levels. Although he admitted that such a change might benefit some of these migrants, he felt that it would greatly complicate the assimilation and integration of blacks in urban society. He thus argued for improving transport instead.

FAMILY

In March 1965, another white expert on the ghetto poor appeared on the scene: Daniel Patrick Moynihan, the Irish American expert on ethnicity now working in government and ideally situated to apply his ideas on a grand scale. Under his influence, and repeating many of his and Glazer's prior characterizations in *Beyond the Melting Pot*, the ghetto would be discussed not in terms of its run-down and overcrowded facilities or inefficient public transportation, but in terms of its broken families. Like Kain, Moynihan set the stage for new ways of thinking about the ghetto, but while Kain as an individual was never known beyond a small circle of academics, Moynihan became a household name.

On August 6 of that year, President Lyndon B. Johnson signed the Voting Rights Act, whose aims he laid out in his "To Fulfill These Rights" speech at Howard University. There he announced his full commitment to creating conditions for black equality. Drawing on an internal White House report, the president argued that "unless we strengthen the family to create conditions under which most parents will stay together—all the rest: schools, and playgrounds, and public assistance, and private concern—will never be enough to cut completely the circle of despair and deprivation."[37]

The document Johnson drew on, "The Negro Family: The Case for National Action," or the Moynihan Report, as it came to be known, was the work of a thirty-eight-year-old junior policymaker. Moynihan had been raised in a single-parent home in Hell's Kitchen on Manhattan's West Side and had entered City College, where he began a long relationship with his psychology professor, Kenneth Clark. A year later, he joined the navy and transferred to Tufts, outside of Boston, where he completed his B.S. in naval science in 1946, as well as a B.A. in history in 1948. After a stint at the London School of Economics on a Fulbright, he went back to Tufts for its doctoral program in international relations at the Fletcher School of Law and Diplomacy. In 1961, he completed that degree with a historical dissertation titled "The United States and the International Labor Organization, 1889–1934."

Moynihan had entered government service as an aide to New York governor Averell Harriman and soon joined the Kennedy administration as assistant secretary of labor. In 1963, the year he and Glazer published *Beyond the Melting Pot*, President Kennedy asked him to draft what was to become the Economic Opportunity Act of 1964, which presaged the War on Poverty.[38] He had already advocated a color-blind national family income support and full-employment policy.[39]

Moynihan's report was a study of statistics on the black family. It was meant for President Johnson, who intended to use it as the basis for Great Society programs to help poor blacks. It was labeled "For Official Use Only," but its contents were leaked and ultimately published by the U.S. Department of Labor in March 1965. Although Moynihan had little training in the social sciences and little contact with blacks, he replaced Myrdal as the most influential thinker on the problems of blacks in America, at least in policy circles.

Moynihan declared that the family structure in ghettos such as Harlem (his prime example) was reaching complete breakdown: "There could hardly be a more dramatic demonstration of the crumbling—the breaking—of the family structure on the urban frontier."[40] He pointed to the relatively large number of illegitimate births and a matriarchal family structure, which, he proposed, was holding back both black men and women:[41] "At the heart of the deterioration of the fabric of Negro society is the deterioration of the Negro family. It is the fundamental source of weakness of the Negro community. . . . Unless this damage is repaired, all the effort to end discrimination and poverty and injustice will come to little."[42]

Moynihan also argued for the centrality of the family on the grounds that its role in shaping character and ability was so pervasive as to be easily overlooked. The family was the basic social unit of American life and, as such, the basic socializing agent. By and large, adult conduct in society was learned in childhood.[43] The breakdown of the black family had thus led to a "startling increase in welfare dependency."[44]

Taken on its own terms, his analysis had coherence. He traced the problems of the black family to the lingering effects of the American system of slavery, which, especially when compared to the Brazilian variant, had dehumanized and "vitiated family life."[45] He also saw the importance of the Reconstruction and migration eras, two historic moments that had hindered black social mobility and further disrupted traditional social patterns. These phenomena, as well as subsequent unemployment, had worked against "the emergence of a strong father figure," according to Moynihan.[46] As a result, the many black fathers who could not support their families were led to "dependence on the mother's income [which] undermines the position of the father and deprives the children of the kind of attention, particularly in school matters, which is now a standard feature of middle-class upbringing."[47]

For Moynihan, such a family structure made black men incapable of assuming their proper place in society. He argued that black unemployment reflected not merely a "lack of training and opportunity in the greatest measure, but . . . also . . . a certain failure of nerve."[48] He presented his original data on this point in the form of an anecdote:

"Are you looking for a job?" Secretary of Labor Wirtz asked a young man on a Harlem street corner.
"Why?"

Moynihan also cited a report that suggested that "[black men] react as they do because they are not equal to the world that confronts them, and they know it."[49] While recognizing the historical roots of the problem he defined, Moynihan found in the black family a single-factor explanation for the complex social circumstances of the black ghetto: "Once or twice removed, it will be found to be the principal source of most of the aberrant, inadequate, or anti-social behavior that did not establish, but now serves to perpetuate the cycle of poverty and deprivation."[50]

Moynihan's report explicitly urged that data on the black family inform any proposals to help the inner city. Questions had to be raised as to whether any policies could help poor blacks before their family lives were improved. As Moynihan stated later that year, the question is "whether the impact of economic disadvantage on the Negro community has gone on so long that genuine structural damage has occurred, so that a reversal in the course of economic events will no longer produce the expected response in social areas."[51] This turned out to be an unfortunate formulation, incendiary in many circles, from a man who had forcefully advocated for both full employment and a national family-income policy.

When the Moynihan Report was released, a firestorm ensued among both intellectuals and activists. Christopher Jencks, a Harvard professor known for his sober and balanced approach to social policy, noted in *The New York Review of Books*, "The guiding assumption [of Moynihan's analysis] is that social pathology is caused less by basic defects in the social system than by defects in particular individuals and groups which prevent their adjusting to the system. The prescription is therefore to change the deviants, not the system."[52] Within the civil rights movement, Martin Luther King rose to the defense of the black family in a speech to Planned Parenthood of America titled "Family Planning—A Special and Urgent Concern."[53] While acknowledging the seriousness of the problems raised by Moynihan, he argued that blacks could not solve very many of their economic or political problems through birth control, which he took the Moynihan Report's emphasis on illegitimacy to be implying; the issues were far more complicated and extended to economic security, education, discrimination, and housing. All the same, if family planning was adopted in a rational manner, it could help resolve or at least alleviate some serious problems, King agreed. While acknowledging that the troubles that black families faced were a "cruel evil they urgently need to control," King did not allow the occasion to pass without challenging the Moynihan Report's stigmatizing tendencies or its argument that family disorganization was the single most important cause of the ghetto's problems. He insisted that poverty lay at the root of the problem: "Negroes of higher economic and educational status actually have fewer children than white families in the same circumstances."[54] Ironically, Moynihan acknowledged this same point in his report, but made less of it.

Reviled by blacks and the left more generally, the Moynihan Report— and the consternation it caused those on the left—led to its author's ascendance in conservative government circles. After the Republican Richard Nixon won the 1968 presidential election, Moynihan remained in his administration as a policy adviser. In this position, with Nixon relying on him regarding issues of race, he generated more controversy. On March 1, 1970, a front-page story in *The New York Times* appeared with the headline "'Benign Neglect' on Race Is Proposed by Moynihan." In a memo, Moynihan had suggested to Nixon that "Negro problems had been 'too much talked about,' and 'too much taken over to hysterics, [and] paranoids . . . on all sides.'"[55] The best way for the administration to make progress on racial inequality, he proposed, was to speak less about it. Such a tactic would disempower radical groups such as the Black Panthers and would make it easier for ordinary citizens to appreciate the great gains that had been made in the past decade.

Throughout the second half of the 1960s and in the 1970s, Moynihan took great umbrage at the fact that the report with his name attached to it had seemingly destroyed his reputation in many progressive circles, though he was not unhappy that he was now regarded among whites as the go-to expert on blacks in the United States. He made tireless efforts to reach out to and recruit the support of eminent intellectuals and experts whose work had been more widely accepted. In a letter to Gunnar Myrdal, now living in Sweden, he expressed hope that the organized black response to his report had run its course, but also let Myrdal know that the response was not all bad: "I continue to get an important response from White America. *LIFE* magazine, for example, devoted an article to the subject in a year-end issue on cities. This idea *reaches* middle class Americans: they see the claims of family as legitimate. Somehow, claims made in the name of abstractions such as unemployment do not excite us."[56]

Moynihan went on to tell Myrdal that his now-infamous report had simply drawn on the concepts developed in *An American Dilemma*: "As you will quickly perceive, my methodology, or rather my analytical concept, is taken wholly from your principle of cumulation. You might recall in Appendix 3 listing 'stability in family relations' as one of the variables which affects the Negro plane of living both in its own right and through its secondary effects on the other variables."[57]

In fact, the spirit of Moynihan's report was diametrically opposed to that of Myrdal's *American Dilemma*. By arguing that the cycle could

only be broken if national efforts were directed toward one variable—
the black family—Moynihan had missed the boat and the spirit of
Myrdal's thinking. Myrdal had been skeptical of all single-factor explanations. He said that "one-factor theories" always end up being
overly fatalistic and make it difficult for people to understand the interdependence of factors and how they come together in "cumulative causation."[58] Myrdal was also impatient with the idea that racial progress
depended on slow, gradual change. Myrdal had urged social scientists
to focus on variables such as employment, which could immediately
affect standards of living, rather than factors that might take generations to change. "The scientific ideal," he had argued, was "not only
to define and analyze the factors, but to give for each of them a
measure of their actual quantitative strength in influencing other
factors. . . . The time element becomes of paramount importance
in these formulas."[59]

CULTURE

In 1965, Moynihan was by no means the only famous American intellectual whose work was understood to blame poverty on the pathologies
of the poor. Nor was he the first. By the time he emerged on the scene,
Oscar Lewis, a white anthropologist at the University of Illinois, was
already an established expert on lower-class family life because of his
work on impoverished housing settlements in Mexico City. Lewis's research on these communities began with his first visit to Mexico in 1943
and became the basis for his controversial thesis about "the culture of
poverty." Simply put, Lewis argued that poverty creates a distinctive
subculture that crosses both national boundaries and the rural-urban
divide. For those embedded in it, the culture of poverty is similar in
both rural and urban settings, and whether in advanced industrial
countries such as the United States or in less-developed countries such
as Mexico. His fieldwork ultimately led to his study of one hundred typical families in four slums in San Juan, Puerto Rico, and fifty families
related to them in New York City. He published the last of his great
works based on this Puerto Rican fieldwork, *La Vida: A Puerto Rican
Family in the Culture of Poverty*, just a few months after the Moynihan

Report came out. Lewis's study received the National Book Award in 1967 for "giving a voice to people who are rarely heard."[60]

Lewis argued that the culture of poverty had its own structure and rationale. A coping mechanism for those consigned to an essentially hopeless existence, it was an inherited way of life.[61] Among the typical characteristics of the culture of poverty was an inability to defer gratification and a consequent focus on the present. Family life was characterized by "early initiation into sex; free unions or consensual marriages; a relatively high incidence of the abandonment of wives and children; a trend toward female- or mother-centered families, and consequently a much greater knowledge of maternal relatives."[62] An artful writer, Lewis's depictions were vivid: whether admiringly or not (and most of it was admiring indeed), he brought his subjects to life.

Lewis argued that those mired in the culture of poverty were socially isolated from the institutions and values of mainstream society and thus constituted a population apart. They were not so socially distant, however, as to be unaware of what was taking place in the wider society. Though hostile to the institutions of that society, they spoke as if they believed in middle-class values even if they did not actually try to live up to them. For Lewis, the wide discrepancy between what people said and what they did was a significant dimension of the culture of poverty.[63] In such a milieu, he claimed, childhood did not exist as others know it because of extreme violence, early initiation into sexual activity, and a mother-centered family stemming from marital instability.

Despite Lewis's emphasis on the destructive tendencies of the culture of poverty, he saw the fatalism and sense of resignation among the poor as a source of psychological health given the concrete deprivations of their lives. Some on the left complained that this meant "being poor is terrible, but having a culture of poverty is not so bad."[64] Nor did they like his claim that from generation to generation the culture of poverty perpetuates itself as one generation transfers it to the next. What rankled them most, however, was the idea that once children of six or seven have "absorbed the basic values and attitudes of their subculture, [they] . . . are not psychologically geared to take full advantage of changing conditions or increased opportunities which may occur in their lifetime."[65]

All in all, Lewis believed that because the culture of poverty took on a life of its own, it was far more difficult to eradicate than might be supposed by reformers stressing other bases for change.[66] At the same time, Lewis did not believe that larger institutions should be off the hook. He suggested that the culture of poverty flourished in particular types of societies, namely, capitalist countries with high unemployment and underemployment, wage labor, and nuclear families (as opposed to extended kinship systems). For a culture of poverty to prevail, the dominant ideology of the society had to uphold thrift and blame failure on the personal flaws of individuals. Indeed, Lewis did not feel that a culture of poverty could be found in all societies.

Citing a wide range of examples—from Cuba and medieval Jewish ghettos to the sweepers of India—he pointed out that it was certainly possible to be poor while maintaining a self-sufficient culture. Even in places such as the United States, where a culture of poverty did exist, he speculated that 80 percent of the poor did not participate in it. Those who did tended to be low-income blacks, Puerto Ricans, Native Americans, and Southern poor whites—a large group to be sure, but still a subset of the total population of poor people. Lewis wrote little about American blacks. From what little he did actually say, it seems he believed that the culture of poverty in the continental United States was less entrenched than in Puerto Rico, where it was characterized by politically conservative leanings among the impoverished. In the United States, racial discrimination had created a basis for protest that could not be found in these other areas.[67] The hope that such protest gave to poor blacks had the potential to "destroy the psychological and social core of the culture of poverty."[68] Lewis suspected that the civil rights movement had accomplished more by improving the self-image and self-respect of blacks than by winning economic gains, even if these two effects reinforced each other.[69] These progressive ideas were less noticed by Lewis's critics than his emphasis on what was lacking in some of the world's poorest places.

As with Moynihan's, Lewis's ideas were taken up by conservatives. Whereas Lewis had argued that the culture of poverty was adopted by the poor to help them cope with their difficult situations, conservatives proposed that poverty was the effect of a culture of poverty rather than its cause.[70] In particular, they latched onto the idea that those living in some cultures had different concepts of time, focused on sensual gratification of the present instead of accomplishments for the future. An inability to plan ahead might be caused by a particular culture, but such a culture gives rise to poverty, rather than the other way around.[71]

Ironically, Lewis became known for dwelling on the negative aspects of the culture of poverty despite the fact that he also saw many virtues in it. Among left-wing critics, Lewis's theory came to be seen as the middle-class intellectual's rationale for blaming poverty on the poor and thus side-stepping the need for substantive social change. Much of what he became known for was therefore at odds with the details of his own argument, which strongly critiqued the institutions that set the terms of poor people's lives.[72] Also missing was acknowledgment of Lewis's palpable respect for poor people's strengths and ability to cope. Lewis was a Marxist who saw poverty as destroying individuals, rather than seeing individuals as self-destructive. He regarded the people whom he studied as victims damaged by the poverty into which they had been born. Rather than blaming them for their condition, Lewis argued that it was necessary to focus on the key local contexts in which the poor were embedded—the slum community and the family, as well as the capitalist system. Lewis emphasized the "lack of justice, the suffering, the inequities, the abuses, the exploitation, and the repression of the poor."[73] He was an anticapitalist, responding to those who blamed poverty on failures of individual character.

His Marxism took the form of eliding race as an explanation, whether as put forward by crude racists or those, like Moynihan, who focused on only one racial group as having the problems associated with all poor people's lives. Writing in *Scientific American* a few months after the Moynihan Report appeared, Lewis explained the implications of the culture-of-poverty thesis for those who believed that the behavior patterns of black Americans were distinctive to that group. He argued that to attribute the high number of female-headed households to anything distinctive in the black American experience, whether it be slavery or migration, was incorrect. Such households were typical of the culture of poverty and existed all over the world, including among peoples with no history of slavery.[74] In both its timing and its content, this piece by Lewis can be read as a subtle rebuttal to Moynihan's race-based perspective.

Lewis denied that the problems of blacks could be attributed to life in the ghetto. On the contrary, he argued in the same *Scientific American* article that problems found in the U.S. ghetto are prevalent in countries with no segregated minorities.[75] A strong implication of Lewis's work was that the problems that some would attribute to racial segregation were instead a broader phenomenon of poverty and the culture of poverty. The tendency to attribute fatalism, helplessness, and feelings of inferiority in U.S. blacks to racial segregation was misleading. Lewis had observed these same traits in the slum dwellers of Mexico City and San Juan.[76]

Between the end of World War II and the onset of the war in Vietnam, *An American Dilemma* was the dominant influence on scholarly literature dealing with race and minority relations.[77] By the mid-1960s, however, the book had begun to lose its relevance. The explosions in the North led intellectuals to feel that Myrdal had been wrong in arguing that white goodwill would solve the race problem in America. As Charles E. Silberman remarked in 1964, the twentieth anniversary of the book's publication, "Myrdal was wrong. The tragedy of race relations in the United States is that there is no American Dilemma. White Americans are not torn and tortured by the conflict between their devotion to the American creed and their actual behavior."[78] Instead, he claimed, they were much more upset that "their peace is being shattered and their business interrupted."[79]

For many, the emergence of a black-led movement for black civil rights had made Myrdal's approach to race relations seem as irrelevant as Robert Park's. The framework of Myrdal's book was rendered obsolete by the fact that the change in American race relations had arisen from peaceful resistance among blacks in the South rather than from white America's conscience.[80] Kenneth Clark summarized his own views in Myrdal's presence at a 1964 symposium on "Liberalism and the Negro" sponsored by *Commentary* magazine: "With all due respect to my friend and former colleague and boss, Professor Myrdal, I have come to the conclusion that so far as the Negro is concerned, the ethical aspect of American liberalism . . . is primarily verbal."[81]

In a sign of how much the pendulum had swung, during the *Commentary* symposium Kenneth Clark chastised Myrdal by supporting the novelist James Baldwin, who was also present. Baldwin had been criticized for his skepticism toward any political program whose success hinged on people not discriminating against each other—that is, on the kind of goodwill Myrdal had envisioned. "I don't care if you don't love me," he argued, "I just don't want to be kept in a ghetto."[82]

By 1969, when *The New York Times Magazine* ran its feature article by the Stanford historian Carl Degler titled "The Negro in America—Where Myrdal Went Wrong," Myrdal's irrelevance was widely accepted. Degler argued that he failed to recognize that change would result from pressure from blacks rather than from white America's conscience: "One would have thought that his many researchers would have given him some inkling of the long history of anti-Negro attitudes and practices in the North which are still reflected in contemporary intransigency among Northern whites."[83]

The astonishment summarized by Degler's *Times* article would become the lasting consensus on Myrdal's work. With the benefit of the archival materials, we can see how Myrdal never came to fully appreciate the significance of Northern racism. He had certainly tried to do so, but this was the price Myrdal paid for failing to make a deal with Cayton to fund the publication of a book for which Cayton would receive full credit. For all the money the Carnegie Corporation had put into Myrdal's massive study, it seems in retrospect that they had been "penny-wise" with the wrong person.

Only when America's black inner cities erupted was the country suddenly forced to focus on poverty within the urban community—an issue that Myrdal had essentially shelved after Cayton's refusal to hand over the Chicago materials. Thus, Northern racism and the circumstances of the "ghetto" were not even on the list of numerous interdependent factors that Myrdal had argued merited consideration for an understanding of the social position of blacks in America. Even as Myrdal brilliantly argued that in theory Northern residential segregation was basic to all other forms of discrimination (inferior schools, hospitals, and playgrounds, to name just some examples), he spent little time assessing the actual impact of segregation. As he assessed the complex interrelations of health, family stability, education, and employment, he paid little attention to their connections with the ghetto.

Looking back at *An American Dilemma* now, after seven decades, one can see that it was both a great and a very flawed book. Myrdal cannot be blamed for his failure to anticipate the massive migration that made cities so much more important to blacks. Certainly he cannot be faulted

for failing to predict all the ways in which cities were neglected in subsequent decades. Even today his book is a brilliant and unparalleled
compilation of the social situation of blacks in the United States
before World War II. The data it publicized on the damage caused by
separate institutions were powerful enough to serve as grounds for the
Supreme Court's *Brown* decision.

Had Myrdal simply delivered this information without further argument, the book would have remained a classic. But Myrdal's faith in the
ability of whites, and particularly Northern whites, to resolve what he
called their ethical dilemma opened him to charges of naïveté and even
accommodation. Most unfortunately, social scientists and others neglected Myrdal's valuable notion that the situation of blacks was caused
by "a great number of interdependent factors, mutually cumulative in
their effects" rather than by any single factor.[84] Instead, as we have seen,
in the mid-sixties, the ghetto was reconceptualized in a variety of ways,
each of them emphasizing individual factors.

The exception was Kenneth Clark's *Dark Ghetto*. By 1965, the year of its
publication, it had been two decades since any important book-length
work of social science on the U.S. ghetto had appeared. Clark now believed that the psychological and experimental approach typified by his
earlier doll study was too narrow for understanding the problems that
confronted Northern blacks in their communities. For one thing, the
brief that he had coauthored with the other social scientists had claimed
that segregation produced feelings of inferiority *only* when it was mandated by law. The lessons taken from his doll experiments, however
helpful in shaping the 1954 Supreme Court ruling that separate but
equal was inherently unequal, were primarily applied to jurisdictions
practicing de jure segregation. Now Clark needed to confront the de
facto segregation of the urban North and argue that it had the same
psychological consequences, far beyond schools and in a pervasive way.
He was also shifting how he wanted to conduct his remaining time in
the academy and in the community. From his lifelong immersion in
Harlem, as a resident and in his work with its Northside clinic, he no
longer aligned himself with "the cool, objective approach" of an experimental paradigm. "In a very real sense . . . ," he acknowledged, "*Dark*

Ghetto is a summation of my personal and lifelong experiences and observations as a prisoner within the ghetto long before I was aware that I was really a prisoner."[85] Yet the book was neither autobiography nor memoir. Drawing heavily upon *Youth in the Ghetto*, his massive report published by HARYOU a year earlier, he now broadened out to write about segregation, racism, and exploitation, while still recognizing the suffering of the people he had known for forty years. Because he wrote such clear and moving prose, the work was comprehensible to social scientists and the public alike.

Although Clark began by vaguely relating the black ghetto back to the precedent of Italy's Jewish ghettos, he also had the Jewish Holocaust on his mind. In sizing up the intellectual task before him, he compared himself to Bruno Bettelheim and Viktor Frankl, "who used their skill and training to provide us with some understanding of the nature of the horror and the barbarity of the German concentration camps."[86] Stipulating that he would refuse to avoid feelings in the name of scientific objectivity, he argued that "if a scholar who studied Nazi concentration camps did not feel revolted by the evidence . . . [people would] fear for his sanity and moral sensitivity."[87] Clark would take a similar stance toward the black ghetto.

For Clark, the black ghetto was more meaningfully a North American invention, a manner of existence that had little in common with anything that had come before in Europe or even in the U.S. South. More specifically, it differed from the entity that Drake and Cayton had written about in the forties. Gone was the semi-flourishing of life symbolized by the Bronzeville of the 1930s and 1940s. Clark's book makes no reference to the spirit of the community, to the enjoyment of life, to praising the Lord, to people's sense that they could get ahead. Whereas Drake and Cayton had barely mentioned the word "control," for Clark the ghetto was about the larger society's successful "institutionalization of powerlessness."[88]

Wirth's original ghetto formulation came with the idea that ghettos were to some extent voluntary and self-imposed. Even Drake and Cayton had taken the middle ground, claiming that blacks would not have minded living together had the ghetto not been forced upon them. Now, twenty years later, on the basis of the doll study and so much more, Clark rejected this perspective altogether.[89] To the extent that blacks might prefer to live apart, the ghetto reflected—at least in part—one of the cruelest characteristics of racial segregation: its victims come to seek one another's company as respite from others' denigration, ending up believing in their inferiority and preferring to remain apart. Exclusion, rejection, and stigmatization were neither desired nor imposed by healthy human beings. "Human beings who are forced to live under ghetto conditions and whose daily experiences tell them that almost nowhere in society are they respected and granted the ordinary dignity and courtesy accorded to others will, as a matter of course, begin to doubt their own worth."[90]

Like Drake and Cayton, Clark saw the ghetto as a neighborhood fundamentally different in kind (rather than degree) from other neighborhoods of the city. It was different in its formation through the migration from the U.S. South to the U.S. North of so many poor blacks in such a short time. It was also different in the social psychological understandings of its residents. And finally, it was powerless. Like Drake and Cayton, he referred to ghetto dwellers as a "subject people," but drawing on his earlier analysis in *Youth in the Ghetto,* he went much further by turning a phrase into an argument about what made the ghetto distinctive.[91] He saw Harlem as a "philanthropic, economic, business, and industrial colony of New York City."[92] His understanding of ghetto blacks as a subject people pervaded his discussions of political leadership, social agencies, schools, business, and real estate, all of which, he claimed, were controlled by forces outside the community.[93] For Clark, the purpose was external control, and the psychology of the ghetto was one of complete helplessness and suspicion.

This extended to the ghetto's politicians, including the long-serving (and long politically dominant) Congressman Adam Clayton Powell, Jr. Clark argued that ghetto politicians were not merely narrowly self-interested but also incompetent when it came to obtaining power or patronage. Their political power rested on a limited economic base, and they were rarely involved in important deals, such as multimillion-dollar construction projects. Instead, they tended "to compete among themselves for the available crumbs; and this struggle, in turn, [made] them more vulnerable to manipulation by real political leadership—i.e. white leadership."[94] Rather than focusing their energies on civil rights or larger issues, black politicians kept their eye on the sort of local concerns that made it impossible for them to rise to higher positions.

If politicians were essentially inconsequential in the power they wielded, where did the true power of the ghetto lie? Not in the black press, which exploited anti-intellectualism and sensationalism, and whose power was dissipated because it failed to take responsibility to bring about "sustained fundamental social change."[95] The social and community agencies did not create power because their money came from outside the ghetto. Controlled by whites, their power was not transferable to blacks. Social change in the ghetto was thus not controlled by blacks. Indeed, Clark saw the social agencies of Harlem as reinforcing its colonial status and dependency on New York City. The subservience and inferiority that the average ghetto dweller experienced in other ways were reinforced by political and institutional structures controlled by outsiders. Such powerlessness could only be compensated for in a few places, among them the street corner, the bar, and the church—settings somewhat beyond the control of whites. Only in places such as these could blacks have a feeling of personal worth. And among these settings, the church was the one that appeared to have an element of power.

All the factors combined to create behaviors that surfaced as pathological, again different not just in degree, but of such intensity and frequency as to make for a qualitatively different reality. In white immigrant neighborhoods of the city, it might be appropriate to deal with social deviance by thinking in terms of reforming or curing individuals. But ghetto pathology was of a different order. Deficits of education, employment, and political capacity were interconnected and tended to self-perpetuate while feeding on each other. Clark's approach to thinking of the ghetto as a vicious cycle was more comprehensive than Drake and Cayton's. He systematically analyzed each sphere of life as its own vicious cycle and developed a theory about how each one reinforced the others in a "tangle of pathology" (a phrase that Moynihan had borrowed from Clark's earlier writing).[96] Whereas the optimistic Myrdal believed that vicious cycles could unwind and turn around, Clark was unconvinced that the principle of cumulative causation could ever reverse. Although he acknowledged that better jobs could help surmount dependency, crime, and disease, he, unlike Myrdal, doubted that

enough jobs would ever be forthcoming.[97] "Nothing short of a concerted and massive attack on the social, political, economic, and cultural
roots of the pathology is required if anything more than daubing or a
displacement of the symptoms is to be achieved."[98]

When Clark referred to the pathology of the ghetto in 1965, drug
addiction—not family life—occupied most of his attention. Harlem had
become a major center of heroin distribution: with the increase in street
people, many turned to crime to support their habits. Many of the people
he met while writing his book told him that they had nothing to live
for save their shot of heroin. "All I can look forward to is what I can get
out of this bag, and that's nothing really," one man acknowledged to
him.[99] The few who were able to quit found that if at some point they
had been imprisoned, it was nearly impossible for them to find a job.
For most, however, treatment was largely ineffective. In *Dark Ghetto*,
Clark became an early advocate for drug legalization. He fervently
argued that drug addicts in the ghetto should not be abandoned, and
that a Harlem Institute for Narcotics Research needed to be set up. It
should advocate for the medical rather than penal treatment of drug offenders and also focus attention on the root causes of poverty, always his
principal concern. He lamented the tendency to imprison lawbreakers
rather than destroy the roots of crime within the community.[100] In addition to establishing treatment programs focused on detoxification
and rehabilitation, the institute should track the Harlem blocks where
drug dealers were active and post alerts wherever heroin could easily be
secured.

In the realm of sexuality, Clark claimed, the ghetto's troubles originated in an enslaved past, where the male had served as a stud for breed-
ing but had otherwise been humiliated and dehumanized. Even after
emancipation, the black male was incapable of joining the labor market
and supporting a wife and family. He adopted a compensatory swagger
and unreliability that led to high numbers of desertions and a pattern of
women running the family unit. Lower-class girls and boys knew the
script from an early age. Neither sought class status because that avenue
was closed; instead, the girl looked for affirmation in sex, while the boy
measured his power solely by the number of girls he slept with. When
the baby arrived, the reputation of neither parents nor family suffered.
On the contrary, the infant received full acceptance, and the mother

gained from having a dependent of her own. The child's father had nothing to lose because he was going nowhere, as all paths to a better life were closed to him. Though Clark's argument echoed Moynihan's, his focus was not on the family per se, but on the ways family instability was a result of pathological conditions imposed on ghetto people.

The book had two notable absences: Jews and women. When it came to the relations between blacks and Harlem's many Jewish store owners, teachers, and landlords, Clark offered little in the way of data or analysis, and this was likely a conscious choice. For Clark was hardly oblivious to the sometimes tense relations between blacks and Jews. His first major publication two decades earlier had been a study of that very issue for *Commentary* magazine, the flagship publication of the American Jewish Committee. In *Dark Ghetto*, he focused briefly on the troubled relationship between white liberals and blacks, skirting over the fact that in New York City, the whites he was referring to were mainly Jewish: "The white liberal must be prepared, in this turbulent period of transition, to accept the fact that even his closest Negro friends will feel some hostility towards him. For if the white liberal can delude himself into believing himself color-blind, the Negro of insight and sensitivity cannot."[101] The formulation is notably similar to (if more benign than) the things James Baldwin and Harold Cruse were writing about relations between Harlem's blacks and Jews.

In discussing the life experiences of women in the ghetto, Clark started out with a potential advantage over Drake and Cayton. Not only were six out of seven of his research assistants female, but he had Mamie Phipps Clark by his side. Yet despite this opportunity, *Dark Ghetto* generally adopts a male perspective and even blames women for certain of the ghetto's problems. In a book composed principally of the words of its male author, 80 percent of the quotes come from men, and nearly half of them appear to have been collected by one of the male researchers on the team. While the mid-1960s were a crucial moment in the genesis of the U.S. women's movement, its ideas were still at an early stage. Further, its founding books, notably Betty Friedan's *Feminine Mystique*, saw "the problem with no name" as one focused on the dependency and angst of middle-class white housewives, rather than the problems of poor black women.[102] Not for at least another decade would black feminisms and third-world feminisms become prominent, and

Clark did not show particular prescience in anticipating their arrival. He did not depict women as having much influence in the ghetto, not even in institutional spheres such as churches, where female presence was strong. He rarely discussed anything beyond women's roles as shoppers, domestic workers, mothers, wives, or sexual partners. Truly not in tune with gender arrangements soon to gain wide acceptance, he saw the two-parent working family as a problem for children, since it left them to fend for themselves. He even cast some blame on black women, lamenting the large number who left their families behind in the ghetto while tending children in white homes. Regarding black men, he said the opposite, regretting that they were denied jobs outside the ghetto as well as within it.

In Clark's view of the ghetto's problems, the public school system held the most critical place. "As long as these ghetto schools continue to turn out thousands and thousands of functional illiterates yearly, Negro youth will not be prepared for anything other than menial jobs or unemployment and dependency; they will continue the cycle of broken homes, unstable family life, and neglected and uneducated children. The tragic waste of human resources will go on unabated."[103] Clark made a forceful case that in the 1930s, young blacks had entered New York City schools with IQs equal to those of whites, but thanks to the low expectations of largely incompetent teachers, their scores dropped over time. The solution to improving schools lay in attracting the best teachers to Harlem, paying them better-than-average salaries, and demanding that they hold the children of the ghetto up to the highest standards and expectations.

Although Clark continued to advocate school desegregation, he predicted that the proposed busing of black and white students into each other's neighborhood schools would end in failure, with whites withdrawing from the public schools—a sound prediction.[104] Rather than hold his breath and wait for the schools to desegregate (and risk negative reactions to such tactics as "forced busing"), Clark broke with many of his strongest allies in the civil rights movement, arguing that blacks should change their political strategy and demand excellence in ghetto schools. This, he stated boldly, was not some sort of "acquiescence in segregation. On the contrary, it is, given the intransigence of the white community and the impossibility of immediate integration, a decision to save as many Negro children as possible now. . . . These

children, Negro or white, must not be sacrificed on the altars of ideological and semantic rigidities."[105]

In concluding the book, obvious in its dialogue with Myrdal, Clark
stated, "Certainly the Negro cannot hope to argue his case primarily in
terms of ethical concerns. . . . If moral force opposes economic or political ends, the goal of moral force may be postponed."[106] This did not
stop his patron from supporting Clark by writing a foreword to the book
in which he ignored that point.

Like *An American Dilemma, Dark Ghetto* was celebrated. The philosopher Bertrand Russell, in a jacket-cover blurb for the book, remarked, "The insight of Dr. Clark into the subtleties of the Negro's
experience in white America brings to our notice the measure of what
has happened and the necessity for radical, indeed, revolutionary action."[107] A few months later, the president of Columbia notified Kenneth and Mamie Clark that the university—Harlem's great academic
neighbor—would confer upon them in 1966 its Nicholas Murray Butler
Medal for contributions to philosophy and education. Among the previous recipients were Alfred North Whitehead and Bertrand Russell himself. Kenneth Clark replied to the president on behalf of himself and
Mamie: "We must confess that we were somewhat surprised at the decision to award this medal to us. We hope that its acceptance will mark a
closer relationship between the University and ourselves in working for
the benefit of our community."[108] This, however, would never come to
pass, not in an academic appointment for either of the Clarks, and not in
any partnership between them and Columbia to study or improve the
neighborhood.

For a long time to come, critics pushed back against Moynihan, Lewis,
and Clark. It wasn't simply that the bleak images of ghetto life were ste-
reotypical or "blamed the victim." Rather, they seemed to present the
psychological dimensions of ghetto life only in terms of degradation. In
all of Clark's work, for example, where were the large number of Harlem residents who went to see Duke Ellington or Thelonious Monk at
the Cotton Club (and Carnegie Hall), the people who took the train
downtown every day to work and who shopped in the same department
stores with whites? Where was the intellectual life of Harlem, and the

style that was the envy of white people around the world? Where were the ordinary people struggling to live in accordance with standards of moral worth? The critique was often overstated, particularly as it pertained to Clark, who frequently got lumped with Moynihan. But nevertheless, the critique had a legitimate point.

This was the response to Clark from Albert Murray, a Harlem novelist and critic of literature and jazz whose 1970 book *The Omni-Americans: Black Experience and American Culture (Some Alternatives to the Folklore of White Supremacy)* argued that social science had missed the boat because it failed to comprehend the actual texture of life in the ghetto. His concern was not merely that the images of the ghetto in Moynihan's report and Clark's book justified white supremacy, though that possibility was hardly lost on him. Murray believed that Clark's revival of the word "ghetto" stemmed from an off-key conception of black life that was inappropriate to the social situation of Harlem's residents. "What useful purpose is really served by confusing segregated housing in the U.S. with the way Jewish life was separated from the gentile world in the days of the old ghettos?" Murray asked. "After all, in addition to physical segregation, the real [Jewish] ghettos also represented profound differences in religion, language, food customs, and were even geared to a different calendar. It is grossly misleading to suggest that segregated housing anywhere in the United States represents a cultural distance that is in any way at all comparable to the one that separated a Jewish ghetto from the life styles of various European countries." Murray argued, "Segregation in New York is bad enough. But it just isn't what it used to be. The national headquarters of NAACP is at 57th Street on Broadway, and the office of the NAACP Legal Defense Fund is at Columbus Circle."[109]

Though the differences between Murray and Clark were significant, they also shared similar concerns. Just as Clark saw the ghetto as a colony, Murray was deeply concerned by the "ill-conceived and condescending benevolence" that "seems to be the way of American welfarism when dealing with Negroes."[110] But whereas Clark placed the blame on white racism, Murray had other primary concerns. He lumped Clark with Moynihan and argued that the condescending welfare system was "of a piece" with their intellectual work.[111]

Other prominent responses came from white anthropologists who saw any version of the culture-of-poverty idea as anathema: poor people, black or white, did not have a problem of consciousness.[112] Nor was family the culprit. Instead, there were good reasons why poor people would, at least to a casual observer, come across as lacking commitment to children, wives, and employment. To get to something deeper, Elliot Liebow, a doctoral candidate at Catholic University, immersed himself in the social world of a group of black men in their twenties and thirties on the corner of Eleventh and M Streets in the Shaw neighborhood of northwest Washington. As described in his book *Tally's Corner* (1967), some of the men's behaviors had simple explanations, such as physical disabilities that made them ineligible for the only kinds of jobs available to them, hard manual labor primarily. More important, perhaps, Liebow argued that similarities in the behaviors of poor blacks from one generation to the next were not the product of cultural transmission. Rather, they resulted as sons experienced the same defeats as their fathers.[113] Once a man experienced these failures, he lost all confidence: "Sometimes he sits down and cries at the humiliation of it all. Sometimes he strikes out at [his wife] or the children with his fists, perhaps to lay hollow the claim to being man of the house in the one way left open to him, or perhaps simply to inflict pain on this woman who bears witness to his failure as a husband and father and therefore as a man."[114] For Liebow, these behaviors did not arise from a disbelief in conventional values, but rather an inability to live up to those values. So a substitute system of "shadow values" arose where special conditions could be invoked—such as having too much love for women to stay with any one of them. This permitted them to be "men once again provided they do not look too closely at one another's credentials."[115]

Throughout, Liebow compared what his subjects related to the wider context of what he had learned about them. He focused not only on what they told him, but also on what they did not say, the topics that never surfaced in spontaneous conversation, and the things that they did not admit. He opposed what the men on the street claimed they wanted to do with their lives to a more realistic appraisal of what was possible for them to do, given their particular abilities. He compared what his subjects said in one conversation to what they said in another. He pointed out the ways in which the men's explanations of their behavior were based on common presumptions and narratives that—if scrutinized—did not bear up to reality. He was sensitive to the way in which both their bravado and their modesty could be self-serving. He compared their declared intentions to what they actually wound up doing. And he spoke to their partners, both male and female, measuring what they said about their relationships against what their wives and lovers disclosed. Throughout all of this, he described a social world in which economic constraints made it all but impossible for many people to live up to the most basic of society's expectations, let alone their own ideals.

However effective and comprehensive these various scholars aimed to be, they all shared liabilities of gender bias: they were men writing, for the most part, about men. The major departure came from the anthropologist Carol Stack, whose 1974 book *All Our Kin* offered a portrait of the women, the sisters, aunts, girlfriends, and those "just like" family among those making their lives in the ghetto. She attended to the children, the relatives who stepped in to care for those children, and the impact of absent, unemployed fathers on the lives of their lovers and family. She showed how residents of the Flats, an African American ghetto community, adapted to their poverty by forming large, resilient, lifelong support networks based on biological family and fictive kin whose presence and mutual support were intrinsic to household and community functionality. Not least, she demonstrated just how powerful, highly structured, and surprisingly complex these networks were.

All Our Kin updated and added significant insight to earlier scholarly studies of reciprocity and forms of adaptation in the black family. Like the type of men studied by Liebow and others, the women of Stack's world "know that the minimal funds they receive from low-paying jobs on welfare do not cover their monthly necessities of life: rent, food, and clothing."[116] Stack introduced a poor black woman named Ruby Banks, a single parent, and described the daily life and survival strategies of her family in the Flats. She found that "friendships between lovers and between friends are based upon a precarious balance of trust and profit."[117] Exchanges included manipulation and exploitation; "wherever there are friendships, exploitation possibilities exist."[118] Stack revealed how the support system of family and friends, which included both mutual exchange and exploitation, enabled people to cope with poverty.

Stack as critical scholar overlapped those such as Moynihan, who was concerned with pathology among the ghetto poor. The difference, however, is that while Moynihan presented the black family as a uniform social configuration that, void of male presence, had reached "total breakdown," Stack showed capacities. She traced *how* families functioned from day to day—how a poor black matrifocal family provided a warm, supportive environment that prepared a child for life within or beyond the ghetto. No less than Moynihan, Stack believed in the importance of active parental engagement in the upbringing of children, but she showed how it was done through substitute mechanisms, including the uncles, brothers, and stepfathers who were indeed present—along with close-in friends and neighbors. And finally, while Moynihan argued that the rise of single-parent families was the most important cause of higher rates of welfare dependency, social deviance, and criminality, Stack saw welfare as a lifeline in light of poor job opportunities. But she also showed that the way welfare was organized—rules against cohabitation, for example—helped undermine long-term relationships between fathers and mothers. This was also true, she argued, because it discouraged the poor from inheriting property and thus gaining equity in home ownership, as occurred for the middle class.[119] For Stack, family deterioration, lack of wealth, and welfare policies were mutually reinforcing. Again, no single focus would do.

The ghetto was not quiescent—as first signaled by the Watts upheavals of 1965 in Los Angeles, then replicated in most other major U.S. cities in the next few years—Chicago, Baltimore, and New York among them. In 1967, the Newark ghetto went up in flames. Soon after the riot's climax, Kenneth Clark was asked by a black television anchor to accompany him and his crew into Newark and share his thoughts on the event.[120]

As Clark later recalled in a journal entry I found in his archives, amid the devastation, they came across ammunition shells in the debris—shells later determined to be from guns fired by police and from rifles of National Guardsmen. The anchorman broke his silence and asked Clark, "Are you ready to say anything? . . . What do you think?"

"There is nothing that I feel I can say," he replied. "This devastation looks like a war."[121]

Finally, he compared what he was seeing to what was going on in Vietnam: "This is America's Vietnam within our own cities." He began a commentary that was not publicly aired. "America has a more insidious Vietnam within its own borders: The incipient, the potential Vietnam, which is within Newark's and other American ghettos, has now become clear. This is a war; these windows were bombed out," he kept repeating, even though he knew that the panes had simply been smashed.[122] The image of guerrilla warfare in the urban ghetto, he later recalled, had blurred his reason; his response had been emotional rather than rational. Having never witnessed the devastation of any war in person, he thought that, however exaggerated, Newark fit the scenario, that this was military invasion.

What also struck Clark was the calm after the storm; the riot seemed to continue on a psychological level even though the barricaded area of the ghetto was now silent. He clearly saw that this war was strangely one-sided. Whereas the Vietcong had ammunition and guns that made it possible for them to fight the enemy, urban ghetto residents had no military weapons, only bricks and rocks. Facing the police and the National Guard, the residents of the ghetto did not stand a chance. As Clark pondered this contrast, he thought that the United States would never be victorious in Southeast Asia because the Vietcong were armed. An army could subdue such a people only by annihilating them. In urban warfare of the sort that had occurred in the Newark ghetto, however, the troops—army, police, National Guard—could squelch the riot and control bouts of violence and aggression. Casualties here were one-sided, making it impossible for ghetto residents to achieve any sort of victory.

Clark described the area as full of broken glass and dismembered mannequins from looted stores. Speaking into the television microphone, he drew a parallel between the broken torsos and amputated arms and legs on the street and what had befallen the residents of the area. He described the scene as surreal, a modern artist's dystopian creation. But he understood it was neither art nor a product of imagination. Clark gazed blankly at what seemed to him the ultimate essence of the ghetto. Now joined with the presence of state violence, this was what the ghetto was and would continue to be; regardless of whether more riots would occur, it was what he called "the day-to-day riot of the human spirit," and he believed it would never come to an end.[123]

Military trucks full of National Guardsmen passed by. Clark noticed that the men were all white. Many were teenagers, the oldest not past their early forties. These were average Americans decked out in military garb. They appeared nervous, fearful as they tried but did not quite succeed in looking vigilant. Not trained as soldiers and merely feigning power, hostility, and authority, they wanted to be elsewhere and were simply playing the role. Most of them would never get any closer to war than this. As their trucks drove by the television cameras, they assumed military poses.

The TV crew and Clark also entered a black public housing project that had been erected as part of an urban renewal campaign the previous decade. The night before, a black man had been shot to death in his apartment, allegedly by police, who had blamed the death on snipers firing from the roof. No snipers had been spotted, however, and the bullets discovered at the site were all identified as police ammunition.

Parked close to the housing project, the crew and Clark came across two black policemen in a squad car. Speaking to Clark and his team, they did all they could to disassociate themselves from the white police and their attacks on the black community in the last forty-eight hours. They insisted that the only snipers in the neighborhood were white policemen. Ashamed of their uniforms, they wanted people to know that they were in the car only because they had been ordered to keep guard. Although they did not openly say it, they intimated that in a showdown, they would protect the blacks to the best of their ability. They were close to tears. Identifying with their dilemma, Clark stopped the crew's white cameramen from approaching, thereby creating a bit of distance between the two cops and the only whites in the group.

Clark also remembered that as he and the crew passed through the streets, they could hear clusters of blacks discussing events, particularly the shooting of the previous night. All concurred that this had been a wanton and deliberately hostile act. Suddenly someone cried, "There is Rap Brown!" It was, in fact, Brown, the former minister of justice of the

Black Panthers, with a band of followers, all looking rather festive. To Clark's inquiry, "How are you? What are you doin' here?" Brown replied, "I am here because this is the beginning of the revolution, you know."[124]

Brown smiled, saluted Clark, and sauntered away with a militant swagger. Clark later noted that here on this war-strewn street, amid the "war-like devastation . . . in the inescapable pathos and the bitterness of the Black police, emerged the mindless jauntiness and pride in violence and rhetoric." For Rap Brown, a "symbol of some delusional vision,"[125] Newark was a place to play at revolution, to perform a kind of unintentional satire. Yet Clark felt that this was no play but a reality destined to repeat itself. This particular experience, in fact, prompted Clark to turn his attention to the Newark ghetto of the 1970s and a final book—which he was never to finish.

In 1969, Stanford University hired St. Clair Drake as professor of anthropology and founding director of its undergraduate program in Black Studies. Stanford and similar universities were under great pressure from student activists and existing faculty members to establish programs in Black Studies and to hire black faculty to research and teach courses in the field. The social sciences now heard much talk of a black sociology conducted by blacks, as in the case of *Black Metropolis*. Competition to hire Drake, a professor at Roosevelt University in Chicago, grew so rapidly that *The New York Times* took note, reporting that he was being "courted with the diligence most schools usually reserve for speedy halfbacks."[126] The article then quoted Drake's response to being offered a job at Harvard after he had accepted the position at Stanford: "I felt like telling them, why didn't you ask me twenty years ago, when I really could have used the research facilities and support? I would have jumped at it then. But they wait until the kids are ready to burn the place down before they ask me."[127]

In his mere seven years at Stanford, Drake became a fixture at the university, generous with his time, encouragement, and ideas. His course Black Communities, USA, was tremendously popular among undergraduates. Teaching on the West Coast brought him into contact with black students from that part of the country. As he came to feel the

inadequacy of studying ghettos according to a one-size-fits-all model—
based on Harlem or the South Side of Chicago—he saw a need for new
research that would take him beyond the large Northern ghetto that he
had spent most of his career investigating. He thus began observing
small, dispersed populations of blacks in towns or cities that were predominantly white, and majority-black settlements outside the inner city.
Working with his students, he looked at tiny black populations in the
states of Utah and Washington and planned to examine other black
ghettos outside urban centers, all of which he hoped to compare to the
already intensively studied classic black ghetto. He also planned to work
in depth on the cluster of two thousand blacks in the urban community
of Eureka, California, as well as on Compton, an incorporated settlement in Los Angeles, where 70 percent of the forty thousand residents
were black. Yet Drake was so absorbed in teaching and campus politics
that he was unable to take any of these studies very far by 1976, the year
of his retirement.[128]

In 1975, when the university announced that Daniel Patrick
Moynihan, now U.S. ambassador to the United Nations, would deliver
the commencement address, the campus erupted in controversy, and
students and colleagues turned to Drake for leadership. By this point,
Moynihan had succeeded in rehabilitating his public image. Persona
non grata on many campuses for a decade, he was now being welcomed
by Stanford—and awarded an honorary degree—as an intellectual hero.
In addition to defending Israel with great fanfare at the UN, he was increasingly being viewed as a man who drew attention to social problems
that only the naive could ignore.

As the director of the renamed African American studies program,
Drake wrote a letter on behalf of fourteen anthropology faculty expressing "regret" over the administration's decision and explaining the
reasons why many blacks would be offended by Moynihan's presence at
graduation. Pointing out that Stanford was more than ever a multiracial
university, he insisted that the organizers of commencement should
have taken into account the feelings of black students and parents when
choosing a graduation speaker. Inviting Moynihan to deliver the address at Stanford amounted to bestowing legitimacy on "what he stood
for" and granting him academic bona fides that he did not deserve.[129]
Drake cited the Moynihan Report as an example of bad scholarship, in

part because it had misused statistics. In particular, he took Moynihan to task for stating that even if blacks could find better employment, they would probably not be capable of improving their condition. He argued that the Moynihan Report had legitimized the belief that the black community was nothing but "a tangle of pathology," and that Moynihan's subsequent call for "benign neglect" on issues of race would be offensive to any blacks who attended the ceremony.

As Moynihan arrived on campus to deliver his address amid protests, his defenders at Stanford responded by comparing him to Gunnar Myrdal. Drake countered this claim directly, arguing that the comparison had overlooked the fact that Myrdal had hired thirty-seven scholars when preparing *An American Dilemma*, twelve of whom were black, while Moynihan had hired no blacks at all.

By the early seventies, Clark's argument that Harlem was an economic, political, and social colony was clearly generating new ways of thinking. The colonial metaphor had been significant for the Black Power movement and was now becoming important for radical scholars as they attempted to make sense of America in the wake of the civil rights movement. In his groundbreaking book *Racial Oppression in America* (1972), Robert Blauner built upon Clark's ideas to provide a badly needed conceptual apparatus for distinguishing between black ghettos and immigrant enclaves, elaborating a concept of "white privilege" that was much needed as intellectuals tried to make sense of Myrdal's failure to understand U.S. whites.

Blauner was cautious in his use of the colonial metaphor. He urged his readers not to believe, for example, that the generally high standard of living in the United States was due to either the legacy of slavery or the conquest of the Indians. A numerical majority cannot live off a numerical minority, he emphasized, also acknowledging that important distinctions were to be drawn between classic European colonialism and the U.S. version. But he argued that while social science could find all kinds of logical reasons for sidestepping the colonial metaphor, doing so would only lead to the opposite error. It would obscure connections between the American experience and European expansion and colonialism. "The colonial order in the modern world has been based on the dominance of white Westerners over non-Western people of color; racial oppression and the racial conflict to which it gives rise are endemic to it, much as class exploitation and conflict are fundamental to capitalist societies."[130]

Blauner argued that by seeing colonization and immigration as opposite processes, we can truly understand the differences between blacks and immigrants. While some immigrant groups settled in places that had ghetto-like characteristics, black ghettos were different due to blacks' colonized status. First, white ethnic enclaves came about through voluntary choices to emigrate to the United States (even when the immigrants were victims of hard times or repression), while black ghettos did not. Colonized groups have no choice; they are enslaved, conquered, or forced to move. Second, white ethnic enclaves usually contained the same families for no more than two generations, after which they typically assimilated through upward mobility. Exceptions, as in the cases of some Jews and Italians, were matters of voluntary choice. Third, white ethnic enclaves remained subject to outside control for brief periods, while black ghettos remained powerless.

In the colonial order, privilege is the most important feature of the relationship between the white minority and the colored majority.[131] The "racist restrictions that strike at people of color in America result in a system of special privilege for the white majority." By privilege, Blauner meant "unfair advantage, a preferential situation of systematic 'head start' in the pursuit of social values."[132] In the United States, restrictions placed upon blacks by whites (including but not limited to the imposition of a ghetto) had resulted in an entire apparatus of special advantages enjoyed by whites. Blauner argued that it was immaterial whether whites consciously follow racist practices or even consciously benefit at the expense of blacks. "Whatever the intent, the system benefits all strata of the white population," including the working classes, who generally live with the expectation that they can avoid the most servile kind of work.[133]

White privilege leads to advantages in residential options and connected educational opportunities. It also leads to advantages in the labor market as whites go through life expecting not to do dirty work. This is a hallmark of a colonial society, one in which people of color take the servile jobs while whites go through life assuming they can avoid them. White privilege also entails nonmaterial advantages, including the psychic benefits of having jobs and living conditions that make it possible to always have someone at least one step below.

Though not framed as an answer to Myrdal, Blauner's examination of white privilege highlighted why it was naive to think that blacks could depend on whites to resolve the contradiction between the American Creed and the reality. Rather than viewing whites and blacks as moral beings, Blauner viewed them as interest groups. Whites understood that by resolving moral contradictions they would first have to abdicate their racial privileges. Whites could never be counted upon to do more than protect what was theirs.

Blauner emphasized also that even though blacks and whites live in accordance with their racial interests, understanding how races and classes intersect was important. "Race affects class formation and class influences racial dynamics in ways that have not been adequately investigated," he argued.[134]

By the 1970s, the term "ghetto" came to be deployed by yet another oppressed group in their struggles for rights—gays. Drawing inspiration from the black civil rights movement, they used the term to call attention to the communities they were forming in New York, San Francisco, Chicago, and L.A.

A crucial figure in this development was Harvey Milk, the San Francisco supervisor who ran three times for public office before being elected as the first openly gay official in California. Before his assassination in 1978, he and the neighborhood he represented, the Castro, granted the ghetto a powerful new meaning in the context of the gay rights movement.

When today's students watch the Hollywood movie about Milk's life (with Sean Penn in the main role), they are usually surprised to hear him refer to his gay San Francisco neighborhood as the "ghetto." Likewise, when they read Edmund White's semiautobiographical novel *The Beautiful Room Is Empty* (1988), they are struck by how White speaks of New York's West Village as the "gay ghetto." That this generation of students are unaware of the term is not surprising, for they were all born at a time when these neighborhoods were on the brink of losing their special gay identity.

Milk believed that gay people could achieve political and social power only through visibility, and that this visibility could occur only though mass residential mobilization within a defined physical space. Calling the Castro a ghetto, just as Jews had once referred to the Lower East Side, Milk helped turn the ghetto into a vehicle for winning the political power that gays have begun to achieve today.

All this occurred in an era when gays were taking to the streets and seeking inspiration in the black civil rights movement. Gay organizations based their early organizational models and programs in education, social service, and legal defense on those of the National Urban League and the National Association for the Advancement of Colored People. Articles in black and gay periodicals, such as W.E.B. Du Bois's *Crisis* or Harold Call's *Mattachine Review*, often seemed to echo one another, albeit on wholly different planes.[135] In the late 1960s, gay activists and intellectuals took the next step and began referring to their residential enclaves as ghettos. As Carl Wittman stated about San Francisco in his "Gay Manifesto," which was broadly disseminated across the American gay community in 1970, "We have formed a ghetto, out of self protection. . . . We came not because it is so great here, but because it was so bad there."[136] This disturbed the parallel between the black and gay ghettos. Like the earliest Jewish quarters, but unlike the black ghetto, the gays saw their enclosures as protective. And gays' use of the term typically had a wink to it—a hint of irony, even camp.[137] The term's black and gay uses were ultimately very different.

In the wake of Martin Luther King's assassination in 1968, America had passed the Fair Housing Act (as Title VIII of that year's Civil Rights Act), outlawing discrimination on the basis of race, color, religion, or national origin. But whereas Kenneth Clark had once believed that such a focus on individual acts of discrimination in housing was crucial, now he was focusing more and more on the capitalist system and the federal government itself. Deeply affected by the Newark riots, he came to feel that the destruction he saw there was wrought by forces that went far beyond those individual acts of discrimination targeted by civil rights legislation—forces he had hardly recognized when he'd written about Harlem in *Dark Ghetto*. Although he had presented the ghetto as a colony, he had never explicitly examined how the ghetto had become a site for the pursuit of profit by capitalist entrepreneurs. Nor had he emphasized how much of this was set in motion during the 1940s and 1950s.

His references to higher-order powers, particularly as they related to capitalism, were previously vague. He had barely scratched the surface of the historical, political, and economic forces that had given rise to Harlem. Nor did he reckon with the fraught politics of housing. A reader of *Dark Ghetto* would not have guessed that new housing projects in Harlem would be opposed because they led to tenant displacement,[138] or that James Baldwin had, in a PBS interview with Clark, referred to this as "Negro removal."[139]

All of these issues were especially apparent in cities such as Newark, where changes, albeit rooted in a longer history, had occurred within the lifetimes of the rioters. Now in his sixties, Clark began writing a detailed historical study that was explicitly meant to explain the Newark ghetto as a phenomenon of political economy and history; he wished particularly to examine how political and business elites had developed the inner city for their own benefit and thus created the alienation that had led to the riots. His reach was well beyond the city of Newark, coming to include urban America in general, including its suburbs (White Plains as one example), which were increasingly becoming zones of ghetto residence. His unpublished manuscript and notes, also found among his papers, demonstrate that he was at work on a pathbreaking study, one that anticipated the approach and findings of subsequent scholars.

He used urban renewal and, in particular, federal policy as a vehicle for analysis. As indicated by the manuscripts, Clark held that two stories were to be told about the federal housing projects. The first, commonly accepted, was one of good intentions gone dismally awry. The other—which was to gain significant traction later on—was one of overt racist policymaking:

> Unlike blacks, [white ethnics] could get loans from the Federal Housing Administration, which effectively denied black men

the same opportunity by refusing to approve financing in older neighborhoods characterized by mixed uses and "inharmonious racial groups." The FHA recommended race restrictive covenants near the mortgage-insured housing developments. After World War II, it encouraged open occupancy but made no attempt to control private practices in the absence of a violation of state law. Thus the federal government contributed to ghettoization even in the reformist New Deal.[140]

Although Clark had always been wary of Marxism, he now considered racist government and capitalist political economy as handmaidens in creating the abject conditions of ghetto life. He also came to see that federal policy in the forties and fifties set the stage for later developments. Clark thus anticipated the now widely accepted position that was painstakingly and brilliantly worked through in later celebrated books such as Arnold R. Hirsch's *Making the Second Ghetto: Race and Housing in Chicago*, Kenneth Jackson's *Crabgrass Frontier*, Thomas J. Sugrue's *Origins of the Urban Crisis: Race and Inequality in Postwar Detroit*, and John Logan and Harvey Molotch's *Urban Fortunes: The Political Economy of Place*. Clark also identified zoning ordinances as crucial mechanisms through which many suburban areas "held the line" against black migration, anticipating contemporary work by urban sociologists such as Douglas Massey.[141]

Clark showed that through federal agencies and their influence on private lenders, the government legitimated redlining policies that channeled mortgage funds away from black neighborhoods. At the same time, it constructed large public housing projects in the neighborhoods where blacks had long been forced to live due to restrictive covenants. These projects had vast bureaucracies that assumed the task of "managing the poor" for decades to come.[142] Whereas the restrictive covenant approach to segregation was weakened once the courts determined that government could not legally enforce it, the federal public housing programs became the mechanism to accomplish massive segregation. With their high-rise projects, the housing authorities created a previously unknown degree of social isolation in a highly unequal society.

By now the story has been well documented. Never very costly (only

2 percent of the Federal Housing Administration's resources were used to fund new black public housing), the projects had massive impacts on the urban ecology as well as the lives of poor people. Highways were routed through their communities; centers of high culture rose where they once lived. Federal housing projects were nearly always constructed in historically black neighborhoods, thus furthering rather than eroding segregation. As put more forcefully by Hirsch, the building of the projects can be understood as "the ferocious application of a domestic 'containment' policy."[143]

There had always been that other urban renewal, the one with the lofty goals of raising up cities—building new parks, concert halls, hospitals, and universities. But as Clark and his successors came to realize, these improvements were covers for massive relocations of the urban poor, including stacking them up in high-rise structures that were, in so many ways, unsuitable for making a living, raising a family, or developing linkages to structures of power and influence. Troubles began even before a shovel touched the ground. Demarcation for urban renewal, especially for public housing, led property owners to give up on buildings they knew would eventually be seized through eminent domain and razed to the ground. By the time the government did act, the poor people living there were blamed for failing to maintain "their" properties—a classic blame-the-victim dynamic that we know goes back to the original ghettos. In Newark, Chicago, and so many other U.S. places, residents were then evicted, often with no help for relocation, in a housing market made worse by the removal of so much supply. In many cases, neighborhoods were cleared before construction started. Some city lands were to lie fallow for decades.

By the mid-fifties, about two hundred thousand dwellings for the poor had been demolished, with little to replace them.[144] Those new units that *were* built were constructed within existing poor neighborhoods, a practice that led to their still greater overcrowding.[145]

Whereas initially Clark had used the metaphor of the war in Vietnam to explain the riots, he eventually came to see urban renewal itself as a metaphor for understanding the riotous destruction he had witnessed:

The methods, the means of rioting were not dissimilar from urban renewal, however unlike the goals may have been. Both demolished and razed. Both left barren land littered with its debris. One burned, the other led to burning. Both displaced ghetto residents from their homes. Both left a no man's land or buffer zone between ghetto residential and business areas and the revitalized commercial and civic core. Both were responses to perception of urban decay, loss of pride, disrepair.[146]

Newark was a good case in point. It had been a catalyst in the lobbying for the national legislation that made urban renewal a reality, and its own program had received special acclaim as the most efficient in the country. But, true to form, it was aimed at elite interests. One was to expand the commercial center of the city and surround it with Rutgers University–Newark buildings that would create a buffer zone between downtown and the ghetto. The university paid no property taxes. But as Clark noted, the tax revenues lost through this buffer zone were supposed to be more than offset by the tax-paying business interests and consumers that it would attract, and the stability that it would bring to the decaying urban core. Newark's urban renewal again followed a standard script in its residential construction: the good payoff would be to "attract the white middle and upper classes back to the city rather than provide housing for displaced poor Blacks."[147]

The black population did not second the glowing accounts of benefits from urban renewal. When Clark read the reports and then interviewed residents, it looked like two entirely different worlds. For him, it was these two worlds that collided in the riots of 1967. The first was the white world, exemplified by public officials, the real estate industry, and finance. The second was the world of the ghetto, articulated by spokesmen for the black community who protested at City Hall. Both claimed that saving the city was their priority. But Clark found that their means, ends, and perceptions greatly diverged. Clark's research demonstrated to him that ghettoization was enhanced and reinforced by urban renewal, with public housing playing its own perverse role.

Clark's unfinished manuscript highlights what the ghetto had come to mean to him by the end of his career. It was not merely a dependent colony, but a vehicle through which both the state and capitalism pursued continued growth at the expense of the most vulnerable. In this sense, he anticipated the work of a new school of Marxist urban sociology that arose in the 1980s. These thinkers showed how real estate elites saw ghettos as targets of opportunity, and their residents as dependent or superfluous. As Clark summarized this governing ideology, "The strength of the city lay in its commerce and its weakness lay in its ghetto population."[148]

Kenneth Clark had begun as a psychologist who focused on the individual perceptions of black children. Through the force of his own thinking and the evolution of events as he witnessed them, he broadened out as both a scholar and a practitioner, becoming a social scientist at the intersection of politics, economics, and sociology.

Clark's thinking evolved out of experimental data, gathered in the flowering of a social science not always committed to applications aimed at social betterment, particularly for those living under severe disadvantage. With sophisticated psychological ideas, he helped convince many whites, including with such great consequence those on the Supreme Court, that new and better ways existed to think about the meaning of equality and the mode of its implementation.

But, as he increasingly realized, psychology was not enough. It would not do to take on one "variable" or one kind of institution or another when the problems were, as Myrdal had himself proposed, cumulative. They needed to be addressed in a way that recognized the interpenetration of problems with one another. Kenneth Clark may have been a protégé of Myrdal's, but he brought direct and indirect experience of the lives of those whose cause was being invoked. He broke new ground, becoming the first to understand ghettos as the result of vicious cycles occurring within a powerless social, economic, political, and educational landscape.

In 1974, he announced that he was retiring from teaching at the City University of New York. That year, Gunnar Myrdal shared the Nobel Prize with the libertarian economist Friedrich von Hayek, and both were cited for their "penetrating analysis of the interdependence of economic, social, and institutional phenomena."[149] Myrdal accepted the award during a semester when he had come to the City University of

New York to coteach a final seminar with Clark. The constant theme of their discussions was the enormous change that had occurred in the South while the North had been left behind, as well as the disappointment each felt about the deterioration of Northern ghettos.

May 17, 1954, the day the Supreme Court handed down its historic decision in *Brown*, had been one of the happiest days in either of their lives—Clark said that on that day he felt more American than on any day before or maybe since. By the time Clark retired, he had come to see that for Northern cities, the *Brown* decision was not much more than a verbal victory.[150] While some positive developments had occurred in the South with the elimination of de jure segregation, Northern racism had revealed itself to be deeper and more insidious, and Northerners had proven to be more hypocritical. During the civil rights movement, Northerners had spoken of themselves as being superior to Southerners, but the past quarter century had demonstrated to Clark that this was simply a posture.

W.E.B. Du Bois, who studied at the University of Berlin, said that his travels around Europe and his later visit to the Warsaw ghetto led him to a more complete understanding of "the Negro Problem." (Photographs and Prints Division, Schomburg Center for Research in Black Culture, The New York Public Library, Astor, Lenox and Tilden Foundations)

Gunnar Myrdal, a renowned economist, was recruited by the Carnegie Corporation from his native Sweden to write the definitive study of the U.S. racial situation, *An American Dilemma*. His book assembled an extraordinary amount of evidence to show how segregation hurt blacks in the South, but it also mistakenly argued that racial progress would result primarily from the awakening of white America's conscience. (Arbetarrörelsens Arkiv och Bibliotek)

When Myrdal asked the University of Chicago graduate student Horace Cayton to share his research on the black ghetto of Chicago, Cayton set conditions on his co-operation. Myrdal's failure to make a deal left him without a perspective that would ultimately be essential for understanding the obstinacy of Northern whites. (Horace Cayton Papers, Photo 037, Chicago Public Library, Woodson Regional Library, Vivian G. Harsh Research Collection)

St. Clair Drake, originally from New Orleans, collaborated with Cayton on their study of Chicago's South Side, *Black Metropolis*. The book was published in 1945, at a time when the Nazi ghettos were discussed in the black press and blacks were increasingly using the word "ghetto" to make a moral claim on America's conscience. (Courtesy of Roosevelt University Archives)

Kenneth and Mamie Clark were the first African Americans to receive doctorates in psychology from Columbia University. When Mamie could not find an academic job, they cofounded the Northside Center for Child Development in Harlem. Kenneth drew upon Mamie's work to study how segregation brings about a sense of inferiority in black children, ultimately influencing the Supreme Court in *Brown v. Board of Education*. He later turned his attention to studying the ghetto. (Kenneth Bancroft Clark Collection, Library of Congress)

William Julius Wilson's *The Declining Significance of Race* influentially argued that the experiences of middle-class and poor or working-class blacks were increasingly diverging. His pessimistic assessment of white America's conscience led him to call for "race neutral" antipoverty policies that would, by his calculations, still disproportionately help blacks. (Courtesy of the University of Chicago Library, University News Office Collection)

In the 2000s, Geoffrey Canada became well-known for his Harlem Children's Zone, an organization built on the assumption that schools, counseling, family services, and job placement services should be tightly integrated and directed at residents of a particular neighborhood. It was an ambitious idea, but insofar as it relied on wealthy donors, it marked a retreat from the idea that government had a responsibility to the inner city. (Alex Tehrani)

Despite the anti-Semitism and difficult economic circumstances that Jews experienced in interwar Poland, Jewish life nevertheless flourished in small towns and big cities. The Jews of Warsaw and Kraków engaged in a vibrant cultural, intellectual, and political life. The post-Holocaust view of Poland has largely eclipsed this era in popular consciousness. (Narodowe Archiwum Cyfrowe)

African American soldiers view corpses at the Buchenwald concentration camp. Black ghettos were constructed in the name of racial purity at home—an irony that was not lost on black ghetto residents whose sons encountered the Nazis abroad. (United States Holocaust Memorial Museum, courtesy of William Alexander Scott III)

Chicago's South Side, 1941. Drake and Cayton's *Black Metropolis* depicted a ghetto that by today's standards was semi-flourishing. Their book demonstrated the spirit of the community and a widespread belief in the possibility of getting ahead. Yet the life expectancy of the men in this photo was about fifty-nine years, at a time when white men could be expected to live to sixty-six. (Russell Lee, Library of Congress)

Chicago's South Side, 1947. Drake and Cayton's interest in the role of women in the ghetto set them well ahead of their time. Even today, there has yet to emerge a comprehensive conception of the ghetto that takes into account the female experience. (Wayne Miller / Magnum Photos)

"Harlem Rooftops," 1948. Kenneth Clark argued that one of the most salient aspects of ghetto life is its ugliness. Clark believed that a run-down physical environment intensifies the feelings of inferiority that residents acquire from discrimination in the school and the workplace. (Photograph by Gordon Parks / Courtesy of and copyright © by The Gordon Parks Foundation)

A Harlem family at the Poverty Board, 1967. Kenneth Clark's understanding of blacks as a subject people pervaded his discussions of social agencies, schools, and businesses. The subservience and inferiority that the average ghetto dweller experienced were reinforced by political and institutional structures controlled by outsiders. (Photograph by Gordon Parks / Courtesy of and copyright © by The Gordon Parks Foundation)

Chicago's South Side, 1986. In the 1980s, William Julius Wilson argued, social isolation, combined with joblessness and a poor marriage market, created a new kind of ghetto. Poor blacks lived with far fewer opportunities than poor whites. (Ovie Carter / Chicago Tribune)

Ferguson, Missouri, 2014. After a protest over the killing of Michael Brown by a Ferguson police officer, tear gas was used on this kneeling woman. Residents of today's U.S. ghettos experience more intrusive control than before. (Scott Olson / Getty Images)

Baltimore, 2015. In April 2015, a black man named Freddie Gray died while in police custody, leading to weeks of protest and civil unrest in Baltimore. (Devin Allen)

4

CHICAGO, 1987:
WILLIAM JULIUS WILSON

When blacks used the idea of the ghetto to frame their experience at the time of World War II, they tied their political case to that of the Jews. In doing so, they were not making a literal comparison between the black and the Jewish experiences, but they *were* making a claim that their experience was of comparable importance for Americans to that of Jews in Europe and should not be eclipsed by the horrors of Nazism. This claim on America's conscience was all the more legitimate to blacks because black soldiers had been fighting the Nazis while black neighborhoods were being constrained by restrictive covenants in the name of racial purity. By tying their experience to that of the Jews, blacks were putting forward their predicament as a moral issue for America. "America's Jews," as it were, were entitled to a place of *priority* in America's conscience.[1]

That way of thinking was also a hallmark of the civil rights era—but it would go into decline during the presidency of Ronald Reagan, a period of retreat from the programs of social change characteristic of the 1960s. For social scientists and the general public alike, the ghetto was no longer an idea that was immediately associated with the priority of the black experience for America's conscience. As support for alleviating racial inequalities declined, some social scientists turned toward a new definition of the ghetto that stressed class instead of race. In one influential definition, the ghetto was any area where 40 percent of the residents lived in poverty, regardless of their race. In this usage, the ghetto did not provide a conceptual apparatus for explaining the different residential situations of blacks and whites. And for the first time since the early Chicago School, the ghetto once again became a concept that could be defined without reference to external control from the wider society.

On February 28, 1978, an article titled "Poor Blacks' Future" appeared on the op-ed page of *The New York Times*. In it, the author, William Julius Wilson, summarized the thesis of his book *The Declining Significance of Race*. A relatively unknown forty-two-year-old University of Chicago sociologist, Wilson was initiating a debate that was to influence the intellectual landscape of social science for years to come. He argued that one of the unnoticed results of recent economic transformation in the United States was the decreasing importance of race and, therefore, the growing significance of class for understanding the life chances of blacks. In the new American economy, well-paying jobs increasingly required education, and this development could be seen in outcomes experienced by the black population.[2]

Wilson argued that opportunities were increasing in the corporate and government sectors for those who were educated, but those who had little training remained confined to a low-wage secondary labor market. College-educated blacks benefiting from the impact of state-mandated affirmative action programs were now doing as well as whites with similar qualifications. But those without educational credentials faced increasingly limited prospects and rising unemployment, and more and more relied on welfare.

Wilson urged his readers to rethink the conventional wisdom. The outcomes for blacks living in the ghetto could no longer be understood by looking only at racial discrimination. Outcomes were now, more than ever, connected to the transformation of the economy. While acknowledging that discrimination had created the large population of poor blacks, Wilson claimed that those poor blacks were *really* in jeopardy because of technological and economic changes that had left the unskilled and uneducated behind. He also argued against the conventional view that traditional forms of racial segregation and discrimination still dominated the labor market; this view, he charged, could not be squared with the success of the black middle class. Indeed, he claimed that even blacks' own sense of group identity was now based in class as much as in race—likely for the first time in the country's history.[3]

The few people who actually knew of William Julius Wilson prior to 1978 would not have considered him likely to produce such a column or book. As a graduate student at Washington State University, and later as an assistant professor at the University of Massachusetts Amherst, he had shied away from controversy. Completing his dissertation amid the civil rights movement, and starting his first job the year that *Dark Ghetto* and the Moynihan Report were released, he seemed to have deliberately avoided getting swept up by the events of the time.

Wilson had grown up in Bairdstown, a small mining community in rural western Pennsylvania, not far from Pittsburgh.[4] His father, who died of a lung ailment when Wilson was thirteen, had worked in the mines, while his mother had served as a part-time domestic. Since the town of Bairdstown had few blacks, Wilson grew up around white children of Irish, English, German, and Italian stock. While he could recollect some explicit discrimination and racist slurs—including being called a "nigger" and fighting over it with older boys in his school— Wilson remembered that he and his five brothers and sisters had generally interacted with these children without incident.

The first person in the family ahead of Wilson to attend college was his aunt, Janice Wardlaw, who became a psychiatric social worker in New York City. As a boy, he visited her and her husband in the summers, when they would take him to museums and libraries. When Wilson entered college, she provided him with additional assistance to supplement the church scholarship that he had received to attend Wilberforce University in Ohio, where W.E.B. Du Bois had taught early in his career. Like Du Bois, Wilson had a theoretical and conceptual mind. He studied sociology with Professor Maxwell Brooks, one of the first blacks to graduate with a sociology degree from Ohio State University, a leading producer of black Ph.D.'s. After serving two years in the U.S. Army, Wilson received his master's from Bowling Green State

University, followed by his doctorate from Washington State. At the latter he joined a legacy of black graduate students who had been recruited by the university. Indeed, more blacks received doctorates in sociology from Washington State in the 1960s and 1970s than from any other graduate program.[5]

Despite entering Washington State with the intention of studying social inequality, Wilson became fascinated by the philosophy of science and wrote a dissertation on concept formation and the scientific status of sociology. By the time he was hired by UMass, nothing in his work or résumé indicated that he was black. Wilson later told people that when he was hired, no one had questioned whether it was because of his race.[6]

Yet events on the outside gradually began to make their mark. At UMass, Wilson became a respected teacher, and his course The Black Man in America resulted in what would become his first book on inequality, a theoretical study titled *Power, Racism, and Privilege: Race Relations in Theoretical and Sociohistorical Perspectives* (1973).[7] Comparing racial regimes in the United States and Brazil, Wilson came up with a grand synthesis of existing theories to explain racial inequality in both countries. Yet despite his ambition, his first effort to write on race was a highly abstract text of limited interest to all but a few specialists. Nothing in it might have set up expectations for the monumental book that was soon to follow.

One of Wilson's senior colleagues when he was at UMass was an eminent scholar of immigration, Milton Gordon. In the mid-1960s, Gordon had put out the book *Assimilation in American Life*, claiming in part that in American society the intersection between race or ethnicity and social class was fast becoming a crucial dimension of "social space." He argued that "with a person of the same social class but of a different ethnic group, one shares behavioral similarities but not a sense of peoplehood. With those of the same ethnic group but of a different social class, one shares the sense of peoplehood, but not behavioral similarities. The only group which meets both of these criteria are people of the same ethnic group *and* same social class," which he called the ethclass.[8] Gordon argued that "the prognosis for America for a long time to come is that its internal social structure will consist of a series of ethnic sub-communities criss-crossed by social class."[9]

Wilson's *Declining Significance of Race* was the logical extension of his former colleague's book. Wilson applied Gordon's argument specifically to the black community. At first, Wilson's book led to a rather simple-minded debate, focusing on whether race or class was now more important in determining the life chances of blacks. As some reviews at the time pointed out, however, an increase in the predictive power of class did not necessarily imply a decrease in the predictive power of race; it was not a question of one *or* the other but rather of a changing configuration in which race had come to matter in various ways. After all, poor blacks were still much worse off than poor whites, and many middle-class blacks were not doing nearly as well as middle-class whites.[10]

The Declining Significance of Race, however, was far more complicated and ambitious than the race-versus-class debate implied. A book of great historical sweep and imagination, it covered the history of U.S. race relations from the end of the Civil War to the contemporary era.

While the book certainly received more attention than it would have had its title been *The Changing Significance of Race,* much of interest and value was lost in the ensuing debate. Little attention was paid to Wilson's extension of Gordon's argument: race was intersecting with class, and in a new way. In the past, it had not mattered as much what class position blacks occupied. Even though class divisions had long existed within ghettos, middle-class blacks had good reason to feel that their fate was bound up with that of poor blacks because from the perspective of the wider society, they were simply black. Now that blacks could move out of the ghetto and their "job ceiling" had been lifted, larger economic dynamics that influenced their social position within society at large had to be comprehended. Wilson believed that these economic or class dimensions had assumed greater importance than racial discrimination. But it should not have been necessary to accept this part of his argument to appreciate his more important idea: the intersection of race and class created distinct social spaces within the African American population.[11]

Wilson also argued that economic conflict between blacks and whites had been replaced by conflict in the sociopolitical sphere. After the Civil War, black workers had been used by Northern industrialists as cheap labor to undermine white unions, but in the modern industrial era working-class whites were no longer threatened by the black poor. The former were now safely ensconced in better-paying blue-collar and white-collar jobs that required superior education and skills, while the latter were segregated in low-wage jobs that nobody else would take. The new interracial conflicts now arose not over jobs but in the political sphere, as poor blacks competed with those working-class whites who had no choice but to remain in the city. These two groups were essentially squaring off over the response to rising crime rates, the control of public schools, and access to housing. On the larger political scale, the debate over affirmative action was driving working- and middle-class whites to the political right.

A segmented labor market also divided poor and middle-class blacks. Black adult unemployment rates were twice as high as among whites. This coincided with a vast increase in the number of unemployed black teenagers, due to a population explosion in that age category. Still, the black middle class's massive upward mobility had enabled this group to separate from the black poor. Wilson argued that these developments had their roots not only in macroeconomic change but also in the civil rights era, a protest movement dominated by middle-class blacks. Biased in favor of middle-class interests, the movement, as Wilson pointed out, had never focused on the subordination of "ghetto blacks," or on de facto segregation.[12] The legacy of that failure could now be seen in the conditions of the black poor.

Ill-suited to addressing the lives of unemployed workers in the low-wage labor market, affirmative action programs that grew out of the civil rights movement did help qualified blacks get jobs in the expanding corporate and especially government sectors. The government jobs were available thanks to the increasing need for social services among poor blacks. Many employees in both these areas were the first in their families to attend college and had done so through affirmative action programs developed in response to the civil rights era. As Wilson wrote in his op-ed article, it was difficult to reconcile the success of the black middle class with the traditional forms of racial discrimination in the labor market.

The response to Wilson's claims was explosive. Though Kenneth

Clark had retired three years earlier, he now suddenly resurfaced. Within days of the appearance of Wilson's op-ed piece, Clark published a response in the same section of *The New York Times* titled "No. No. Race, Not Class, Is Still at the Wheel." Despite progress, he argued, the major factor in blacks' life chances was still race.[13]

Like many at the time, Clark largely ignored Wilson's arguments about the black poor and focused mainly on what he had to say about the black middle class. Clark refused to accept Wilson's contention that college-educated blacks now had job opportunities that were "at least comparable" to those of whites with similar accomplishments. When you looked at blacks in government and corporate America, tokenism prevailed. The number to be found in managerial positions was still tiny.[14] Clark claimed that the hostile reactions of white ethnic groups and the rise of reverse discrimination lawsuits demonstrated that blacks were a perceived threat to working- and middle-class whites. Since segregated education remained inferior, blacks were mainly dependent on white goodwill in the form of special uplift programs.

Clark's response was a sign of things to come, particularly from black intellectuals. After Wilson's book won an award from the American Sociological Association, the Association of Black Sociologists made an unprecedented public statement, protesting that *The Declining Significance of Race* was insufficiently factual to merit such recognition. "It is the consensus of this organization that this book denies the overwhelming evidence regarding the significance of race and the literature that speaks to the contrary."[15]

By the late 1970s, black communities had changed considerably from those of the civil rights era. During that earlier period of mass social protest, it seemed to knowledgeable observers that ghettoization would extend into the coming decades. Blacks talked more and more about what the future of community life would be like as these ghettos continued to increase in size. The assumption of the best-informed analysts was that, without major improvements in job opportunities and income inequality, poor blacks would continue living a segregated existence.[16]

But now, rather than just a few middle-class blacks "trickling" into the suburbs, large numbers of them were departing the ghetto for mixed-race urban neighborhoods and suburbs. The increasing isolation of poor blacks raised the specter of a new generation of unstable slums. At the same time, in the metropolitan areas of cities such as Washington, D.C., Detroit, and Atlanta, middle-class black communities had developed on a scale barely imaginable in previous decades.

In the Northern ghetto of the late 1970s, there were more black students in segregated schools than there had been in 1954, when *Brown* was handed down. In the South, where school segregation could not possibly have increased, the record of improvement looked better. But even there, some of the biggest cities had given up on desegregation completely. In what became known as the "Atlanta compromise," Maynard Jackson, a black mayor, worked with the white business establishment to maintain his city's white tax base by not pushing for the desegregation of the city's schools.[17]

After the passage of the Voting Rights Act of 1965, Atlanta became one of many increasingly black cities in the South and the North that had elected black mayors and black city councils and would come to appoint black school boards. Mayors such as Kenneth Gibson (Newark), Coleman Young (Detroit), Richard Hatcher (Gary), Carl Stokes (Cleveland), and Tom Bradley (Los Angeles) rounded out a growing list of big-city mayors whose elections were sources of pride for many blacks, who had long felt powerless in their own cities. This also meant that for the first time the authorities regulating the ghettos were also black.

The classic studies of ghetto life written in the 1960s had been conducted mainly before President Lyndon B. Johnson's massive extension of federal benefits in the form of food stamps, jobs programs, and public assistance. But in the late 1970s, black ghettos were receiving between two and three times more money from social welfare programs than at the time that Johnson had assumed office. Moreover, not only the desperately poverty-stricken were receiving aid—as had been the case before the civil rights movement—but also the working poor. Aside from offering jobs and educational programs, the government had also increased Social Security, public assistance (AFDC), and unemployment insurance and had established food stamps, Medicaid, and Medicare. It seemed that everyone in the ghetto was receiving some sort of check. This made for a very different social and political context than the one that Clark and others had described at the time of the riots.

As the number of U.S. residents grew by half between 1950 and 1980,[18] government programs were extended not only to the kinds of people who had traditionally received assistance since the 1930s, but also to whole new demographics within the country.[19] In these three decades, in constant dollars, health and medical costs rose by 6 times; public assistance by 13 times; education spending by 24 times; social insurance outlays by 27 times; and housing costs by 129 times.[20] Not all of this spending had been directed at the ghetto, but the ghetto was absorbing far more than its proportionate share.

What was noteworthy about Wilson's argument in *The Declining Significance of Race* was not merely the controversy that it provoked, but also the controversy that it did not provoke.[21] On the first page of the book, Wilson used "underclass" to describe the large population of poorly educated people who are either on welfare or subsist on menial jobs that don't pay a living wage.[22] The concept of the underclass, previously used by Gunnar Myrdal in the Swedish context to describe a subproletariat mired in intergenerational poverty, was very much in the air at this moment—and it came with a set of meanings associated specifically with the black population of the United States. A *Time* cover story six months earlier had been titled "The American Underclass: Destitute and Desperate in the Land of Plenty." The underclass was defined as consisting mostly of unreachable and antagonistic poor blacks.[23] By describing the ghetto poor as an underclass on the first page of his book, Wilson gave new scientific authority to the "underclass" label. He described the population in behavioral terms, as a people disconnected from behavioral norms of the wider society. Although his treatment was somewhat unsystematic (he defined the underclass as both "permanent"[24] and "semi-permanent"[25] at various points of his book), the magnitude of the problem was unquestioned; like the author of the *Time* article, he argued that it represented a third of the black population, an astounding number by any measure.[26] He claimed that the underclass relied on welfare and illegal activities as profitable alternatives to low-wage jobs.[27] He cited data showing that more and more Northern-born urban blacks were living off public assistance.[28] Due to rising expectations, younger blacks were less willing to accept menial work. Even poor blacks who did accept low-paying jobs did not value them and were prone to absenteeism and high turnover. They knew that they could quickly find other employment, and Wilson placed particular emphasis on welfare as a substitute for low-wage and menial employment.[29] In writing about the underclass, he cited a study of the previous decade indicating that 20 percent of Harlem's residents lived on illegal income. Many of those interviewed for the study saw drug sales, prostitution, and gambling as a more desirable way to achieve success and status than the low-level jobs available to them.[30]

Although scholars debated the relative merits of Wilson's race-versus-class analysis, they paid little attention to his description of the underclass or his claims about its dependence on welfare or deviant activity. Yet Wilson's take on these issues anticipated other important works, such as the journalist Ken Auletta's *The Underclass*, which would bring even greater attention to the group's problems.[31] Meanwhile, the political right believed it needed a conservative black intellectual who could enunciate a compelling vision of what had gone wrong in the ghetto. When Ronald Reagan was elected president, no weighty study existed to support the conservative agenda of cutting back on welfare payments. From the standpoint of Reagan and his backers, who rose to power in a landslide victory over Jimmy Carter in 1980, American social welfare spending had once promoted equality of opportunity but now sought equality of outcome; that is, it had moved "from the dream of ending the dole to . . . permanent income transfers."[32] Although conservatives would appropriate Wilson's claims that the impoverished ghettos were full of people avoiding work through criminal activity and the dole, and that race had diminished in importance, he insisted that he was a person of the political left, a "social democrat." Indeed, in 1981, when Ronald Reagan took office and invited him to a meeting with black conservatives at the White House, Wilson replied, "Take me off that list," a move that could not stop them from invoking his data.[33]

Enter Charles Murray. A native of the small town of Newton, Iowa, where Maytag appliances were manufactured, he had attended Harvard and received a doctorate in political science from MIT. Murray had the kind of personal history that may have raised eyebrows in academia but that conservative foundations found attractive. After graduate school, he had worked in Thailand for the American Institutes for Research (AIR), a contractor that operated under the umbrella of the Department of Defense and the CIA and supported preventive U.S. counterinsurgency efforts to protect the Thai government. Subsequently, he went on to work for AIR in Washington, D.C. But as he told *The New York Times*, by his late forties he was tired of writing research reports that were read by a few people at most. And so he set out on his own to write a book that would make a difference.[34]

When the Manhattan Institute, a wealthy conservative think tank in New York City, got wind that Murray was writing a critical study of the impact of government spending, its leaders saw it as an opportunity. Here was a work that could affect U.S. domestic politics in a major way. The institute offered generous support to the project, and the effort paid off. *Losing Ground*, a history of social welfare programs from 1950 to 1980, was published at the end of Reagan's first term. The book was consistent with William Julius Wilson's claim that many ghetto dwellers were rejecting low-wage jobs in favor of illegal activity and welfare cheating, but it took the argument one step further. Murray argued that these behaviors were rational.[35] Two decades of well-intentioned government spending had unwittingly encouraged these behaviors and values.

Murray claimed that things had deteriorated considerably for the black poor since the massive expansion of the welfare state. Participation in the labor force, for example, had declined for young black men—those born in the early 1950s—but not for their fathers or older brothers. Nor had it declined for white male adults of any age, who should have been equally affected by any large-scale reduction in the need for labor due to deindustrialization. Why then, Murray asked, were poor young blacks the only ones who had stopped working? He claimed that this decline in the young black labor force had begun in the late sixties, just as "federal efforts to improve [blacks'] position were most expensive and extensive—efforts not just in employment *per se*, but in education, health, welfare, and civil rights as well."[36]

Why did men born after 1950 fare so much worse? Murray argued that despite government efforts to increase employment, changes in incentives had made living without a job for the long term easier than ever before. Changes in welfare policy had kicked in at precisely the moment when the oldest of these boys were about eighteen, the age at which most people begin looking for jobs. Rather than search for stable employment with the intention of sticking to it, they had given up. Claiming that the state of the poor could not be blamed on structural change in the economy or racism—and ignoring the fact that single men were ineligible for Aid to Families with Dependent Children, the program that epitomized welfare—Murray offered a clear alternative both to Wilson and to Wilson's critics. What needed to be examined, he stated, was the trap that had been unintentionally created by the federal government when it sought to ameliorate poverty. This trap could only be understood by studying how the new incentive structure interacted with the ghetto itself. Whereas Wilson had little to say about the ghetto as an institution in *The Declining Significance of Race*, Murray offered a view of social welfare policy that came with an analysis of the ghetto as such.

Murray claimed that the pivotal change in the post-1965 U.S. ghetto had been the introduction of social welfare programs such as food stamps, which, by 1980, had become available to more than 21 million Americans. Recipients included most ghetto dwellers, who, according to Murray, were stripped of their sense of pride. They no longer felt obligated to remain true to their long-standing ethos of family independence. As soon as the government created benefits that were widely available to anyone below a certain income level, the moral presumption that poor people would not accept charity from anyone outside the family was jeopardized.[37]

Murray claimed that under the new welfare dispensation, the working poor, who had once felt a certain status advantage over those who did not work, no longer felt superior, while the unemployed did not feel stigmatized. With so many working families receiving public support of various kinds, young people could not understand why anyone should work at a poorly paid job. A sibling born before 1950 might have done so for the sake of respectability alone. But once that motive disappeared, low wages and disrespect on the job could not be compensated for by rewards from the family or community. With neither income nor status rewarding those who take jobs, "the man who keeps working is, in fact, a chump."[38]

If this was the case, then why did older adults, even brothers and sisters only a few years older, continue working while the younger generation opted out of the labor market? The answer, according to Murray, was that once people moved up at their jobs, they were no longer working for entry-level wages, and public assistance could no longer compete with their salaries. Moreover, once they were part of a peer group that valued self-sufficiency, they felt reinforced by that ultimate value rather than threatened by a newly formed status system. Unfortunately, those born after 1950 no longer had any sense that hard work pays off. "The network of social service agencies . . . existed to help the least provident and least able. . . . The way to get something from the system was to be sufficiently a failure to qualify for help, or to con the system."[39] Murray's was not simply a theory of how individuals respond to incentives, but also of how communities and even generations respond collectively.

Murray ended his description of the ghetto by speculating that if such conditions existed in any poor white community, its youth would most likely adopt the same attitude and not join the labor force. However, he said that the data on Appalachian whites were not good enough to demonstrate this, and anyway, "the white elite never could rouse the same passion for excusing the white disadvantaged as it did for excusing the black disadvantaged."[40] In other words, liberal policymakers were failing to expect anything from blacks and were thus ultimately racist— practicing an intellectual/moral variant of reverse discrimination.

Murray saw his argument as a basis for doing away with much more than the AFDC program. He called for the elimination of the "entire federal welfare and income support structure for working-aged persons, including AFDC, Medicaid, Food Stamps, Unemployment Insurance, Workers' Compensation, subsidized housing, disability insurance, and the rest."[41] As became increasingly clear in his later work, Murray was a radical libertarian who opposed the general growth of the modern state since the New Deal.[42]

When Christopher Jencks reviewed *Losing Ground* in *The New York Review of Books*, he accepted Murray's argument that AFDC had undermined work incentives. In at least seven states, he noted, a mother of three was worse-off if she accepted a minimum-wage job over welfare. But he also engaged in a withering attack on many of the other arguments in *Losing Ground*, most importantly that the material welfare of the poor had not improved since the massive expansion of the welfare state. To the contrary, argued Jencks, there had been substantial improvement, and if this had occurred more slowly than expected, it was because of the loss of industrial jobs, stagnant wages, and other changes since the 1970s. That the poverty rate had actually gone down under unfavorable economic conditions was evidence that government policies had achieved many of their desired results. Jencks also questioned whether incentives had the effects on families that Murray assumed. Citing data from his Harvard colleagues David Ellwood and Mary Jo Bane, he pointed out that states with high benefits actually had a lower rate of out-of-wedlock childbearing than states with low benefits.

Jencks also accepted Murray's assumption that high AFDC levels cause women to set up their own homes, end bad relationships with their children's fathers, and hold back on new relationships. But whereas Murray saw this effect as evidence of moral decay, Jencks argued that the benefits that came from women's independence far outweighed the costs. Jencks was assuming that the poor black men in the lives of these women were unable to fulfill breadwinner obligations and were often abusive. Referring to the hypothetical couple Phyllis and Harold introduced by Murray in *Losing Ground*, Jencks argued that "taking collective responsibility for Phyllis's problems is not a trivial price to pay for liberating her from Harold. Most of her problems, after all, remain intractable. But our impulse to drive her back into Harold's arms so that we no longer have to think about her is the kind of impulse we should resist."[43]

Jencks emphasized in conclusion that Murray was incorrect to argue that the government programs of the 1960s hurt the poor. If he did not dismiss *Losing Ground* completely, it was because he believed that changes in social policy were needed. Like many liberals of the time, he hoped to restore status to those who chose work over welfare and "strike a balance between collective compassion and individual responsibility."[44]

In the decade after *The Declining Significance of Race* was published, the MacArthur Foundation awarded William Julius Wilson its coveted "genius" grant, which provided five years of generous no-strings-attached funding. In 1987, he reappeared with another book, *The Truly Disadvantaged: The Inner City, the Underclass, and Public Policy*. This work took Wilson's earlier observations about the new racial and class demographics of the central city as a starting point, asking how they expressed themselves in space. Wilson believed that the recent rise in joblessness in the ghetto was due to nonracial factors, particularly economics. Resurrecting John Kain's spatial-mismatch hypothesis (an idea that played a minor role in the earlier book), Wilson also argued that the mismatch between the skills necessary for the kinds of jobs that were migrating to the central city and the qualifications of the poor black population was growing. The number of jobs for poorly educated workers had declined as those available to the best-educated had risen. This left black men, and particularly black youth, with a catastrophic rate of unemployment. Wilson also dropped his earlier contention that black unemployment was a result of a revolution in expectations. Nowhere in his new book did he continue to claim that poor blacks eschewed low-wage, degrading work or that they saw welfare as a substitute for it. He thus made his case that any policy directed at resolving ghetto problems must be economic and called for universal programs that would help all working-poor Americans but would end up helping blacks disproportionately, since they were disproportionately disadvantaged. More specifically, he called for a guaranteed jobs program that would put the unemployed to work cleaning parks and playgrounds, assisting the elderly, cleaning graffiti off subway walls, and the like.

What's perhaps most fascinating about this book from the perspective of the black ghetto's intellectual history is the way in which Wilson positioned himself, both implicitly and explicitly, with regard to the three most controversial thinkers of the previous generation, Gunnar Myrdal, Oscar Lewis, and Daniel Patrick Moynihan. Three decades had passed since the publication of *An American Dilemma*. Whereas Myrdal had argued that whites could be trusted to act in accordance with their ideals, Wilson's attitude in *The Truly Disadvantaged* was exactly the opposite—that is, completely cynical. Writing during the presidency of Ronald Reagan, he sought to imagine "race-blind" solutions to the problems of the ghetto on the grounds that whites would only buy into social policy that helped *them* as well. As Wilson observed, though such policies would have a disproportionately positive impact on the black population, any effort to help the ghetto had to be targeted at all groups, albeit with an ulterior motive. He had originally wanted to call his book *Hidden Agenda*, but changed the title prior to publication.[45] As he explained to Bill Moyers in an interview on public television, "It's important how you describe policies if you want the American people to support them. If you just throw up the red flag and say, 'We've got to do something about the underclass,' they're not even going to listen to the opening sentence, because there is an element of racial hostility that will surface and get in the way of rational thinking about ways to improve our society."[46] Wilson was not making a principled argument on behalf of race-neutral assistance. He was not arguing that both poor whites and poor blacks were doing badly and thus deserved help, even if the black poor were on average worse-off than the white poor, and even if racism helped make that so.

At the heart of Wilson's conception of the ghetto was its own real dilemma about race, the significance of which had not sufficiently receded. Wilson believed that the situation in which blacks found themselves at the time was primarily due to historical discrimination and contemporary economic forces, and not contemporary racism. However, the amount of racial hostility in the country made it unlikely that the American electorate would listen to his argument for aiding the black poor to contend with this history of racism. Concluding that Wilson felt compelled to advocate a kind of "hustle," Moyers summarized Wilson's views as coming down to "We can't do anything for the truly disadvantaged unless somehow we fake it."[47] Though Wilson made no reference to Myrdal's thesis, which was now largely forgotten, Wilson's presumptions about the white conscience could not have been a stronger rebuke to it.

While *The Truly Disadvantaged* took social science far from the era of Myrdal, Wilson also sought to return it to the Moynihan era. A key argument of his book was that the liberal perspective on race and poverty had become less persuasive in public discourse because many liberals had seen what had happened to Moynihan and had thus grown afraid to address the serious problems of deviance and pathology. This was also the reason, he argued, that so little attention had been paid by social scientists to the ghetto in the past several decades. Wilson particularly took on those who rejected the use of the term "underclass"—which he had used in *The Declining Significance of Race* to describe the ghetto dwellers whose behavior was so at odds with that of mainstream America. He claimed that no matter what word one used, the behavior of many inner-city families undeniably stood in sharp contrast to the mainstream.[48] He argued that though a stigmatizing label might carry risks, a failure to use it might obscure what had to be seen and debated.[49]

To grant Moynihan greater legitimacy, Wilson conflated his writing with that of Kenneth Clark, who, he claimed, had likewise placed great emphasis on family deterioration. Notably, as Wilson refashioned himself as the new liberal voice on the ghetto, he saw it desirable to embrace Moynihan. He pointed out forcefully that conservative arguments had become ascendant because the right had filled the gap that remained after the left stopped discussing ghetto deviance in the wake of the reaction against the Moynihan Report.[50]

Wilson had a far less charitable view of Oscar Lewis, whom he used as a major foil in the book. He objected to Lewis's claim that the "culture of poverty" tends to take on a life of its own and reproduce itself from generation to generation. To highlight the difference between his own concepts and Lewis's, Wilson stated he was *not* claiming that ghetto culture "went unchecked" with the emergence of social isolation and the concentration of poverty.[51] He also rejected Lewis's claim that by the time slum children reach the age of six or seven they are not psychologically geared to take advantage of changing conditions. Rather, Wilson believed that people's motivation to learn and work was connected in an ongoing way to the urban economy. Descent was not destiny, though ghetto inhabitants' options were terribly foreclosed all the same.

Trying to become the spokesman for a reinvigorated liberal approach to the ghetto, Wilson took Charles Murray to task for suggesting that welfare caused women to forgo marriage. Arguing that Murray had neglected the issue of male joblessness when explaining the rise of single-parent families, Wilson claimed that there was no link between benefit levels and the rising number of births among unmarried women. Wilson introduced the concept of the "male marriageable pool index," which referred to the number of men who could support a family.[52] He claimed that the rise in welfare dependency had been caused by a loss of jobs, not an increase in benefits.

Wilson attributed the contracting black male marriageable pool to economic changes caused by a shift from the production of goods to the production of services, and by the relocation of industry from the North to the South as well as from the urban core to suburbia. Jobs had disappeared in areas where blacks were most heavily concentrated, and in places where they had moved after whites had migrated out of the city. As Wilson noted, in the three decades after 1950, more than 9 million whites had departed the central cities while 5 million blacks arrived, including many rural blacks.[53] He also pointed out that the decline in jobs had been most severe in wholesale trade, manufacturing, and retail—areas that required the least education. The problem was thus not merely a geographical shift in jobs, as had originally been stipulated by John F. Kain in the 1960s, but also a mismatch between skills and available employment. Although new jobs were appearing in the central city, these required far more education than poor blacks could obtain. Deviating from his typically hardheaded analysis, Wilson speculated about whether those jobs that allegedly required higher education *really* did so. Was it possible, for example, that the new high technology was sufficiently "user-friendly" to be operated by people who had simply mastered the three Rs?[54] He suspected that the association between formal skills and such jobs was false and kept many poor blacks out of the labor market.

Although Wilson referred to the ghetto throughout *The Truly Disadvantaged*, he only defined it by implication—that is, as an area of concentrated poverty. Noting what he called a major trend in the decade between 1970 and 1980, he showed that in the nation's five largest cities (New York, Los Angeles, Chicago, Philadelphia, and Detroit), all of which had seen a decline in population, the number of poor residents had increased by an average of 22 percent. Even more striking was Wilson's discovery that the number of people residing in high-poverty areas had increased by 161 percent.[55] He blamed this concentration of poverty on the flight of middle-class blacks, who had enjoyed an increase in economic opportunities as a consequence of the reforms initiated by the civil rights era. The distinctive middle class and the underclass that had emerged had a particular spatial expression. Neither demographic group could be found in large numbers in the same communities.

Viewing the ghetto as a place with "a disproportionate concentration of the most disadvantaged segments of the urban black population," Wilson's underlying conception of the relationship between physical space and disadvantage was summarized by the idea of "concentration effects."[56] His ideas drew heavily on Drake and Cayton's portrait of the black community, which Wilson revived to show that prior to the 1960s, the middle class had been an important social buffer in communities with high unemployment. Serving as role models for the poor, they not only reinforced mainstream values but also helped sustain the churches, recreational facilities, stores, and schools in these communities.[57] With the departure of the middle class, which had been central to Drake and Cayton's account, poor blacks were now left without this bulwark.

Writing four decades later, Wilson now saw little interdependence between the ghetto and wider society. For blacks in the 1980s, social isolation, combined with joblessness and a poor marriage market, created an ecological niche in which the average poor black individual lived with far more restricted opportunities than did the average poor white. Reviving the kind of ecological (or spatial) analysis that had been central to Drake and Cayton's account, Wilson argued that while poor whites rarely lived in poor, isolated urban neighborhoods, poor blacks could frequently be found in such communities. Comparisons of impoverished black and white communities often mistakenly presumed that different results stemmed from racial difference, drawing attention away from the actual cause: the inferior ecological niche that poor blacks occupied.[58]

The extreme social isolation of poor black neighborhoods meant that in comparison to poor whites, poor blacks had little contact with the working and middle classes. Not only did they have limited access to networks of people who could help them find better jobs, but they also had few role models. Wilson pointed out that the situation was best understood through comparison to the stable black communities of the past, in which a youngster growing up would typically observe many more employed and law-abiding adults, more working and professional two-parent families, and more youngsters completing school with opportunities at the end of the line.[59]

By contrast, in the ghetto of the 1980s, according to Wilson, children did not regularly encounter employed individuals or families supported by a working person.[60] The dual problem of unemployment and embeddedness in neighborhoods with a concentration of unemployed families had become critical. It had led to a vicious cycle that worked its way through other institutions such as schools, where graduation rates plummeted. As he had earlier argued in *The Declining Significance of Race*, when institutions became tainted by the ghetto's decline, they came to be increasingly avoided by outsiders, a situation that created further social isolation, and thus another vicious cycle.

What, one might ask, was Wilson's conception of the relationship between self-selection into the ghetto and the effect of the ghetto itself? Did he view the ghetto as a social context that brought about the problems of the people living there, or did he believe that people likely to have such problems were the ones left behind in the ghetto in higher numbers? Nowhere in *The Truly Disadvantaged* did Wilson acknowledge this latter possibility. Instead, like some (though not all) of the original Chicago School sociologists, he seemed to see the ghetto as a context that was far more determinative than the personal characteristics of the individuals themselves.

He did not think this was because people prone to out-of-wedlock childbearing or unemployment had remained in the ghetto in higher numbers. Rather, he believed that their situation was brought about directly by larger economic factors such as deindustrialization. But there was a tension in his analysis between the large-scale outside forces (such as deindustrialization) that he emphasized and the neighborhood dynamics (such as a decline in role models) that sometimes appeared to take on a life of their own.

An important response to Wilson came from two demographers, Douglas Massey and Nancy Denton. Their book, *American Apartheid* (1993), reprised Wilson's focus on the interrelations of space, race, and poverty, though it took issue with his explanation of how their convergence had come about. Both Drake and Cayton in the 1940s and Kenneth Clark in the 1960s had begun with the assumption that racial segregation was the ghetto's defining feature. Massey and Denton were essentially reasserting that claim. For them, segregation was supported by both contemporary and historical racist forces; whites, they claimed, were not only implicated in its creation but continued to be implicated in its maintenance. Thus, unlike Wilson, they viewed the ghetto as a creation of societal power.

Everything that Wilson (and Murray) had written, they argued, was incomplete without an understanding of the significance of racial residential segregation—an issue, they asserted, that had disappeared from the radar screen of U.S. social scientists. They were among the only prominent American sociologists to grant Murray his point that welfare policies helped facilitate the rise of the ghetto underclass, but they maintained that segregated groups were the only ones that were actually harmed by welfare payments. This was because segregation results in the spatial concentration of welfare recipients, thus bringing about a niche in which welfare dependency is the norm. This leads to prolonged urban poverty, and even "intergenerational transmission."[61]

Massey and Denton claimed that Wilson overstated the importance of middle-class outmigration as a cause of increased poverty concentration; it had been occurring for a much longer period than he implied, and more importantly, his argument obscured the fact that the persistence of racial segregation in housing markets made poverty concentration and black social isolation inevitable. The concentration of extreme poverty would have occurred even without middle-class outmigration. While Wilson was correct to focus on the transformation of the urban economy, the devastating effects of growing black poverty were actually caused by segregation, which "confined the increased deprivation to a small number of densely settled, tightly packed, and geographically isolated areas."[62]

Whereas Wilson had placed a lot of stress on the legacy of past discrimination, Massey and Denton were arguing that blacks, especially poor blacks, still enjoyed little residential mobility because of present-day barriers. Therefore, it was not merely the history of restrictive covenants, housing project construction, and federal mortgage policies that had led to the ghettoization of blacks and the spatial mobility of white families. One also had to recognize discrimination in the present, as the real estate industry continued to create residential advantages for whites and disadvantages for blacks. Because of discrimination against black renters and buyers, even those with the necessary means lacked the residential options of whites in better neighborhoods. Whereas

Wilson argued that employment policies that targeted the bottom of the labor market were needed, Massey and Denton argued that segregation was based on white prejudice, rather than market forces. The deleterious effects of white racism would not recede even if the right employment policies were instituted.

Massey and Denton's conception of the ghetto as a vicious cycle was consistent with that of earlier generations of scholars. They argued that by manifesting itself in residential segregation, racism has indirect as well as direct consequences. Segregation further differentiates groups and thus perpetuates discrimination by the majority against the minority. In a section of *American Apartheid* titled "The Language of Segregation," they illustrate this point by discussing the divergent dialects of English that have emerged among blacks and whites. The "speech gap" between the two races has fostered widespread ideas about their supposed differences and been used to uphold white supremacy. Yet the "speech gap" itself was the result of racial isolation.[63] The Africans who were brought as slaves to North America spoke many different languages and were often unable to understand each other. Settled on various plantations, they developed a distinct way of speaking that endured well after abolition. The language that blacks brought with them when they migrated from South to North during both World Wars did retain certain generic Southern features, but it also had elements that were not shared by whites from either the North or the South, but only by other blacks who could trace their heritage to the plantations and ultimately back to Africa.

Massey and Denton drew on research conducted by the linguist William Labov, who had studied the speech of African Americans living in Northern cities for five decades. His startling finding was that the speech of many blacks in high-poverty urban neighborhoods had become more distant from the speech of whites than it was in earlier decades—including the eras of slavery and Jim Crow. This had in turn fostered both presumptions of racial difference and faith in white supremacy.[64] Labov has shown that while blacks did speak a distinct dialect during slavery and Reconstruction, the most salient features of what modern linguists refer to as African American Vernacular English emerged in the decades of residential segregation after World War II— that is, in the black ghetto.[65] African American Vernacular English as it is known today is not a remnant of four hundred years of overt racial and economic oppression, but a product of the extreme spatial and social isolation of black Americans in the second half of the twentieth century.

Those who speak Black English are generally regarded as speaking bad English or slang; they are often deemed lazy or incapable of learning so-called Standard English or are said to be self-consciously rejecting mainstream society. Thus, a dialect that emerged through the sustained spatial isolation of the people who spoke it came to signify inherent inferiority. In short, spatial isolation produced distinctive behaviors, which were then stigmatized, seen as innate, and used as evidence to justify continued spatial isolation and socioeconomic marginalization. Once again, we see the ghetto as a vicious cycle.

Massey and Denton defined a ghetto as a "set of neighborhoods that are exclusively inhabited by members of one group, within which virtually all members of that group live." By this definition, there would be no black ghetto today, though the actual long-term impact of Massey and Denton's work was to equate the ghetto with residential segregation and housing inequality for blacks. By refocusing attention on this problem, they provided the intellectual foundation for contemporary arguments that the Fair Housing Act must systematically be enforced. The effort to overcome segregation cannot simply rely on countering individual acts of discrimination.[66]

Discussions of residential segregation often overlook daily interactions between blacks and whites. Demographic studies, which rely mainly on data about where people live, were not intended to be informative about what happens as people circulate throughout the city. Those studies could give the impression that blacks and whites barely interact at all.

One sociologist produced a steady stream of books in counterpoint to that conclusion. In his 1990 classic, *Streetwise*, Elijah Anderson captured the intimate experiences of blacks and whites and painted an informative picture of the role of race in everyday social interaction and public space. In the Philadelphia of the late 1980s, whites were starting to gentrify black neighborhoods, and blacks and whites were increasingly living in closer proximity. But the murder tally was approaching five hundred per year, higher than any tally subsequently recorded in that city.[67]

Anderson argued that the key symbol of the ghetto during the 1980s was the anonymous poor black male who tended to dominate space. "The black males take in all the others and dismiss them as a lion may dismiss a mouse," Anderson wrote in a controversial formulation. For virtually all whites, the key goal on the street was to avoid these potential "predators," and when that was not possible, they tended to show deference.[68]

But not only whites "clutched their pocketbooks," "walked stiffly," and averted their eyes. Even many middle-class and older blacks lived in fear of the anonymous black male. When younger black men dressed in the "urban uniform" of sweatsuits, sneakers, caps, and sunglasses, they were often trying to be intimidating enough to avoid becoming victims.[69] Yet they also needed to be able to avoid being so scary as to cause whites to panic. Thus, black males had to master code-switching to survive on the street. Anderson described the phenomenon of "getting ignorant," whereby any black man could abandon his mainstream interactional style for a street orientation. Being able to switch back and forth made these black males feel more secure, Anderson argued, and was a part of what it meant to be streetwise.[70]

For both blacks and whites, being streetwise also included the ability to differentiate between different kinds of black men (e.g., law-abiding youths versus gang members, as an extreme example). Being streetwise required a mastery of interactional dynamics—such as knowing how to alter one's pace to walk the right number of steps behind a suspicious person or how to bypass bad blocks at various times of the day. Urbanites with such skills, the ones Anderson called "streetwise," did not rely on gross stereotypes; rather, they had a more refined understanding that allowed them to distinguish between different kinds of people in public space. According to Anderson, only a rare white was "streetwise" enough to know the difference between a dangerous black male and one with benign intent. All of these interactional dynamics indicate how much work it takes to exist on the city streets. City dwellers, and especially black men, are attentive to all public interaction because getting it wrong in any particular interaction could have dangerous consequences.

Consistent with the work of psychologists who study stereotypes,

Anderson noted that when a bias is strongly held, it is hard to disconfirm it with facts or data from interactions on the street. Thus, even when an interaction is positive, it is easy to believe that it is just an exception. Racial stereotypes are resilient because they resist disconfirming data. Whites enter social interactions with negative stereotypes of blacks. When some blacks go walking through a neighborhood intimidating whites verbally or physically, according to Anderson, white fears are reinforced. "Blacks and whites thus become increasingly estranged," in yet another "vicious cycle of suspicion and distrust between the two groups."[71] Thus, a particular wariness of anonymous black males arises. "If a stranger cannot pass inspection and be assessed as 'safe' . . . the image of predator may arise."[72]

Like Wilson, Anderson argued that deindustrialization had left many residents of the ghetto without any opportunity. But this was a superficial similarity. What was important about his book was that it highlighted the sense of powerlessness that whites—so used to being in control—now felt on the city streets.

Some, in challenging Wilson, argued that it was no longer possible to think of the urban economy in terms of black and white. The question was: If the work that replaced industrial jobs required more education, how could one explain the fact that uneducated immigrants were flourishing and even prospering? Why, in fact, were they doing so much better than blacks? In his 1996 book *Still the Promised City?*, the sociologist Roger Waldinger argued that Wilson's theories had come up short in answering such questions.[73]

While Wilson insisted that significant job losses had occurred in the industries most open to urban minorities,[74] Waldinger demonstrated that, at least in New York City, blacks had never enjoyed access to these positions. Based on a careful study of the industrial economy of the city in the heyday of manufacturing, his study revealed that native-born blacks had long worked in the service sector, as domestic maids, taxi drivers, launderers, and hotel employees. Even in World War II the industrial economy had not incorporated blacks to any significant extent, Waldinger showed. By 1950, blacks were working primarily in public hospitals, transportation, and post offices. While Wilson's study might explain conditions in certain Rust Belt cities, such as Chicago and Detroit, where blacks had been deeply entrenched in the industrial economy, it failed to account for the economic decline of blacks and the success of immigrants in many other areas. Indeed, given the success of immigrants, Wilson's explanation was only partly satisfying even for the country's Chicagos and Detroits.

Waldinger's argument was not inconsistent with many of the claims that Wilson had initially advanced in *The Declining Significance of Race*. For example, Waldinger's interviews with blacks suggested that they believed jobs in the garment and hotel industries were not worth fighting for since wages were dropping. Young blacks were no longer even applying for the kinds of stigmatized service jobs to which their parents had been relegated.[75] Although Waldinger saw race and even racism as a significant dynamic in the situations he described, he also presented certain findings that the Wilson of *Declining Significance* could have put to use. He demonstrated, for example, that black immigrants were just as successful as whites in finding jobs in the postindustrial economy. In and of itself race was therefore not determinative. Furthermore, the fate of middle-class blacks diverged from that of lower-class blacks. Like immigrants, those with higher education used their social networks to find jobs in the municipal economy. As one labor relations director told Waldinger, "Our biggest recruitment is by word of mouth." Similarly, a black union leader admitted, "You'll find that many people are relatives."[76] Waldinger thus showed how middle-class blacks had developed a lock on jobs in the municipal economy, just as poor immigrants had done in the garment and hotel industries. The poorest blacks, meanwhile, had essentially been shut out of the labor market.

What Waldinger added was that the low-paying jobs that blacks were now turning down were being actively taken by a new generation of immigrants from Latin America, the Caribbean, and China, whose social networks created "ethnic occupational niches."[77] Waldinger argued that the immigrants had initially arrived at these occupations through self-selection rather than decisions made by employers, but his interviews in the hotel industry indicated that once established, employers became partial to immigrants over blacks. He also found that they heeded the biases of their workers, who often wished to exclude blacks.

Waldinger's effort to explain the divergent fortunes of poor blacks and immigrants differed markedly from previous works on the subject. The many earlier studies in this genre tended to focus on the cultural differences between blacks and immigrant groups, particularly with regard to their work ethic and the value they placed on education. But like Liebow in *Tally's Corner*, Waldinger argued that poor blacks had no desire to repeat the lives of their fathers, who had been blocked from rising beyond the lowest rungs of the economy by their own poor skills. (Waldinger also added racism, which had not been a focus of Liebow's.) Nothing in this claim was cultural.

Waldinger ended on a pessimistic note. Whereas Wilson had depicted the situation of middle-class blacks in a reasonably positive light, Waldinger questioned how long their position in the municipal economy would protect them from competition from migrants. His comparison of the 1980 and 1990 censuses indicated that, at the time of his writing, migrants were already moving into the public sector. Thinking in particular about Puerto Ricans, about whom he otherwise had little to say in his book, Waldinger predicted that the public sector would be the next battleground for these two long-standing antagonists in New York's economy. Given that New York's municipal economy was then in a fiscal crisis, Waldinger saw the supply of public-sector jobs dwindling even as migration would increase the number of people competing for those jobs.[78] And indeed, after some recovery, public-sector employment dwindled across the United States as part of a general retrenchment and the privatization of public services.

While early books on the ghetto such as *Black Metropolis* occasionally sought to grasp the female experience of poverty and spatial restriction, they were written before any feminist movement had systematically addressed the lives of black women. Even the women's liberation movement of the 1960s was primarily concerned with the boredom of middle-class suburban housewives and their dependency on men. As the feminist critic bell hooks summed it up, "To want to work and to have to work are two very different matters."[79] By the 1980s, however, the bar for serious analysis of black women's lives was raised by a new generation of scholars and activists.

The year before Wilson published *The Declining Significance of Race* (1978), a group of black lesbian feminists published "The Combahee River Collective Statement," a major analysis of the situation of black women.[80] Just as Wilson built upon the idea that the social structure of America had become a series of racial "subcommunities crisscrossed by social class,"[81] so too these black women proposed an analogous feminist theory, arguing that the intersection of race, gender, and social class corresponded to the actual identities, behavior, and material conditions of women. They thus laid out what they termed a theory of "intersectionality," claiming that interlocking racial, sexual, and class oppressions needed to be understood as operating simultaneously.

The black feminist response to Wilson was respectful but critical, particularly toward his diagnosis that the problems of the inner city lay partly in the lack of "marriageable" black males. The implication that major problems could be alleviated by giving men more jobs appeared sexist to the core because it expected that black women would be dependent on black men. In *Black Feminist Thought*, Patricia Hill Collins argued that Wilson was far more concerned with issues afflicting black men—for example, the availability of black male role models for black boys—than he was with those affecting women. Others felt that Wilson's embrace of the Moynihan Report, which black women viewed as demeaning and disempowering, would contribute to their further marginalization. Yet even as she argued that Wilson placed too much emphasis on the rise of female-headed households, Collins differentiated him from Moynihan, stating that Wilson was "exemplary in linking patterns of family organization to the changing contours of economic opportunities in black urban neighborhoods."[82]

What some have also argued was that spatial mismatch created even more challenges for women than for men. Single mothers with child-care responsibilities had to avoid long commutes and work shifts that required traversing desolate, unsafe neighborhoods, especially at night. As the urban sociologist John Kasarda argued the year that Wilson published *When Work Disappears* (1996), spatial mismatch was a gender issue: "Job options for these women tend to be much more restricted spatially and temporally, often limiting them to low-paying and part-time work closer to home. These constraints no doubt pose strong work disincentives."[83]

Whatever the criticisms of Wilson's analyses, his focus on poverty concentration and the spatial fix of poor blacks' lives gained huge attention in policy circles and indeed became the basis of one of the most important social programs in the history of urban America. In the early 1990s, the Clinton administration embarked on a new program called Hope VI. The Department of Housing and Urban Development would tear down severely distressed public housing throughout the urban areas of the United States, a process that had begun two decades earlier, most famously in the case of the Pruitt-Igoe project in St. Louis. Under the Clinton-era planning, such housing would then be replaced with revitalized mixed-income housing in which poor families could live among middle-class families drawn back into the city. The government spent as much as $660 million per year in redevelopment grants in the late 1990s. In the current debates over the significance of poverty concentration, an even more important program was a rental-voucher program whose federal expenditures of up to $16 billion per year dwarfed the redevelopment grants.[84] This program made it possible for nearly 2 million families to move out of the projects, often to other neighborhoods of the city.

Although Wilson's work was clearly having enormous influence, after a quarter century at the helm of the illustrious University of Chicago Department of Sociology, he said that he was feeling isolated. Speaking to the New Yorker editor David Remnick, he noted that he felt cut off from national policy debates, which mainly took place on the East Coast. Around that time, he had been invited to Cambridge, Massachusetts, for dinner at the home of Henry Louis Gates, Jr., the famed chair of African American Studies at Harvard. Seated around the table were all of the luminaries of the department at that time, including Cornel West, Kwame Anthony Appiah, Orlando Patterson, Leon and Evelyn Higginbotham, and Charles Ogletree. "That was one of the most exciting evenings of my life," Wilson later told Remnick. When the group tried to persuade Wilson to join them, it was not a hard sell. A short time later, articles in newspapers and magazines across the country carried the story that the most influential black social scientist in America had accepted Harvard's most distinguished faculty position.[85] The University Professorship he would occupy entitled Wilson to teach anywhere he wanted in the university, and Wilson settled on homes in the Department of Sociology, African American Studies, and the school of public policy.

The impact of Wilson's work on public policy meant that his underlying conception of the relationship between space and disadvantage, as it occurred through concentration effects and social isolation, was now at the forefront of the nation's approach to fighting poverty. With support from over half a dozen of the country's leading foundations, he had now completed another project that employed not only a generation of the best graduate students at the University of Chicago, but also a number of colleagues. Not since Myrdal had any scholar been able to command the kind of massive resources that made it possible to hire eminent faculty alongside graduate students. The result, *When Work Disappears: The World of the New Urban Poor* (1996), was researched while Ronald Reagan was in the White House and published during the first term of Bill Clinton's presidency.

While in *The Truly Disadvantaged* Wilson had defined the ghetto underclass but not the ghetto, here he was quite precise in defining the ghetto, and he did so in demographic rather than behavioral terms. He had begun his earlier book with the assumption that a ghetto was a neighborhood with a high concentration of people with so-called underclass behavior. Now he systematized a definition by referring to census tracts in which 40 percent or more of the population lived below the federal poverty line.[86] This definition was generated in the early 1980s by two social scientists who had worked for the federal government. After driving a car around certain blighted neighborhoods, they reported that the 40 percent criterion tended to identify "areas that looked like ghettos in terms of their housing conditions." They became more confident about their claim when they found that these were the same areas that local officials saw as ghettos. The investigators were white, though their article revealed nothing about their race.[87]

In his push for race-neutral policies, Wilson implemented a race-neutral demographic measurement. He went against the prevailing conception of the ghetto by eliminating race from the equation and using the term to describe *any* concentration of 40 percent poverty. As his work was directed primarily at the inner-city neighborhoods of Chicago, most of the people he studied were African American by default. As a result, his project tended to focus on the lives of poor blacks. Because the neighborhoods he studied included many of the same ones discussed by Drake and Cayton, it was lost on many readers that he was not defining the ghetto as racialized poverty but as poverty per se. By Wilson's definition, he could just as easily have been talking about inner-city Latino, Asian, or white neighborhoods, which he barely discussed at all. His definition was consistent with his ideological commitment to promoting public policies that could be embraced by a multiracial coalition.[88]

Wilson paid far less attention than did Massey and Denton to the lower property values and substandard housing caused by ghettoization and instead placed greater emphasis on the disappearance of role models and nearby manufacturing plants. He saw concentrated poverty as a phenomenon of economic restructuring and depopulation: the communities that he studied, which had been demographically robust when Drake and Cayton were writing in the 1940s, had lost half of their residents between 1970 and 1990.[89] These demographic shifts were accompanied by a major decline in the resources that contributed to neighborhood vitality.[90] Abandoned buildings became crack houses and spaces for other illegal activities. Finding it difficult to maintain a sense of community, the more conventional working-class residents followed the middle class to other neighborhoods.

In addition to his demographic analysis, Wilson sent teams of assistants to the inner city to interview residents and business managers. One of the most valuable parts of his study was a survey of employers, who revealed their negative views of ghetto residents and the extent to which this influenced their hiring decisions. Page after page, Wilson gave voice to employers' perspectives, such as "They don't want to work, they don't want to do anything. I think that's a big part of it. I don't think anybody wants to admit it, but I think that's primarily it."[91] The author of *The Declining Significance of Race* was willing to acknowledge that race was still a factor in many hiring decisions, but not racism. Ironically, in the controversy surrounding that earlier work, he had claimed that despite saying that the significance of race had declined, he had never argued that racism in his day was not a problem. Now, despite his acknowledgment that race was a factor, he wrote that the issues were too complex to be "reduced to the simple notion of employer racism."[92] He discouraged readers from interpreting the comments of employers as a problem of white racism, since one could also observe black employers expressing negative views about ghetto blacks, as in this example from an insurance agency:

> There is a perception that most of [our] kids . . . don't have the proper skills . . . they don't know how to write. They don't know how to speak. They don't act in a business fashion or dress in a business manner . . . in a way that the business community would like. And they just don't feel that they're getting a quality employee. . . .
>   Interviewer: Do you think—is that all a false perception or is something there or—?
>   Respondent: I think there's some truth to it.[93]

By the time he published these interviews, Wilson was no longer maintaining—as he had earlier on—that employers were illegitimately requiring higher levels of education for work that in fact required nothing more than reading, writing, and arithmetic. Rather than viewing the low place of blacks in the labor market as a function of unfair requirements, he accepted employers' claims and argued that their hiring practices were not usually based on unreasonable expectations or racism. Nor did he argue that the rise of unemployment among poor blacks was the consequence of lost jobs. Instead, he advanced a far more complex theory of a vicious cycle that linked the views of employers and employees to the urban skills mismatch. Ironically and despite its title, *When Work Disappears* did not hinge mainly on an assumption about the supply of jobs. Instead, the problem was that blacks were ill-suited for the jobs that were currently available. The drop in traditional blue-collar jobs in Chicago had done more than merely increase unemployment among black men in the inner city or force them into low-paying, often short-term service-sector jobs. Stuck in a ghetto environment and surrounded by social networks and homes that did little to help them find employment, these men could not keep up with their white and Hispanic counterparts, especially when the labor market was slack. Since Hispanics were integrated into migrant networks, they more readily got referrals from current employees and found jobs in manufacturing.

Blacks, on the other hand, embittered and resentful at having to take on hard, often dehumanizing, poorly paid jobs, ended up expressing their frustration in the work setting. Their attitude and behavior, combined with their erratic performance in high-turnover jobs, led to the common belief that they were unreliable employees. This made it increasingly difficult for them to find solid and satisfying work, not only because employers were relying more on immigrant and female labor, but also because service jobs were steadily on the rise. Their immersion in a ghetto environment with poor schools, a culture of nonwork, and few professional role models made them particularly ill-suited for a new economy in which employers were looking for workers with hard skills (literacy and numeracy) and soft skills (interactional ability). The reputation they had acquired over time thus had a negative impact on employers' hiring decisions, especially when the economy was slow.

Again, Wilson focused minimally on the problems of black women, pointing out that they too faced problems in the labor market. Socially isolated in poor neighborhoods, they had few employment prospects. Although employers in Chicago preferred them to black men, women had an equally hard time making connections of the sort that allowed them to move into white-collar jobs. The environment in which they lived did not enable them to develop the language and job-related skills demanded by an economy that favored those who could work and communicate effectively with the public.

Ultimately, the vicious cycle Wilson conceptualized began with a single cause: economic restructuring. His response was still a WPA-style federal program that would increase employment prospects for all Americans and thus have a positive social impact on the ghetto. The problems caused by unemployment in ghettos, he insisted, could not be tackled separately from those caused by unemployment in general. As more people found jobs, crime—including violent crime—and drug use would drop, family bonds would grow stronger, and the number of welfare recipients would fall precipitously. Wilson never addressed the question of whether poor blacks would continue to live together in the same physical space, but the problematic behavior that was so prevalent in the ghetto would gradually disappear as it would no longer be sustained or nurtured by chronic unemployment. As more people became gainfully employed and accumulated work experience, their chances of finding available jobs in the private sector would improve. Employers too would change their attitude toward inner-city workers, who would now be entering jobs with more experience and references from previous employers and managers.

Wilson did not claim that all unemployed individuals in the ghetto would take advantage of this improved situation. Those who had already succumbed to drug and alcohol abuse thanks to chronic unemployment might not be able to live up to the basic requirements, such as showing up for work regularly and on time. But these amounted to only a fraction of the inner-city population. Most workers in this sector were ready, willing, capable, and eager to take on a steady job if there was one.

In 1994, Charles Murray coauthored a book called *The Bell Curve*, which initiated an explosive debate on the connections between inequality and intelligence.

Among other things, Murray argued that members of the "underclass" were characterized by lower IQs than the rest of American society, thus contributing to their social position. Murray became increasingly subject to attacks and charges that he was a white supremacist. Orlando Patterson asserted that Murray's arguments were "no different in principle" than the hereditarian views that undergirded the genocide of the Nazi Holocaust. Patterson said that the popularity of such views led him to wonder "whether supporting gun control is a socially intelligent policy for underclass Afro-Americans, or for that matter, Afro-Americans in general."[94] These and other attacks did not stop Murray's earlier *Losing Ground* from continuing to be influential in policy circles.

Wilson's strong effort to rebut Murray helped define Wilson himself as a liberal—a strong turnabout after the confusion and denunciations *The Declining Significance of Race* provoked on the left. Stressing larger economic forces, Wilson did not include fixing a broken welfare system in his larger policy agenda or his conception of the ghetto. Nor did he implicate welfare as a system while he focused on "social isolation" and "underclass neighborhoods."[95] That intellectual work ultimately was taken up by other liberal scholars who would end up having a major impact on the transformation of the welfare system after Bill Clinton took office in 1993. These included researchers from Harvard's Kennedy

School, the Institute for Research on Poverty at the University of Wisconsin–Madison, and the National Poverty Center at the University of Michigan, often doing work that was supported by the Russell Sage Foundation. With a brain trust of liberal scholars now informing his plans, Clinton came into office promising "to end welfare as we know it." Though the president diplomatically paid his respects to Murray, which no doubt played well to conservatives ("He did the country a great service," Clinton said to NBC News about Charles Murray. "I mean, he and I have often disagreed, but I think his analysis is essentially right"),[96] his agenda was completely different from Murray's.

The Clinton policy initiatives were guided by a group of liberal advisers, including David Ellwood and Mary Jo Bane of Harvard's Kennedy School, Peter Edelman of Georgetown Law School, and Donna Shalala of the University of Wisconsin. Unlike Murray, who was a radical libertarian and opposed social provision across the board, these advisers were part of a larger community of liberal academic social scientists who were critical of welfare and believed that social policy could be recast to promote work and well-being and to be more consistent with American values. They roundly rejected Murray's major claim that the rise of long-term dependency could be blamed on the welfare system. The actual causes of rising dependency, they argued, were economic, primarily slow wage growth since the 1970s.[97] But in an influential work of the period, *Poor Support*, David Ellwood argued that while jobs were as scarce as Wilson claimed, single mothers should ultimately be expected to work at least half-time. His logic was that absent such requirements, "welfare will still be seen as the refuge for those who are not willing to work."[98]

In 1996, three years after Clinton had passed a large increase in the Earned Income Tax Credit—the biggest expansion of an antipoverty program since the 1960s—he signed a bill passed by the Republican Congress that made good on his campaign promise to reform welfare. It imposed strict work requirements and time limits on AFDC—cash assistance to the poor—but it left intact the other major safety-net programs, including food stamps and Medicaid, which Republicans had sought to curtail in two earlier bills that Clinton had vetoed. The combined effect of the expansion of the EITC and the limits on AFDC was to shift assistance to the poor toward policies that promoted work. The effect was also to transfer control over benefits from the states—which set AFDC levels and in the South kept them to minimal levels—to the federal government, which set the levels of the EITC and food stamps. On a net basis, the Clinton years increased aid to the poor, especially in the South, and would have increased that aid further if the 1993 universal healthcare plan had passed.[99]

This offsetting expansion of social policy was contrary to what Murray had called for. Nevertheless, Daniel Patrick Moynihan voted against the bill in the Senate, arguing that while it told people to take jobs, there might not be any jobs to take. Even some of Clinton's own circle, including David Ellwood, Mary Jo Bane, and Peter Edelman, resigned from his administration because they thought welfare reform would gut the safety net needed to transition to the labor market. Edelman had begun his career as an assistant to Robert F. Kennedy and had written the senator's first speech on welfare reform. He had spent his life working on poverty issues and was married to Marian Wright Edelman, the founding director of the Children's Defense Fund. The welfare reform legislation was more than Edelman could take, and he resigned soon after Clinton signed it into law. In March 1997, he wrote a sharp critique of the bill in *The Atlantic* titled "The Worst Thing Bill Clinton Has Done." In it he declared that he hated the welfare system as it had existed because it had led to a chronic dependence on assistance, even among those who would have preferred steady jobs. But, as Edelman and some liberal critics of Clinton saw it, the legislation lacked critical supports, such as child care, which would have enabled mothers to enter the labor force. As a result, it would harm countless poor children when benefits were cut off.[100] The law, in Edelman's view, told former welfare recipients to "find a job" without providing the necessary means for them to do so.[101]

Although the bill did not turn America into Calcutta, we may never truly know what the long-term impact of Clinton's welfare reform has been. One of the lucky breaks that accompanied the introduction of time limits on federal aid was a surge in economic growth and low unemployment. When the sociologist Katherine Newman wrote about a group of low-wage black workers she had been following for eight years, she came up with more positive findings than she had expected. She was inspired to follow them by the fear that welfare reform would dump thousands of low-skilled job seekers into the oversaturated inner-city labor markets and destroy any prospect of stability, much less upward mobility. But the workers and job seekers whom she began observing in the "bad times" of the early 1990s had caught the wave of "perfect weather"—high growth, low inflation, and very low unemployment—of the late 1990s. This was hardly the ideal test of what it meant to shred the safety net. In any event, the effects also proved difficult to study as many people disappeared into the woodwork of doubled-up housing, couch-surfing, and living on the margins.[102]

By the mid-nineties, social scientists were eager to evaluate the impact of another Clinton administration initiative, Hope VI. In particular, they were interested in finding solid evidence for a causal link between improved neighborhood quality and the long-term economic outcomes of those who moved out of the projects.

Concern over the effects of concentrated poverty had been magnified by Wilson's arguments about social ties and the isolation of the poor in his 1987 book *The Truly Disadvantaged*. Interest in these dynamics continued to grow when sociologists analyzed data from the Gautreaux housing program in Chicago. Dorothy Gautreaux had sued the Chicago Housing Authority in 1966, in the wake of Martin Luther King's fair housing marches in Chicago. By 1976, the U.S. Supreme Court allowed a trial court to force the Department of Housing and Urban Development to use the entire Chicago metropolitan area (not just the city) to redistribute over twenty-five thousand people in over one hundred different middle-income, white communities. The results showed much better outcomes for the participants than for those left behind, but because participants were not randomly selected, the results were dismissed.[103]

Thus, however enticing the Gautreaux data and Wilson's theory were, the question remained as to whether the effects of living in a poor neighborhood—over and above one's own family income—were causal or just reflected underlying differences between those who "escaped" and those who got "left behind."[104] This creeping doubt about the causal claims regarding neighborhood conditions was best articulated in 1989 when Christopher Jencks and Susan Mayer weighed in, responding to

Wilson in an article titled "Growing Up in Poor Neighborhoods: How Much Does it Matter?" Jencks and Mayer concluded that assessing the actual impact of living in poor neighborhoods was difficult—because it was hard to distinguish the influence of the neighborhoods per se from the characteristics of the individuals who lived there.[105] If those who moved to (or were unable to leave) such neighborhoods had personal or family traits that disposed them to be poor regardless of where they lived, then it was difficult to prove the independent impact of their physical and social surroundings. Nonetheless, the research tended to assume the causal arrow went in only one direction: the nature of the neighborhood affects those who live there.[106]

Responding to this need to separate out causal impacts from mere associations, in 1994 a group of researchers at the U.S. Department of Housing and Urban Development took up the challenge of sorting out cause and effect. The researchers initiated a long-term study known as Moving to Opportunity (MTO), which was designed to overcome previous criticisms. It followed more than four thousand families living in projects in the most concentrated areas of poverty who had been given federal housing vouchers to move to similar or better census tracts.[107]

When HUD announced the MTO program, people living in public housing in Chicago, Boston, Baltimore, Los Angeles, and New York received notification that they were eligible for housing vouchers that would help them afford alternative domiciles in the housing market. Thousands of people in the target cities grabbed their phones to call the switchboards; most were greeted by constant busy signals. Those who got through to an operator effectively won a lottery—or rather, a chance to be in a lottery.

The "lottery" worked like this: One-third of those selected were awarded a Section 8 housing voucher for the private market (which normally has a long waiting list), but were told that they had to use their voucher to find a rental unit in a neighborhood with a poverty rate below 10 percent—for the first year, after which they could use it anywhere. Another third could move anywhere they could afford with the Section 8 voucher and were not required to move to a higher-income neighborhood for even that first year. A third, "control" group consisted of people who had called the hotline but did not get selected for an immediate Section 8 voucher. (They could still get all the other government benefits they were receiving and get on the regular Section 8 waiting list.) With the help of public housing agencies and local non-profit organizations, only those in the first group were counseled on how to look for housing units in neighborhoods with less poverty.

Save the possibility of disappointment, little was at stake in making the initial phone call to HUD. In the next stage, however, lottery winners were presented with what most people would consider both an opportunity and a risk: a move to a new neighborhood that offered better housing, schools, and proximity to jobs at the cost of giving up everyday contact with friends and relatives who had both sustained them and dragged them down.

The initial results after seven years appeared negative. In particular, young men in the treatment group seemed to fare worse in the new neighborhoods. The desire of scholars to publish studies quickly led to such reports as *The Washington Post*'s "Moving Students out of Poor Inner Cities Yields Little, Studies of HUD Vouchers Say." The implication was that if leaving the ghetto did not help, then the ghetto context did not truly matter:

> Many social reformers have long said that low academic achievement among inner-city children cannot be improved significantly without moving their families to better neighborhoods, but new reports released today that draw on a unique set of data throw cold water on that theory. Researchers examining what happened to 4,248 families that were randomly given or denied federal housing vouchers to move out of their high-poverty neighborhoods found no significant difference about seven years later between the achievement of children who moved to more middle-class neighborhoods and those who didn't.
>
> Although some children had more stable lives and better academic results after the moves, the researchers said, on average there was no improvement. Boys and brighter students appeared to have more behavioral problems in their new schools, the studies found.[108]

But was this the final word? Were all the earlier studies merely reflecting the social sorting of more and less capable people in and out of poor neighborhoods and not the actual effect of living there? The MTO experiment seems to have been stacked against the hypothesis that living in a disadvantaged neighborhood mattered. In response to the early, disappointing results, the sociologist Robert Sampson pointed out that the disruptive act of moving could have a negative impact on social outcomes such as school performance, delinquency, and health.[109] It would therefore be difficult to separate the impact of a move (negative) from the impact of a new neighborhood (perhaps positive), which may cancel each other out.[110]

When people change neighborhoods, they pay a cost in lost network ties, otherwise so valuable to poor people, as documented by Carol Stack. They lose at least some of their support network immediately and most likely cannot take maximum advantage of their new context because they have not yet established social networks there. This is very different from the way migration and immigration usually work, since people most often migrate to places where they know someone who can help them get started—part of the "migration chain" so well documented by immigration scholars.

Furthermore, when the families who received vouchers designated for low-poverty areas moved to higher-income tracts, they moved to ones that were populated overwhelmingly by minorities. The experiment only required that people move to neighborhoods with higher income levels, but did not require them to move into nonblack communities. This was due to Wilson's definition of a ghetto as a neighborhood of any race with a poverty rate of 40 percent or higher; his race-blind definition was now coming back to bite him and others who believed the ghetto context mattered. As the sociologists Susan Clampet-Lundquist and Douglas Massey argued, even if two neighborhoods, one white and one black, have similar numbers of unemployed people living in poverty, the black neighborhood is more likely to have been neglected by public and private services over time, which exacerbates the effects of unemployment and poverty.[111] This argument was, ironically, made by Wilson himself in *The Truly Disadvantaged*, and it remains a particularly poignant point in any comparison of black and white urban middle-class neighborhoods.

Even blacks who have left the ghetto and live in working- or middle-class black communities are often severely handicapped in comparison to whites who live in their own segregated middle-class neighborhoods. Black neighborhoods in this range have higher crime rates, lower property values, and poorer schools than otherwise comparable white neighborhoods.[112] Sometimes they come closer to resembling poor black neighborhoods than white middle-class ones. As Clampet-Lundquist and Massey noted, "Even though middle-class black areas may not themselves display concentrated poverty, because of racial segregation they tend to be located adjacent to or very near areas of concentrated deprivation and often share common service catchment areas."[113] Given all this, one way to test whether black ghettos have a negative effect would have been to move poor blacks to whiter neighborhoods, where they might have enjoyed significantly better services and more interaction with whites. An obvious area in which this could have made a difference was public education, where more interaction with white students who spoke Standard English may have offered an alternative to Black English vernacular, which is highly penalized in both the educational system and the workplace.

As more time passed, some positive effects of "moving to opportunity" did become evident in the realm of health. Substantial results were published in *The New England Journal of Medicine* fourteen years after the MTO experiment began. Measuring the body mass index and markers of blood glucose levels of the people who had moved to neighborhoods with lower poverty rates, investigators concluded that the female participants were significantly less obese and diabetic.[114] One factor behind this result may be violence, which declines in the lives of those who move out of high-poverty neighborhoods, as glycated hemoglobin, body mass levels, and the stress of living in a violent place are linked.[115] It may also reflect the healthier food options available in these neighborhoods or the social norms of higher-income, thinner neighbors exerting influence.

The lottery winners initially reported that they saw little risk in the experiment, simply a great opportunity. While it was impossible for winners to have an objective sense of the actual odds that their lives would get better or worse as a result of the move, HUD assumed that those selected for the treatment had a subjective sense that they were being presented with exactly what the government had advertised: opportunity. In retrospect, one may assume that the factor most responsible for giving them a subjective sense of little risk was the hope that violence in their new neighborhood would be lower. The study could have equally been titled Moving to Safety.

A series of interviews conducted with the subjects revealed that most had experienced a great many random incidents of violence in their former communities. Many of them had grown extremely isolated from spending so much time indoors with their children due to safety concerns. After seven years in their new neighborhoods, however, adults reported substantial improvements in mental health. Among children, girls (who may have felt the most constrained in violent neighborhoods) seemed to fare best in many ways. A subsequent study presented far more polarized results: girls continued to do better while boys showed increased rates of depression and conduct disorders.[116]

So what of the goal of moving people out of ghettos? The progress of boys and girls will need to be continuously tracked. The adults who move seem to experience clear mental health benefits even if their position in the economy remains unchanged. Such individual effects have great value for people, even if they merely make poverty more humane and easier to bear. Nobody would argue that people living in historically black American ghettos have inherent characteristics that make them and their children happier in violent and destructive environments or in places filled with disease, not to mention hunger and cold. A team of sociologists' evaluation of the MTO experiment said it best: "Security is essential to leading a decent life even if one must live poor or live poor for a time, and ironically, it is easy to miss this by focusing exclusively on 'opportunity' in education, work, or other domains."[117]

But the MTO story was not over. An even longer-term follow-up conducted by some of the same group of researchers who reported the initial, disappointing results found a ray of hope.[118] The lack of a net positive outcome for the treatment group still held for the adults and for the offspring who were adolescents at the time of the first move. But when the researchers examined the outcomes for younger siblings, they indeed found many of the benefits that policymakers who invested in this massive experiment had hoped to find. Those children who were less than thirteen years of age during that critical first year when families left the ghetto were more likely to attend college and earned wages 31 percent higher than those in the other two groups.

Further bolstering this interpretation that neighborhood poverty mattered for younger children was research by the economists Raj Chetty and Nathaniel Hendren. While these scholars did not conduct an actual experiment, they used IRS earnings data that included 5 million individuals over seventeen years, across the entire span of the country. They looked at families who changed neighborhoods and compared siblings within those families. Since the concern about selective migration in and out of "bad" neighborhoods revolves around savvy versus less capable parents, comparing kids from the same family eliminates that problem and allows for a cleaner estimation of the effects of the neighborhood per se. That is, one sibling who spent more time in a poor neighborhood acts as the "control" for her sister who spent more of her childhood in a higher-income area by virtue of when the family happened to move. Chetty and Hendren found that every year a child spent in a better-off neighborhood increased the gap with his or her sibling's wages.[119]

While the newer MTO results are based on a limited sample and the Chetty and Hendren results do not represent an experimentally "clean" study, in combination they provide powerful evidence that neighborhoods do matter for children's long-term outcomes and that they matter most earlier in life. In retrospect, the new MTO findings and those of Chetty and Hendren dovetail nicely with the growing body of work—led by that of the Nobel Prize–winning economist James Heckman—showing that social conditions matter most in early childhood.

Given such findings, residential-mobility programs hold out great promise in the abstract, but so far they have been attempted only on a small scale. If a massive program was proposed, would white Americans welcome large numbers of poor blacks into their neighborhoods? "It is sad that this approach seems to be acceptable to white society only when it is limited and small-scale," wrote the political scientist Peter Dreier. "In the end, residential mobility plans are only a small part of the unfinished business of reviving old inner cities and integrating America."[120]

In his entire corpus of work, William Julius Wilson has rarely mentioned Gunnar Myrdal. Yet one can detect an implicit if unconscious dialogue with the Swedish Nobel Prize winner throughout Wilson's writing. While he is mainly viewed as someone who de-emphasized racial factors, his major policy framework reflects what should have been learned anyway from Myrdal's failure. That failure was Myrdal's inability to understand Northern racism, and his consequent prediction that America would bring its actions into alignment with its ideals. It was a devastating mistake, because that argument unnecessarily framed the 1,483 pages of his book, overshadowing his larger contribution. As many of Myrdal's critics would be the first to recognize, no other book before or since has so fully documented the inferior place of blacks in American society. The Supreme Court recognized the book's importance in this regard in footnote 11 of *Brown v. Board of Education*.[121]

Despite being so well-known for a book called *The Declining Significance of Race*, throughout his career Wilson has had no confidence that whites would ever willingly deal with blacks' problems for their own sake. His work, much like that of Drake and Cayton, has emphasized over and over that whites will never help blacks out of the goodness of their hearts. There will be no charity for blacks. The "hidden agenda" is to appeal to whites' desire to help others who share their skin color—but in alignment with other whites (the policymakers) who will join in the conspiracy. If ever a message could be seen as a rebuke to Myrdal, this would be it. Yet Wilson's assumption may also demonstrate what turns out to be a potential fundamental misunderstanding of middle-class whites in the United States. Unlike middle-class blacks and poor blacks, who had a sense of shared peoplehood, middle-class whites may simply not have seen themselves and poor whites as parts of a community with a shared identity.

The Truly Disadvantaged caught a wave because it appeared at precisely the moment when many liberals in the Democratic Party sought a deracialized approach to addressing black poverty and the white electorate in general. The party could benefit by not being so closely linked with the ghetto and welfare. Wilson's approach was a way to de-emphasize race while still retaining liberal aspiration. During his presidential campaign, Bill Clinton invoked Wilson's work: "*The Truly Disadvantaged* made me see the problems of race and poverty and the inner city in a different light. It reinforced my conviction that we have to find broad-based economic solutions to a lot of our country's challenges."[122] Wilson had made a forceful case that resonated with the pragmatic goals of Democratic politicians, though his call for robust job creation went far beyond what Clinton or any of those politicians were apt to call for. In that light, Wilson was surely not pandering to the mainstream. The job schemes he advocated were far more radical than many race-conscious policies that were already on the books.

The importance of Wilson's contribution—especially for its time—has frequently gone unappreciated. Even if he himself undervalued the ongoing significance of race, his work marked a clear departure from what had come before. What is different about race in contemporary American society is that it intersects with class in new ways. In the past it didn't matter what blacks' class position was—they were simply consigned to the ghetto by the larger society because they were black. By the time Wilson was writing *The Declining Significance of Race* in 1978, that was certainly no longer true, an idea that required consideration whether or not one accepted his beliefs about the decline of contemporary discrimination. Later, in *The Truly Disadvantaged*, Wilson built insightfully on the notion of separate race-class positions with the idea that these distinctive positions express themselves in space. Unlike the life in the ghetto described by Drake and Cayton in the forties (to which Wilson regularly referred), he showed that poor and middle-class blacks were located very differently. Middle-class blacks were far less likely to be found in the same neighborhoods as poor blacks, and they had very different experiences in part because of that fact. But their fates continued to be linked: after all, the disappearance of middle-class blacks from the ghetto resulted in a greater concentration of poverty.

Wilson's strategic (and cynical) call for race-neutral public policies could have been accompanied by an analysis that highlighted the *continuing* significance of race. But he did not take that tack. Even as he argued that whites would be unsupportive of race-targeted solutions, his insistence on "the declining significance of race" thesis led to the view that he was naive with regard to contemporary racism and discrimination. The ironic result is that many of the same people who criticized Myrdal for his naïveté about the white conscience have scorned the more skeptical Wilson throughout his career.[123]

Wilson rightly argued that the situation of both middle-class and poor blacks at this moment in history could be better understood if greater weight was placed on the intersection of race and social class. But he also went so far as to claim that too much focus on race obscured rather than clarified an understanding of the life chances of individual blacks—an analysis that dovetailed with policy discussions and political dynamics of the time. Prominent progressives thus accused Wilson of giving aid and comfort to politicians who wanted U.S. public policy to downplay the challenges of race. The sociologist Stephen Steinberg concluded, "To be sure, Wilson did not cause the retreat from race that has occurred over the past two decades. He did, however, confer on it an indispensable mark of legitimacy."[124]

From a slightly longer historical perspective, the significance of Wilson's definition of the ghetto stands out. Wilson ushered in a sea change in the way that the ghetto was viewed. If any neighborhood with 40 percent poverty was a ghetto, then use of the concept to draw a distinction between certain black and white neighborhoods was no longer a pivotal agenda. Likewise, if the ghetto no longer symbolized blacks' claims to being a priority of the American conscience, then the moral case for change would be subordinated to appeals to whites' self-interest. Furthermore, for the first time since the Nazi and civil rights eras, the ghetto was now being defined without reference to either race or power. As a result, the idea's history in Europe and America no longer seemed relevant.

5

HARLEM, 2004: GEOFFREY CANADA

Unsurprisingly, this encapsulated history of the idea of the ghetto has not been uplifting. All the programs, projects, and approaches have proven discouraging or problematic, whatever their intellectual source—from Myrdal onward. But some individuals will always care deeply about their communities and refuse to throw up their hands in despair. Seeing their own ghetto as a possible site of reform, some of these individuals will deal with people in the places where they live because moving them elsewhere is hardly an option.

One particular such effort garnered attention, support, and celebrity: the Harlem Children's Zone, founded by Geoffrey Canada. Canada is not a social scientist, and he came on the scene at a moment that was ripe for a new and compelling vision—the neoliberal moment. At this time, even many people who sympathized with the need for social reform came to believe that the free market and privatization, as well as public-private partnerships, had the potential to alleviate problems of the ghetto. With the election of President Barack Obama in 2008, Canada became the most visible symbol of a new set of ideas about the ghetto and how to fix it. Rather than focusing on macroeconomic change or moving people out of ghettos, he believed that the solution was to improve communities from the ground up. On this premise, in the 2000s he founded the Harlem Children's Zone (HCZ), built on the assumption that schools, counseling, family supports, and job placement

services should be tightly integrated and directed at residents of a particular neighborhood.

When Canada came to public attention, social science in the
United States was utterly absorbed by the question of whether the
ghetto was a problem of unemployment, welfare dependency, or racial
segregation. Canada broke through this debate. He advanced the idea
that whereas single-focus efforts did not succeed, a full-court press
would.

Whereas Wilson's analysis of the ghetto was vacillating between
the internal dynamics of impoverished neighborhoods and the larger
macropolitical conditions that determined them, Canada asserted
that the ghetto was a self-contained entity that could be addressed in
and of itself. His initial intervention was to look at the ghetto from the
standpoint of its youth and to argue that its most crucial problems
were violence and fear. Like many others living in the ghetto, he saw
that harsh drug laws and gun accessibility had coalesced to create an
atmosphere of fear and of physical injury. This atmosphere defined
the relationships among ghetto dwellers and between them and the
police.

Canada's outlook reflected his coming-of-age in the South Bronx
during the civil rights movement. As he explains in his 1995 memoir,
Fist Stick Knife Gun, he had grown up in a ghetto that was full of violence but very different from the ghetto that succeeded it. His earliest
memories were of his mother, a single parent, teaching him and his
three brothers about the importance of self-defense. In their neighborhood, institutions could not be counted on to protect children, and
even parents felt powerless to protect their kids from the laws of the
jungle.

In 1959, when Canada was in second grade, his family moved into
a two-bedroom apartment at 1165 Union Avenue in the South Bronx.[1]
In these years, at the tail end of the period between World War II and
the civil rights movement, the "ghetto" was not much in the air. By his
own testimony, he had no idea what it even was and only later discovered that he was living in "the slums." He and his brothers used to sit
by the window and watch the older children play. This pastime seemed
heavenly until one of the largest kids on the block saw the Canada
boys looking down and made a threatening gesture. Thereafter, one

by one, Geoffrey and his brothers learned that if they wanted to avoid a savage beating at the hands of a mob, they had to prove that they could fight with others of their own age and learn to think on their feet without showing fear. Canada's own first fight was pronounced a draw by the other boys on the block. They made the Canada brothers shake hands with them and "be friends." Through such experiences, the Canada brothers showed that they could live up to the code of the street.

During this era, decades before crack cocaine, most street violence consisted of fistfights known as "fair ones," which precluded "dirty" fighting. Those who violated these unwritten rules risked punishment by their peers.

One of the difficult things about growing up in a tough Bronx ghetto in the late fifties and early sixties was that the hierarchy did not remain the same for long. First one had to prove oneself on one's own blocks; then one had to start all over again and fight consecutively for respect and status in one's elementary, junior high, and high school. Each time the stage got larger and the challenges fiercer.

Once Canada entered elementary school at PS 99, he discovered that the fights were a bigger event than ever, usually held after school with audiences of fifty to a hundred children. Children were drawn to their gory details. The good news was that the rules of Canada's neighborhood pertained also to school: the fights had to be between people of the same age and size, or someone bigger would break them up. The cultural norms Canada had learned on Union Avenue continued to apply at PS 99. What was most important was showing that one had "heart"—that is, no fear—and would fight even if victory was impossible.

The struggle for most men on the block was to remain "decent" while appearing tough. This often entailed responding to threats, even when there was no chance of success, and taking potentially life-threatening risks. On the street, status was derived from fearlessness—known as "being cold"—which meant concealing one's humanity.

By the time Canada was a teenager, it was the mid-sixties. The older boys in the neighborhood sometimes carried knives, but generally not guns. Today, Canada claims that he is alive because the one time he

came face-to-face with a handgun, its owner was "a seasoned professional, not a scared kid with a gun." His memoir recalls an era before
the ghetto turned into a "killing field."

Whereas Kenneth Clark evoked a world in which the people of the
ghetto were dehumanized by their power relations with the wider society, Canada's "humiliation" came when others in the neighborhood stole
his baseball glove or basketball. When Canada was twelve he discovered the K55 knife. After finding one on the street, it became his prize
possession. This was the "weapon of choice" among his peers. Though
it was only used when one was accosted with a knife, or outnumbered,
Canada could now confidently saunter through city blocks full of street
kids whom he did not know. This registered on the kids who could see
him staring ahead with his hand in his pocket, and, as he recalls, the
tactic worked.

One summer afternoon, Canada's hand slipped while holding the
knife. The spring snapped the blade shut before he could move his right
index finger out of the way. Afraid to lose possession of his knife, he
chose not to go to an emergency room or even tell his mother. Instead,
he created a splint out of ice cream sticks and told everyone that he had
hurt his finger while playing basketball. Although permanent disfigure-
ment resulted, it seemed like a rational decision because he wanted to
keep his knife.

In 1970, Canada was admitted to Bowdoin College, an elite liberal arts
school in Brunswick, Maine. During his freshman year, Richard Nixon
declared a War on Drugs, setting the stage for the enactment of the
1973 Rockefeller drug laws in New York State. These became a model
for the harsh drug laws passed by many states as well as on the federal
level. Billions of government dollars flowed into urban police departments. Stricter sentencing guidelines were implemented, and the numbers of black men in jail and prison slowly began to rise.

Far away from the newly emerging reality of the ghetto, Canada
had his first substantial interaction with white students. Given that the
environment was safe, it is ironic that he felt the need to purchase a gun.
He obtained it legally in Maine with a Bowdoin College ID to protect
himself on his trips back to the Bronx. By this point his mother had

moved to a new neighborhood, and the Bronx was becoming an ever-tougher, more violent, and drug-infested place.

Prior to his purchase, he had sometimes found himself crossing streets to avoid gangs of kids whom he did not know. Now, transformed by his gun, he felt bolder. Just as his demeanor as a teenager changed when he first obtained his knife, so now he felt himself using his eyes to challenge people to accost him.

Fortunately, the gun was irrelevant back in the peacefulness of his college town. There he had a chance to think about the changes that had overcome him, and he decided to throw it away.

At the beginning of his sophomore year, Canada discovered that Joyce Henderson, a girl he had casually dated back home over summer vacation, was pregnant.[2] She already had a daughter. In February, she gave birth to twins and took care of them while Canada continued his studies at Bowdoin, an absentee father. That winter, one of the twins, Geoff, Jr., died in his crib. Right before Canada's senior year, he and Joyce married, and she and the children moved into his dorm room at Bowdoin. The relationship lasted two more years, after which Joyce took the children to Long Island with her.

In 1975, after obtaining his B.A., then a master's degree from the Harvard Graduate School of Education, Geoffrey Canada took a job in South Boston, at the Robert White School for emotionally disturbed boys. He worked with violent white boys from the toughest housing projects in the city—mainly children who had been expelled from public schools.

This job yielded valuable lessons that would inform his work for years to come. One of the most important things he learned while assessing the violence in the school was the impact of a few bad apples. Canada later referred to them as "program busters," because they could undermine any program if their behavior went uncorrected. Many boys who had been intimidating others since early childhood had ended up at the Robert White School partly because nobody else could deal with them. Soon after his arrival, Canada noticed something that offered a clue to how to control them: they only picked fights when adults were around to break them up. In the Bronx this had been considered "amateurish." Although these boys were intimidating, they were not, in fact, good fighters, especially when compared to those Canada had grown up with.

Once he became director, Canada recalls that he used this insight to transform the culture of the school. He always attempted to identify those individuals with the greatest influence on the school's overall environment. Rather than forbid two boys to fight, he would sit them down and tell them he was going to take them to an empty construction site across the street to fight unsupervised. Given a choice between the construction site and the classroom, they went back to the classroom. In a short time, he recalls, he brought order to the entire school. The lesson that a few bad apples could change an entire school remained with him for years to come.

In the 1980s, social scientists who worked on the ghetto focused mainly on how to improve job prospects for adults. Although William Julius Wilson acknowledged that the demography of the inner city had been transformed by massive numbers of black youth, nearly all of his attention had been devoted to grown-ups, and more specifically to "manpower." Wilson, whose experience of the ghetto was more academic and detached than Canada's, believed that the black family could be stabilized by helping the black male. He thought that even with all of their bitter experiences, black men needed job opportunities above everything else.

Canada, by contrast, was not as concerned with adults and did not assume that if more jobs were created, everything would fall into place. Though he took work into consideration, his main objective was to make a difference in the lives of kids who were growing up in violent neighborhoods. In the early 1980s, he was offered a job at the Rheedlen Centers for Children and Families in central Harlem. The original mission of this organization, founded by the youth advocate Richard L. Murphy about a decade earlier, had been to reduce the number of children dropping out of school, but it had gradually grown into helping their families and finally the entire community. While working in Boston, Canada met Murphy and was inspired to come and work with him. After years of studying at Bowdoin and Harvard, then working with troubled white youth in Boston, Canada felt prepared for the challenge of returning to New York. The new job also gave him a chance to move to Long Island, close to where his children were living.[3]

Canada came on one condition. During his years in Boston, he had received a black belt in tae kwon do, a martial art developed in Korea for unarmed combat. While at the Robert White School, he had discovered that teaching this sport to poor children in the violent inner city was a great way to mentor them in both self-discipline and self-defense. He thus told Murphy that he would take the job at Rheedlen only if he could begin a martial arts school. Luckily, Murphy saw this as a major opportunity for transforming an after-school program that he was already offering at a local junior high school. Thus was born the Chang Moo Kwan Tae Kwon Do Club.

Ironically, between the early seventies, when Canada had left for college, and the early eighties, when he had returned to New York City, guns had replaced physical ability as the principal means of self-defense. The kinds of skills he hoped to teach were thus far less relevant. The city's drug economy had also undergone a major transformation. Crack had become the dominant drug in the inner city, and with it came the guns. Building on the Rockefeller drug laws, the U.S. Congress passed mandatory minimum sentences for drug distribution. The sentences for crimes involving crack were ten times longer than for those involving powder cocaine, the preferred drug among whites.[4]

In the seventies, children had served as lookouts for drug dealers. Now their role increased. Once the harsh drug laws came into effect, adult dealers who wished to avoid long prison sentences put up children to sell drugs for them. Fearful of getting robbed, these minors used some of the money they earned to purchase guns, which Canada believed had changed the codes of street behavior.

Though Canada was not trained as a sociologist, his memoir demonstrates that his skill at pinpointing the changes that had occurred over his lifetime was on par with that of the best social scientists. Having observed the inner city for several decades, he realized that basic norms of interaction were shifting. The "natural checks and balances" on violence among youth, which had once prevented minor scraps from escalating into life-threatening encounters, had broken down. In an era with no guns, an adolescent had been forced to contend with "natural checks." That is, he faced deterrents such as the prospect that he might not win a fight, retaliation by his opponent's friends, or an awareness that even if he won the fight, he might be seriously injured. But now, due to the ubiquity of firearms, the new generation of youngsters was oblivious to the natural brakes on violence that Canada had known as a child. When outnumbered, a teenager on the street was no longer intimidated; he could simply shoot some bullets and scatter a threatening group. The only check on his behavior was his own death.

While before, a youth's reputation (his rep) was determined by the fights he had won, the current "tough" kid was the one who carried the most dangerous weapon and was willing to use it to kill. Many of the two hundred adolescents whom Canada kept tabs on at Rheedlen died young. He remembered them as frivolous, irresponsible, inexperienced youths who had never developed the smarts that had once supported a rep on the streets. As he sardonically observed, "The funeral parlors [became] rich as a result of their poor decisions."

Canada was committed to bringing attention to what the drug trade was doing to the urban environment. What, however, was the solution?

As handguns penetrated the inner city in the 1980s, the federal and local bureaucracies stepped in. They were more determined than ever to manage the violence, if at times only to prevent it from spilling out beyond the ghetto itself. For lawmakers, the most straightforward and rational response was the imposition of severe penalties for users and dealers. In 1994, at the beginning of President Clinton's first term, the federal government enacted the Violent Crime Control and Law Enforcement Act, the most extensive anticrime bill in U.S. history. It included almost $10 billion for the construction of prisons and enough money to hire one hundred thousand new police officers. The law also created new death-penalty offenses for many of the most common crimes in the ghetto, including murder caused by drive-by shootings, carjackings, or drug trafficking. Membership in gangs was likewise outlawed.

Canada was among the first to see this as a giant mistake. To begin with, he argued, the real problem lay not only in the young black men who were being incarcerated at alarming rates, but in the gun industry's campaigns directed at youth. Canada also maintained that the tactics of the crime bill were inappropriate for the inner city. Stationing more police on the streets, he argued, was hardly a solution in this place where they had no legitimacy. Most of the officers did not come from the neighborhood and treated its population the way outsiders usually do—as an undifferentiated mass. Unable to distinguish between the law-abiding and the criminal, they tended to treat everyone with equal disrespect. Failing to establish their authority by gaining genuine respect, they controlled the streets through intimidation and outright corruption. Moreover, as ghetto residents—especially youth—witnessed police corruption, their cynicism mounted.

In 1991, David Dinkins, the black mayor of New York City, was considering the idea of building a series of schools tightly integrated with the neighborhoods they served. Dinkins's youth commissioner was Richard Murphy, the founder of Rheedlen and the man who had hired Geoffrey Canada. Murphy argued that the local school was the best institution for effecting change. Every community, no matter how poor, had schools that could provide all kinds of additional services when not in use. What if each of these schools remained open after hours and partnered with a local community-based organization to provide evening programs for youth and adults? Influenced by Murphy's approach to the ghetto and its problems, Dinkins decided to fund what came to be known as the Beacon Model in ten New York City schools. The principal goal was community development (rather than a mere provision of services).

At the time, nobody was better positioned to assume the directorship of a Harlem site than Geoffrey Canada, now the head of Rheedlen. Echoing Kenneth and Mamie Clark's earlier arguments about that very community, he later wrote, "It's clear that we can't separate violence from all the other problems that plague [Harlem's] youth: educational failure, teenage pregnancy, drug and alcohol abuse, lack of employment, crime, AIDS . . . the list goes on and on. . . . We can't expect to make a difference unless we are willing to talk about comprehensive services for massive numbers of children *and* their families."

To compete successfully for the grant money, Canada and his Rheedlen colleagues first had to find an appropriate venue that could be redesigned as a multiservice center. Countee Cullen Elementary

School on 144th Street near Adam Clayton Powell Boulevard in the heart of Harlem struck them as the right place. The school was located in an extremely poor community with minimal services. Heroin addicts and alcoholics hung out around the building's entrance, and the blocks around it were known for their violence. Canada looked around and saw an opportunity for taking the first serious step toward implementing a comprehensive solution to the ghetto problem. With nearly missionary zeal, he resolved to take over the school, not merely to provide services for the people enrolled in the program, but to transform the community in which it was located.

Just a few days prior to the scheduled opening of Countee Cullen, a teenager was murdered near the entrance to the building. If the Beacon Model was to transform the community, it needed to work first and foremost on switching the neighborhood's vicious cycle of violence into a virtuous one. The first step was to alter the atmosphere around Countee Cullen's own building. Working with a local theater company, the school organized a series of performances on 144th Street. Such a project seemed to fly in the face of common sense, which dictated that for anyone to be out on the street or doing anything other than minding one's own business was foolhardy. Nevertheless, as local residents heard music from their windows and went downstairs to see what was going on, they interacted with others from the community and were introduced to the Countee Cullen Community Center. Building on this initial success, Canada formed the 144th Street block association, which convinced the city to turn the street into a "play street"—that is, off-limits to cars between 8:00 a.m. and 4:00 p.m. The idea was to have a block on which children could be out and about within the range of adult eyes and ears, thus making the entire neighborhood safer.

From that point on, the Countee Cullen Community Center became an inspiring example of a program capable of delivering services that matched the needs of the local community. Funded primarily by New York City's Department of Youth and Community Development, it served (and continues to serve at the time of this writing) over a thousand children and four hundred adults in a single school building—six days per week from 9:00 a.m. to 9:00 p.m. during the school year, and 8:00 a.m. to 8:00 p.m. in the summer.[5] It includes an elementary after-school program open until 6 p.m., and one for middle school children that is open until 6:30 p.m. Both offer classes in dance, arts and crafts, and sports. Most of the adults involved in the center have entered programs through their children, and their participation has reflected Canada's "holistic" approach to thinking about the ghetto and maintaining children in their family and community context. The success of Countee Cullen led Canada to open two more Beacons. At one of those centers he founded the Moving Forward Program for young men and women no longer in school.

In the 2000s, the journalist Malcolm Gladwell's *Tipping Point* became a nonfiction bestseller. Drawing on a number of ideas from the social and medical sciences and synthesizing these with his own stories and principles, Gladwell advanced the argument that "ideas and products and messages and behaviors spread like viruses do." Seeking to pinpoint the climactic moment of an epidemic when everything may suddenly shift, he argued that key individuals were central to the spread of ideas and behavior. Those individuals' unusual qualities enabled them to transform tiny but crucial elements of the environment, with outsize results. Gladwell contended that pressure exerted by certain peers in the community could have more influence than the family on childhood development.

Gladwell persuasively argued that the external environment shapes children, that the streets they walk down and the people they meet—that is, their *"immediate* social and physical world"—shapes who they are and how they act. "It isn't just serious criminal behavior, in the end, that is sensitive to environmental cues, it is all behavior," he claimed.[6] His book departed from other analyses of how the environment influenced behavior. When William Julius Wilson, for example, referred to the environment, he viewed it as a phenomenon also of national economic policy. If one wished to resolve the problem of the ghetto, focusing on the immediate environment of the neighborhood—the lack of role models or the poor motivation among workers—was not enough. While Wilson emphasized these factors, he viewed the issue from the top down; the environment that required change was the entire opportunity structure, including everyday close-at-hand opportunities and hindrances.

By the mid-2000s, Gladwell's book had sold 1.6 million copies. The idea of a "tipping point" that could influence change from the bottom up was in the air. Most of Canada's ideas in this period stemmed from his realization that whatever he was doing was simply not ambitious enough to change the larger community of Harlem. He had previously been obsessed with those children he was unable to reach for humanitarian reasons. Now his reasons were more tactical. As long as the children he was able to help were residing and going to school in a community that also included vast numbers of those who could not be reached, the odds were stacked against them. Canada had concluded that if children who were in his program were overwhelmed by the social cues given off by those who were not, then the program would have but a limited influence, since those who participated in it did not spend all day under its umbrella.[7]

By contrast, and consistent with Gladwell's tipping point, if many children in Harlem joined the program, then the public standards of the neighborhood might change rapidly—as if infected by an epidemic of virtuous behavior. "When you've got most of the kids in a neighborhood involved in high-quality programs, you begin to change the cultural context of that neighborhood," Canada wrote. "If you are surrounded by people who are always talking about going to college, you're going to end up thinking, 'Hey, maybe this is something I could do, too.' You can't help but get contaminated by that idea. It just seeps into your pores, and you don't even know that you've caught the virus." Canada thus essentially applied his own tipping-point theory to Harlem and came to sound much like Gladwell. Canada believed in positive contamination and felt that it would lead young students to do better, while also preventing them from feeling that they had betrayed their neighborhood. Just as things could go from good to bad, so too could the reverse occur.

As he began thinking in epidemiological terms, Canada also became close to Stanley Druckenmiller, a billionaire hedge-fund manager and member of the Rheedlen board. Druckenmiller and Canada had both attended Bowdoin College in the seventies. Druckenmiller later worked for George Soros, who would establish a new model for philanthropic billionaires. In 1993, Druckenmiller met Canada when he joined the board of the Robin Hood Foundation, which funded 108 different organizations. Within an hour Druckenmiller was convinced that Canada was far more impressive than the leaders of the other organizations that Robin Hood supported and decided to develop a special relationship with him. As a hedge-fund manager, Druckenmiller believed in "putting all of your eggs in one basket and watching the basket carefully." He had taken a similar approach as a philanthropist when investing in cancer and brain research as well as environmental activism. With his eyes turned toward poverty, he believed that he could make a similarly significant mark by investing in Geoffrey Canada.[8]

The time they spent together on the Robin Hood board also had an impact on Canada. Perhaps what impressed Druckenmiller most about Canada was his willingness to buy into the strategies of American business. Canada accepted a corporate measuring stick that was then unusual in the world of philanthropy, even more so in NGOs operating in the inner city. Druckenmiller encouraged Canada to hire a management-consulting company to come up with a ten-year plan. The result was significant financial support from Druckenmiller—the Rheedlen Center's budget expanded from $6 million to $58 million and it extended its services to twenty-four blocks of central Harlem, which came to be known as the Harlem Children's Zone. The zone's headquarters was in a brand-new building on 125th Street, Harlem's central thoroughfare.

Canada also wished to focus on the life course of the individual rather than on a limited span of his or her existence. Thus, on top of the Countee Cullen Community Center, he envisioned a prekindergarten class, a tutoring center, and, to cover the earliest part of life, a course for the parents of infants and toddlers. Called Baby College, the nine-week series of classes would teach parents-to-be about brain development and discipline, home safety, asthma prevention, and immunization.

Yet even as Canada conceptualized a fully integrated set of services, he knew that a major roadblock lay ahead of him. Regardless of how well he could integrate services for parents and children, he could do little about the hours the children spent in their regular school. As the Harlem Children's Zone took on a greater role in the community, its efforts to provide tutors, reading services, and computer labs did not meet with great success. School principals were generally uncooperative and often did not want his help.

When Michael Bloomberg was elected mayor of New York City in 2001, he appointed Joel Klein, a former assistant attorney general, as schools chancellor. The Harlem Children's Zone was an obvious target for one of Klein's big ideas—to create new charter schools that would be supported by both nonprofits and corporations. The solution for Canada would be to start a charter school. With help from the Bloomberg administration, the Harlem Children's Zone set out to open Promise Academy in 2004. The school was set to begin with a kindergarten and a sixth grade, with an additional grade to be added each year.

Canada had already been speaking for ten years about rising rates of incarceration and how the country was spending far more money on prisons than on education. Arguing that the United States benefits little from all the money it pours into jails, he pointed out that the money could better be spent on education and youth services. At the time he founded the Harlem Children's Zone, nearly 10 percent of American black men in their thirties were serving time in prison, and 60 percent of black male high school dropouts had served time.[9] Drugs and guns on the street, as well as a rapidly growing prison industry, were all feeding on one another.

By the early 2000s, it had become apparent to many in social scientific circles that Geoffrey Canada was embarking on an important alternative to this punitive approach to poverty. Social scientists and journalists alike wanted to observe this experiment. Paul Tough of *The New York Times* began to cover Canada for the newspaper's magazine section and was granted unrestricted permission to write about him and the Harlem Children's Zone. Tough was on hand for a number of crucial episodes in the history of the HCZ and wrote a book, *Whatever It Takes: Geoffrey Canada's Quest to Change Harlem and America*, about what he observed during the program's formative years. He witnessed what were probably the high and low points of Canada's experiment.

On the rainy evening of April 4, 2004, Promise Academy held a lottery to determine which of the 359 students who had submitted applications would be admitted to the initial classes. Canada and his staff had gone door-to-door throughout Harlem to drum up applications from the neediest and most difficult-to-reach students, many of whose parents would not have known to apply on their own. Technically, students from all of New York City were eligible, so if Canada wanted kids who lived in the zone, he needed to work to get them into the pool.

Tough recalled that Canada walked to the stage and, as the noise level in the auditorium subsided, announced:

> We are calling our school Promise Academy because we are making a promise to all of our parents. If your child is in our school, we will guarantee that child succeeds. There will be no excuses. We are not going to say, "The child failed because they came from a home with only one parent." We're not going to say, "The child failed because they're new immigrants into this country." If your child gets into our school, that child is going to succeed. . . . We're going to have the best-quality education that parents can imagine.

As each name was pulled out of a golden drum, the parent of the lucky winner made his or her way up to the front of the auditorium screaming and crying with joy while receiving a personal congratulation from Canada. As the places were gradually won, only disappointed parents remained. When Paul Tough caught up with Canada at the end of the night, he reported that he had never seen Canada so tired. He was trying to get the families to leave before the last child was selected. It saddened him to disappoint parents who knew that the quality of their children's lives depended on their being accepted into a decent school. Canada seemed aware of how cruel a move this had been.

Paul Tough's reporting on the early years of Promise Academy takes readers inside the daily life of the school with all of its struggles. His account shows teachers and administrators trying to do "whatever it takes" to keep the promises that were made during the lottery drawing. Yet beneath the surface of the goodness and devotion that he observed were some cold, hard facts. When school began the following fall, Canada had exactly what he had hoped for: a student body that was a cross section of the larger Harlem population. The incoming sixth-grade class was 90 percent black and 10 percent Latino. Its test scores were far below the city average. How could Canada have looked out at the parents the previous spring and promised them that their children would succeed? He had expected the kids to be below grade level, but he had no sense of how far below they were: almost everyone in the class was between two and three years behind in math. Nor did they improve much over the year. When the statewide test scores came back the following June, the Promise Academy was one of two charter schools in the city (the other also located in Harlem) that brought down citywide charter school averages. To make matters worse, a sizable number of students tested worse at the end of sixth grade than they had tested the year before. Canada had told the assembled parents that he was guaranteeing the success of their children and that his administration would make no excuses. Now what was he thinking?

But it no longer really mattered what Canada thought, or at least not as much as it once had. By the time that he was confronting these results, he was a very different man from the one who had started the tae kwon do school and run the Rheedlen Centers. Not only did he and his second wife live in a nice house in Valley Stream, Long Island, with their young son, but Canada was taking home a salary in the $400,000-per-year range ($150,000 higher than that of the chancellor of the New York City public schools).[10] Moreover, the Geoffrey Canada who had run the tae kwon do school was his own boss, but the one who ran the Harlem Children's Zone was answerable to the board that paid his salary, including Stanley Druckenmiller and another billionaire, the Home Depot cofounder Kenneth Langone.

When Canada met with these and other members of his board, he discovered that they felt it was urgent that Promise Academy be able to show results to all the funders—the many other wealthy individuals who had committed significant resources to the program. Druckenmiller told Tough that if several years passed and the results did not match expectations, then the donors might question the program and withdraw their money. From the board's perspective, part of the problem lay in a few "bad apples" that could be tossed off, the 30 percent of the student population with learning and discipline problems who were a dead weight on the shoulders of Promise Academy. Moreover, from Druckenmiller's perspective, other charter schools elsewhere in New York City and around the country had met with success educating underprivileged children. Perhaps Geoffrey Canada and the Harlem Children's Zone were better off letting others handle this momentous task.

Until that moment, Canada's worldview had been more or less consistent with that of his board, but it now seemed to be deviating. When its members suggested that his students might do better if he adopted the model of other charter schools in low-income neighborhoods, which prioritized "intense monitoring and shaping of behavioral patterns," Canada resisted them because he believed this approach stigmatized poor black students. He did not feel that it was right to treat these students so differently from American students in general, for that would make the general population believe that something was wrong with them. Such a stand was out of character for Canada, who had never been one to put the brakes on public dialogue about the so-called self-destructive cultural forces that prevail in the ghetto.

Viewing the students in the schools that they were funding as if they were stock picks, the billionaires had the instinct of traders; at bottom they wished to protect the brand name of the Harlem Children's Zone. Perhaps Harlem could be changed later, they thought, but first, would it not be better to dump the losers and begin with a shining success? There was no harm in selecting the most motivated children and demonstrating, from the outset, that a top-notch education made it possible for them to succeed. If the program could boast several examples of students getting accepted by Ivy League schools, would that not lead to more generous donations? And if the children in the program did fail despite the resources of a topflight education, would that not be the ultimate sign to middle-class America that something was, in fact, wrong with these youngsters?

Canada, however, was an extraordinary salesman. Had anyone else attempted to argue against their logic, Druckenmiller and Langone might have pulled the switch on the experiment. However, they decided that Canada deserved another chance to make his vision work and had the decency to give him a bit—but not too much—more time. They let him understand that he had another year and a half at most, but if he was unable to run a successful school by then, they would place Promise Academy in the hands of people with a proven track record.

With such a short deadline, Canada became a tough-minded executive. His first action was to dismiss the school's principal, Terri Grey. She had never had much faith in Canada's promise that every child would go to college. After receiving the scores of the students from the previous

September, she had assumed that their skills were so deficient that they would be lucky to end up in a vocational college. Canada needed a principal who believed in his mission, so, on the recommendation of the New York schools chancellor, he hired Glen Pinder, an experienced black principal with a job in the suburbs. Shortly afterward, the academy's superintendent and a dozen teachers quit. It was time to start over again.

The two crucial matters now were discipline and standardized tests. What Pinder addressed first were the "bad apples" who had already troubled Druckenmiller and Grey. As discipline was a serious problem, Pinder decided to create the position of assistant principal for discipline, to which he promoted Chris Finn, one of the best science teachers at the academy. All of the twenty-nine seventh- and eighth-grade students who had had discipline or attendance problems in the past year were summoned over the loudspeaker to the auditorium. After informing the students that this was their last chance and that they would be permanently expelled if they misbehaved one more time, Pinder told them that they were leaders among their peers and could get attention by doing positive things. By the end of the first month, the strategy seemed to be working to some extent.

Pinder's second idea was to focus much earlier in the year on the statewide tests that the students took in the winter. To help with this, the HCZ hired forty additional tutors and a new director for its after-school program. Both the tutors and the teachers were charged with keeping careful data on each student to coordinate the shift from the school to the after-school program. All the same, by spring it was clear from practice exams that the eighth-graders who had been given continuous test preparation for an entire year were not up to the job.

Even before Canada met with his board and presented the data, he knew what would be demanded of him, but he also recalled his promise to the children. Canada's situation was similar to Kenneth and Mamie Clark's when Marion Rosenwald Ascoli removed her subsidy from their Northside clinic. The Clarks believed her insistence that she knew better what was best for Harlem's children was a clear case of white paternalism. Refusing to allow their organization to be turned into a colonial outpost, they had taken their chances and cut her loose. There are no indications, though, that Canada viewed his board in this way, and he took ownership of the decision. In March 2007, he sent a letter home to the parents of each child indicating that come June, the eighth grade would be terminated and there would be no new entering sixth-grade class.

Although this account of Promise Academy after the lottery relies heavily on Paul Tough's outstanding reportage, he should not be held account-able for the interpretation presented here. Tough never reported the exact size of Canada's salary, did not write about him in the context of the Clarks' earlier efforts and struggles in Harlem, and did not associate Malcolm Gladwell's *Tipping Point* with Canada's ideology.

Tough's portrait is admiring, not least for Canada's remarkable forthrightness. Nothing illustrates this better than what Canada did on the day he sent his letter to parents informing them their children would be returned to the regular public school system the following year. Knowing that the day would be one of the worst in his career, he never-theless invited Tough to accompany him so that Tough could paint a fuller picture of Canada's work.

Tough witnessed what anyone other than Canada might have pre-ferred to have gone unrecorded: how the parents and children reacted when they realized their dream was a lie. Aside from their being kicked out of school, what most upset the eighth-graders was that it was too late in the school year to apply to other high schools. With entrance-exam dates long past, and most spots in good specialty schools filled, many of these kids would end up in the local high school.

"If I go to my zone school, I'm going to lose my life," one boy complained.

"They want to kill my family at that school," another boy claimed to dramatize his feelings.

"Basically, they're kicking us to the curb," another retorted.

In the school auditorium that afternoon, Canada addressed the entire eighth-grade class.

Some teachers in the school were quite vocal among themselves that the fault lay with the children, who had not been working hard enough, but Canada refused to accept this. "When we first talked about opening this school, I made one promise, that we would not have a lousy school," he said. "There are too many times in Harlem when people have allowed schools that aren't doing their job to continue. The kids don't get an education, and later on they can't get jobs and take care of their families. That's what happened in Harlem for a long time. And I promised everybody that we would never do that."

Later, one of the children asked him why he had not given them any advance warning. Canada took the blame, admitting that he had naively believed that things would turn out exactly as planned and had thus not considered other options.

That evening, Canada met with the parents. He acknowledged that he had promised to support their children through high school, and he said that he was not backing out but simply modifying the program. The students currently at Promise Academy would still be eligible for all the other services offered by the HCZ, including after-school tutoring, because helping young people and getting them into college was the key objective of the Harlem Children's Zone.

Canada also addressed the matter of the late notice, which came after all the subsequent year's specialty-school spots and private-school scholarships had already been awarded. He said that he had called everyone he knew, including the New York City schools chancellor, and had put together a team of advocates who would work tirelessly on the children's behalf to find them the best possible schools.

When Canada finished speaking, one of the fathers raised his hand and said, "You said you were going to talk to the chancellor. Well, my son wants to go to St. Xavier. He wants to go to Bronx Science."

Canada explained that the specialized schools required admission tests for which the deadlines had already passed.

"So my son lost his opportunity to get into those schools."

"My understanding is that those schools are closed now."

"That's all I wanted to know," the father replied, turning to his son. "I'm ready to go. I don't have nothing else to say. Let's go."

This was the worst possible outcome for the kids. What kind of diminished futures came to the children for being the last-place kids in the application process for the next school? That Canada "faced it squarely" and took Paul Tough along turned out to be a very small tribute to his capacities.

Geoffrey Canada and his board were now committed to cutting their losses and moving on. They continued to work on raising the performance of the sixth and seventh grades, but their real hope lay in the children in the elementary school.

For most of the second half of the twentieth century, people frequently debated whether poor residents of the ghetto were culturally and psychologically prepared to take advantage of opportunities that came their way. Oscar Lewis argued that by the time children in a "culture of poverty" were six or seven, it was essentially too late to help them change, while William Julius Wilson believed in the individual's potential to change at any age. He argued that when restricted opportunities improve, so do aspirations and habits. Wilson spent much of the 1980s and 1990s arguing that cultural values and the characteristics of individuals could not be altered without addressing the opportunity structure directly. The gulf between liberals and conservatives on this issue seemed impossible to bridge. Generations of students in the social sciences had been reared on the difference. In a left-leaning academy, the enlightened position was the optimistic one: culture was not destiny; it was never too late to help the poor by changing the structure of opportunity.

By the time that Geoffrey Canada dismissed his eighth-grade class in 2007, much had changed. Early-childhood education, a concerted focus on prenatal care, and a variety of other kinds of early-childhood intervention had become central planks in the political agenda of both liberals and conservatives. The psychological and cultural claims that Oscar Lewis made in the 1960s were only slightly different from those now made by a range of liberal social scientists, who were beginning to feel that to make a difference, programs had to reach children early in life before harmful habits were established. Only by focusing on the cultural values and norms of the inner city could change be effected in the environment where these children were raised.

When Canada terminated the eighth-grade class, much that he was doing was consistent with the ideology of those who believe that a child beyond seven years of age is psychologically unfit to take advantage of new opportunities. He had become an advocate for starting even sooner, and he directed his energies to changing the individual characteristics and cultural values of the ghetto poor. This meant teaching the poor the behaviors of middle-class children, which included such basic rules as looking people in the eye when speaking to them and saying "uh-huh" to keep conversation flowing. Beginning with the Baby College, Canada had added another set of parental classes called Three-Year-Old Journey, a preschool for four-year-olds called Harlem Gems, and a kindergarten and middle school in Promise Academy.

In the first year of Promise Academy's kindergarten, 1994, there were barely more applicants than available spaces. As the Harlem Gems had been encouraged to apply, they ended up getting nearly all the slots offered by the lottery. The following year, many more people found out about the lottery, so the entering class ended up including less than half of the eligible Harlem Gems. The students from the outside arrived less prepared. Afterward Canada became more strategic, changing his lottery system to insure that those admitted to kindergarten would also have had the benefit of the earlier programs. The lottery for a spot at Promise Academy was now held two years in advance, and every child randomly admitted to the kindergarten at age five began in the preschool. Canada was talking differently. As he told Tough, "I want to get out of the business of trying to save failing students before their lives are destroyed."

The Harlem Gems prekindergarten program ran from 8:00 a.m. to 5:45 p.m., eleven months per year—exceeding the state requirement of 2.5 hours per day over ten months. The teacher-student ratio was 1:4, as opposed to the statewide average of 1:9. Perhaps most importantly, the pre-K program obsessively integrated language into every aspect of the day, trying to improve the vocabulary of children who came from backgrounds with "restricted codes." Students were exposed to the English language throughout the day and also received regular French lessons. The results appeared quite positive to Tough as he came to the end of covering Promise Academy. He reported, for example, that 18 percent of incoming Gems had begun delayed in their language, while 17 percent had been advanced or very advanced. At the end of their time in Gems, 51 percent were advanced or very advanced, and not one was considered delayed or very delayed.

Similarly, whereas the students who had entered Promise Academy in middle school had not been able to improve their verbal scores, the results for the elementary school were quite different. Like those who had gone through Gems, those who had been enrolled from kindergarten to fifth grade demonstrated significant progress in English language arts. In light of the massive evidence that early childhood is the crucial time for language development, this is hardly surprising. These early successes made clear to Canada what even most conservative critics of antipoverty policies believe: below a certain age, the ghetto poor are prepared to take advantage of the opportunities offered them.

During the presidential campaign of 2007 and 2008, Barack Obama declared that a key strategy of his urban agenda would be to replicate the Harlem Children's Zone across the country:

> And that's why when I'm president of the United States of America, the first part of my plan to combat urban poverty will be to replicate the Harlem Children's Zone in twenty cities across the country. We'll train staff. We'll have them draw up detailed plans with attainable goals and the federal government will provide half of the funding for each city with the rest coming from philanthropies and businesses. We can do it here in Washington, D.C. We can do it in Chicago. We can do it in N.Y. We can do it in Houston. We can do it in L.A. We can do it all across the country.
>
> Now, how much will this cost? I'll be honest with you. It can't be done on the cheap. It will cost a few billion dollars a year. We won't just spend the money because we can. Every step these cities take will be evaluated carefully. And if what they're doing isn't working, if the plans or programs aren't meeting the goals we have set, then we'll stop funding them and we will try something else. But we will find the money to fund the things that work because we can't afford not to.[11]

Skeptics argued that Obama's ideas would be too expensive, but he had no patience with such criticism:

> There is no reason we should spend tens of thousands of dollars a year to imprison one of these kids when they turn eighteen

when we can be spending $3,500 to turn their lives around with this program. To really put it in perspective, think of it this way. The Harlem Children's Zone is saving a generation of children for about $46 million a year. That's about what the war in Iraq costs American taxpayers every four hours. That is something that we can invest in. Let's invest this money. Let's change the odds in urban America by focusing on what works.

By the time he was elected, the economic recession Barack Obama inherited from the end of the Bush presidency had made it impossible to commit billions of dollars to just about any domestic program. Those who were suffering most from the downturn needed direct assistance rather than investment in neighborhoods that might take many years to pay off.[12] Despite the post-recession political mood in the country, President Obama did make a gesture in the direction of such a policy. On April 30, 2010, the Department of Education announced a pilot program under which communities were encouraged to apply to become Promise Neighborhoods that offered "cradle to career" services for their residents. In September 2010, the Department of Education designated 21 of the 339 applicants as recipients of Promise Neighborhood planning grants; in subsequent years it awarded five-year implementation grants of about $25 million to a number of communities. As time passed and support for a large-scale plan was not forthcoming from Congress, the Obama administration began working on interagency collaborations that would develop place-based strategies for dealing with concentrated poverty. The "neighborhood revitalization initiative" was meant to be an "integrated, coordinated" approach to neighborhood transformation that would align the goals of various agencies that dealt with poverty at the community level. As this approach gained traction within the administration, calls increased for rigorous evaluations of programs in Harlem to examine whether they were actually achieving what Geoffrey Canada was claiming for them.

In spring 2009, the *New York Times* columnist David Brooks received an e-mail from the Harvard economist Roland Fryer stating that his own statistical study of the Harlem Children's Zone had changed his life as a scientist. As Brooks reported in an editorial on May 8, 2009, after Fryer and his colleague Will Dobbie completed a rigorous assessment of the Harlem Children's Zone,[13] they concluded, "The effects of attending a Harlem Children's Zone middle school are enough to close the black-white achievement gap in mathematics. The effects in elementary school are large enough to close the racial achievement gap in both mathematics and English Language Arts."[14] Such results, Fryer told Brooks in his e-mail, no longer made him interested in marginal changes.[15]

Those findings certainly seemed like good news to readers and advocates who were looking to replicate the program nationwide. But closer analysis of Fryer and Dobbie's paper revealed a curious twist, suggesting that President Obama had possibly less warrant than originally thought for pumping billions of dollars into efforts aimed at emulating the Harlem Children's Zone model. Those analyses concluded that the high-quality schools created by the Harlem Children's Zone were sufficient in and of themselves to increase student scores, even without the other community services provided by the organization. They pointed out that the children who attended Promise Academy but lived outside the area served by the Harlem Children's Zone did as well as those who were entitled to all the community services. Also, siblings of students who did not attend the Promise Academy but were entitled to the community services did not show academic improvement. This implied not only that the schools had brought about the desired outcomes, but that the epidemic of virtuous behavior that Canada had hoped to initiate was not necessarily taking place. Those young people in Harlem who were in high-quality programs should have been improving the cultural environment of the neighborhood. Yet even those young people's siblings were not sufficiently influenced to improve their own scores.

Why were there so few spillover effects? In 2010, the CUNY sociologist Philip Kasinitz was commissioned by the Harvard EdLab to direct a qualitative study of Promise Academy's first graduating class; his report was to accompany a further quantitative study of the graduates by Fryer, then EdLab's director. Canada initially enthusiastically supported the research.[16] He later apparently changed his mind. For reasons never made clear to Kasinitz, Promise Academy ended its cooperation with him after his researchers were in the field, and the study was not

completed. Yet Kasinitz told me that his preliminary interviews with
Promise Academy administrators, teachers, parents, and children
helped him to understand why Fryer and Dobbie might have gotten the
results they did.

The lack of spillover effects was actually consistent with the goal of
most of the parents: to isolate their kids and see them attain educational
success and upward mobility by getting into good colleges and leaving
the neighborhood. Kasinitz found that the parents felt that they had
been blessed in some sense by having their kids win the lottery. And
with that blessing came a promise: "Your life has been changed. Your
kid is going to college. I, Geoffrey Canada, will guarantee that if your
child works hard and you do your job as a parent, he or she will go to
college." Kasinitz concluded that everything about Promise Academy—
from the fact that the selected families felt blessed, to the extraordinary
resources that they had access to by their children's being in Promise
Academy, to Canada's own charismatic presence—reinforced the notion that the students in the academy were special, and different from
those around them. The fact that they were spending such a large part
of their day in the school and in HCZ after-school activities, as well as
the fact that they were sometimes encouraged by their own parents not
to associate with other kids in the neighborhood, further reduced the
possibility of any spillover effects for other Harlem youth.

Kasinitz noted that while Canada sought to change Harlem as a
community (particularly what Canada referred to as a "toxic" street
culture that romanticized antisocial behavior), for many parents the goal
was less to change the community than to escape it. Like many generations of upwardly mobile blacks before them, they viewed education
as a way out of the ghetto. What they saw in Canada's life story—a poor,
tough young man from the ghetto who went to a good, faraway college, got an important, high-paying job, and moved to the suburbs—was
precisely what they wanted for their own kids. As Kasinitz concluded,
"Unlike Canada, they had far less interest in improving Harlem than in
getting out of Harlem."

Kasinitz also came away from his interviews wondering how to even
think about Promise Academy as a model for national policy. First he
asked, "What success have they documented, other than that they
have been incredibly successful at raising money and selling an idea?"
Granted, now that the first graduating classes from Promise Academy

had finished college, one could no doubt point to some people who might otherwise have become pregnant, gone to jail, or never graduated. "But have the lives of Harlem's young people, other than the small number who attended Promise Academy and benefited from its extraordinary resources, substantially benefited from Canada's work? Has Harlem become a better place to be a kid?" Harlem had, of course, changed during those years, but primarily due to crime reduction and gentrification, neither of which HCZ had much to do with.

Assuming the successes can be documented, there is still the question of whether such an experiment could ever be replicated on a national scale. In Tough's account of the organization, it was not Canada's personal contributions to the program's success that mattered most, but his ideas, which were backed by solid research. "If future replication models can learn from the Zone's accomplishments and avoid its mistakes, I believe they won't just match the level of success he has achieved thus far in Harlem, but they may well go beyond it."[17]

Kasinitz is skeptical. First, there is no real evidence that Canada's ideas are actually more important than Canada himself. For many of the parents whose children attended Promise Academy, it was their personal relationship with Canada that was central to their belief in the entire enterprise. As one parent told Kasinitz, "Joel Klein [the chancellor of the New York City public schools] doesn't know my kid. Mr. Canada knows my kid." Canada's ability to communicate to the parents that he cared, and that he would do "whatever it takes" to help their child, was possibly as important as any of his specific ideas about education.

Second, Canada demanded very high levels of dedication from a staff at Promise Academy that was overwhelmingly young and working long hours. Canada's personal charisma facilitated a level of commitment that would be very hard to replicate when entire systems must be staffed with people who have adult responsibilities (including raising their own children) and who cannot be expected to bring such single-minded zeal to the job. In addition, Canada was willing to tolerate high levels of staff turnover when young, extraordinarily committed, but often inexperienced teachers proved not up to his standards or burned out after some time in the Promise Academy pressure cooker. This would also present serious problems in staffing a larger system on a nationwide basis.

Third, the participants in Promise Academy (both children and parents) were given unusual incentives, such as gift certificates as rewards for doing well. Given that these prizes were funded by private donors, it is not clear that a federal effort to replicate the HCZ could ever spend the kind of money on incentives that was showered on the children of Promise Academy. Nor would Congress necessarily buy into the idea that it is appropriate to give parents prizes for their children's performance.

Fourth, it is hard to know what it would take to replicate Promise Academy. The school's budget comes from multiple sources and is hard to track. The best estimate of the budget comes from Ronald Fryer and Will Dobbie, who estimate that HCZ spent at least $3,000 per pupil more than the median school district in New York State. Their data does not incorporate the privately financed visits to colleges and incentives such as iPads, cash prizes, and trips to France.

One might add that it is not merely Canada who can't be replicated, but his board as well. Harlem is a unique poor neighborhood in that it is located in the upper reaches of a city that houses many of the wealthiest people in the United States. How many poor communities in the United States could count on billionaires to sit on the board of an organization for their redevelopment, no less donate a significant portion of both their time and its operating expenses? Would even Canada have been successful if he had tried to open another Children's Zone in Mississippi or South Carolina, where there are not as many wealthy people? Just as it would be hard to replicate the money that these individuals donated, so would it be difficult to duplicate the vast amount of time they donated in advising Canada and being personally involved with the school.

Yet none of these questions would get answered, because it soon became clear that Barack Obama could not come close to offering the massive funding that he had envisioned during his campaign.

Though Geoffrey Canada has been universally characterized as a unique figure in the history of Harlem, his work actually shows a strong continuity with Kenneth and Mamie Clark's earlier vision of integrated services for ghetto youth and their families. The Harlem Children's Zone continues the legacy of the Clarks' Northside clinic and HARYOU programs. That said, not since the Clarks has anyone demonstrated such organizational capacities and vision for addressing the totality of a resident's experience in his or her local ghetto from cradle to adulthood. Canada's widespread support is evident not only in his impact on the Obama administration's approach to the ghetto, but in the reactions by two scholars who had previously agreed on little: Wilson and Murray.

On May 8, 2009, Murray received a series of e-mails with the subject heading "The Harlem Miracle." People ranging from his son-in-law and wife to colleagues and strangers wanted to know his opinion on the column published that day by David Brooks. That a well-respected conservative columnist from *The New York Times* had endorsed the HCZ caused many to wonder what the most prominent right-wing critic of welfare policy, the one who had done more than any other intellectual to bring about welfare reform, thought of the excitement surrounding Geoffrey Canada.

But Murray was more skeptical. Citing previous claims about several other programs—the most prominent being Head Start—he argued that the results were always the same: "An initial report gets ecstatic attention in the press, then a couple of years later it turns out that the miracle is, at best, a marginal success that is not close to the initial claims." Murray pointed to a number of generic problems with studies of this kind, such as "teaching to the test" and "fade-out"—that is, when large and sudden improvements in test scores fade within several years. All the same, Murray's skepticism ended on an uncharacteristically positive note: "All this doesn't mean that the Harlem Children's Zone isn't terrific. I like the sound of its approach."[18]

Like Murray, William Julius Wilson approved of the overall approach but had some reservations. Endorsing the Harlem Children's Zone as a model for a place-based agenda, he argued that all of the current studies and assessments were focusing too narrowly on school outcomes and insufficiently considering the full impact of the community services provided by the HCZ.[19] Endorsing Canada, Wilson quoted him: "We'll see the impact five or six years from now, when they are working adults and no longer going to prison."[20] Whereas the original aim of the Harlem Children's Zone had been to create and nurture a healthy environment for youth development, the Promise Academy had been directed at getting children into college. Wilson tried to bring the discussion back to Canada's initial and pivotal agenda of pairing healthy youth development with academic progress.

Wilson likewise broadened the discussion to questions that had not been raised by others. Dubious that Congress had funded Promise Neighborhoods at a level sufficient to achieve the kind of success seen in Harlem, he noted that they would have to operate on a much smaller scale and raise more money on their own. "Undoubtedly a much leaner Promise Neighborhoods initiative will struggle to address many of the broader concerns that HCZ is able to tackle," he observed.[21] In a perceptive sociological analysis of the Obama administration's urban initiative, he urged policymakers not to view the Harlem Children's Zone as an exclusive prototype for Promise Neighborhoods, given the significant differences in the HCZ's circumstances and others'. For example, Wilson argued that most Promise Neighborhoods could not be run under the strict control of a single individual in the way that Canada coordinated charter schools, day-care centers, and after-school programs. Since Promise Neighborhoods depended on broad collaborations overseen by nonprofit organizations, they were by necessity a "messier undertaking" organizationally.[22] Because the funding was channeled through these nonprofits, they needed to find a way to ensure that schools were effective. How all this was to be coordinated was for Wilson an open question. While supportive of the overall approach, he was no less realistic than Charles Murray.

By the time Canada started working at the HCZ, each dominant social scientific approach to the ghetto of the nineties was still calling for top-down, one-shot solutions such as ending racial segregation and achieving full employment—solutions with little chance of being realized in a neoliberal era that saw the free market and the withdrawal of state social services as the new common sense. Canada, however, adopted a vision that saw change as something achievable within the community. He perceived the ghetto's problems as an epidemic that could be eradicated through the discovery of its precise tipping points.

William Julius Wilson never said that the Harlem Children's Zone was "the" solution or that he was adopting Canada's agenda to the exclusion of his own. Yet that even he signed on to this agenda shows how influential it had become by the first decade of the twenty-first century. Since the mid-1980s, Wilson had been differentiating his "declining significance of race" thesis from black conservatism by characterizing himself as a progressive social democrat, calling for big government and massive funding to address the problems of the ghetto. This was the first time he had embraced a major solution to the ghetto's problems based on privately run initiatives. Wilson's best-known policy prescription had been a WPA-style employment program that would create public employment for millions of low-income people. Wilson had consistently argued that only change in the political economy of job creation could create incentives for poor blacks to develop their human capital. He had seen few prospects in changing the daily practices of ghetto dwellers without also initiating changes in economic opportunities for them as well. The insight behind these prescriptions was that for young people to be motivated to embrace the goals of school, some reasonable articulation was needed between what people were learning and the opportunity structure itself. Now he was embracing a program with a strong rhetoric about "every child succeeding." Yet surely Wilson knew that even as many beneficiaries of the program went on to college, the vast majority of the children benefiting from the neighborhood services would only be saved by stable working-class employment.

While important contradictions can be seen between Wilson's long-standing approach to the ghetto and Canada's, in one way they are fundamentally in sync: Canada's Promise Neighborhood approach also advanced the "hidden agenda" that Wilson had called for in his 1987 book *The Truly Disadvantaged*. Wilson had always been pragmatic about finding programs that generated widespread political support for helping poor blacks. Canada was clearly generating precisely the kind of support that Wilson had once dreamed of effecting through macroeconomic reforms—albeit through means in many respects at odds with Wilson's prior beliefs.

Wilson's support for Canada echoes Kenneth Clark's call to improve ghetto schools, even when it seemed to many that he was acquiescing in segregation. As Clark had insisted, despite the intransigence of the white community and the impossibility of immediate integration, "children, Negro or white, must not be sacrificed on the altars of ideological and semantic rigidities."[23] Seeing all the cross-racial public support that Canada had generated, Wilson was willing to lend his support. While he still advocated macroeconomic change to generate work for adults, he now sounded like Clark when he argued, "We cannot wait to improve the life chances of inner city residents to upgrade city schools."[24]

Wilson could see that by focusing on schools instead of economic reform, and by creating a program that could inspire the Obama administration to focus on white poverty, Indian reservations, and black ghettos, Canada was generating support for programs that would disproportionately help the black population. Thus, Canada's work could end up supporting Wilson's "hidden agenda." But just as Wilson's ideas had likely "conferred legitimacy" on the liberal retreat from race in U.S. urban policy in the late twentieth century, so too did Canada's emphasis on public-corporate partnerships confer legitimacy on neoliberal solutions to problems of the inner city at the outset of the new millennium.

America seemed further away than ever from recognizing Martin Luther King, Jr.'s observation that "philanthropy is commendable, but it must not cause the philanthropist to overlook the circumstances of economic injustice which make philanthropy necessary."[25]

6

THE FORGOTTEN GHETTO

Diversity of their topics notwithstanding, I hope all the chapters point in the same direction and reinforce one central message: They are all arguments in favor of assimilating the lessons of the Holocaust in the mainstream of our theory of modernity and of the civilizing process and its effects. They all proceed from the conviction that the experience of the Holocaust contains crucial information about the society of which we are members.

—Zygmunt Bauman, *Modernity and the Holocaust*

In the summer of 2013, I brought my students to Warsaw's new POLIN Museum of the History of Polish Jews for a seminar on the ghetto. The museum is an inspiring structure designed by a Finnish architect, Rainer Mahlamäki, and built out of concrete and glass. This is not a Holocaust museum, and there is no gloominess here. Magnificent light shines through most of the public spaces. The museum is located across the street from the monument to the Warsaw ghetto uprising, which was there when Du Bois went back in 1949. After that trip, he would write, "The result of my [visit to] the Warsaw ghetto was not so much a clearer understanding of the Jewish problem in the world as it was a real and more complete understanding of the Negro problem."[1]

Of the more than 3 million Jews who were living in Poland in 1939, only about 10 percent survived, and most of those who remained in

Poland after the war emigrated in various waves up through the 1960s. About 60 percent of the visitors to the museum are Poles, many of whom have never met a Jew in their lifetime. The museum allows Poles to get in touch with their own history and to fill a gap in their knowledge.

Like many Jews of my generation in America, I had grown up believing that the Holocaust took place in Poland because Poles are anti-Semitic. The genocide was a logical end point of their hate. But the museum challenges those assumptions by placing the Holocaust within the thousand-year history of Polish Jews, a history in which Jewish culture had thrived in the midst of anti-Semitism. In answering how it could happen in Poland, the museum leaves its visitors with an understanding that it happened there because of complex religious and economic factors, and also because Poland had the largest Jewish population in Europe and was not a focus of world attention. This made it easier for the Nazis to take the genocide to the Jews than to take the Jews to the genocide.

FLOURISHING, CONTROL, AND THE CONTEMPORARY GHETTO

In one exhibit, the Hungarian artist Peter Forgacs used sheets to screen home movies made by American Jews who had returned before World War II to the provincial towns and cities where they had been born or grown up. Played against music by the Klezmatics, the footage shows the autonomy and fullness of everyday life, even for Jews who were living under the strains of economic crisis and anti-Semitism. The lower level of the building has a replica of a synagogue's roof and painted ceiling that is built almost to scale, re-created using only the techniques that were available to builders during the seventeenth and eighteenth centuries.

Day after day, my students and I saw what it meant to treat the Jewish communities before the Holocaust as worthy of their own memory, a memory separate from the Holocaust. We were struck by the respect the exhibitions showed for how the people in these communities defined their lives without knowing what would come next.

What was most surprising for many of us was that the exhibition seemed to present an uplifting story of Jewish history in Poland. One of my students asked the chief curator, the eminent anthropologist

Barbara Kirshenblatt-Gimblett, whether the museum was intended to be a celebration of Jewish life.

"To be able to say that what you see is an uplifting story is really fantastic," Kirshenblatt-Gimblett said. "Especially since Poland was indeed the epicenter of the Shoah, the genocide. Yes, it is an uplifting story. But that said, I would not call it a celebration because a celebratory approach tends to be boastful and celebrate great achievements. There is a great Jewish tradition of what to do when someone dies. If you want to console a mourner, remember how the deceased lived. This is the way to honor those who died and those who came before them."

One of the most important realizations we had in the museum was that Jewish life in Poland *prior to the Holocaust* has been largely forgotten, overwhelmed as it was by the memory of the Holocaust itself. The Nazis thus blotted out not only the lives of millions of people, but also the history of the culture of a particular people. The new Museum of the History of Polish Jews exists to bring that world to life. Rather than being a Holocaust museum, it revives memories that were almost destroyed by the mayhem.

After the Nazi era, blacks would make the Nazi analogy less and less in justifying their own use of the word "ghetto." A reference to the Nazis became not merely a rhetorical but also a factual problem: In the years surrounding World War II, black ghettos witnessed a flowering of cultural institutions that bore more resemblance to the Venetian ghetto of the sixteenth to eighteenth century or the flourishing of Polish Jewish life than to anything that went on during the Holocaust.

Yet just as the institution that became known as the Nazi ghetto lasted for only a minute of Jewish history, so did the black ghetto of the thirties and forties last for just a minute of U.S. black history. By the 1960s, an uplifting portrait of the black ghetto became harder to draw. Ever since, those left behind in the black ghetto have had a qualitatively different existence. For the U.S. black ghetto has, over time, seen less flourishing and more pathology; it has lost much of its autonomy and become subject to more intrusive forms of control. Recently, scholars, characterizing the ghetto have used metaphors such as "ethnoracial prison" and "the new Jim Crow" to highlight the transformation.[2]

In this book, we have traced the black ghetto through several stages: Cayton and Drake's Bronzeville, in which an autonomous social and cultural life flourished while coexisting with the evils of segregation;

Clark's Harlem, in which human flourishing was overshadowed by self-perpetuating pathology, and autonomy was replaced by a sense of powerlessness; and Wilson's depopulated ghettos, where the loss of jobs and middle-class people gave rise to social isolation. This final phase of ghetto life has been accompanied by the scourges of drugs, violence, and social decay as well as by the War on Drugs, greater intrusion into the lives of black residents, and the delegitimation of state-sponsored welfare interventions—the very conditions that Geoffrey Canada was responding to in setting up the Harlem Children's Zone. Even if we stipulate that these periods are too sharply distinguished or, in the case of Clark's pathological ghetto, too one-sided in conception, the path has led from an initial state of semi-flourishing[3] and autonomy to one of pathology and control.

Today, the idea of the ghetto has become synonymous in the social sciences and public policy discussions with such phrases as "segregated housing patterns" and "racial residential segregation." It signifies restriction and impoverishment in a delimited residential space. This emphasis highlights the important point that today's residential patterns did not come about "naturally"; they were promoted by both private and state actions that were often discriminatory and even coercive. Nonetheless, this conception of the ghetto truncates our understanding. It does not convey the *variations* in degrees of control and degrees of flourishing that the history of the Jewish ghetto from Venice to Warsaw suggests. In Venice, Jews lived in a ghetto characterized by this understanding: We regulate you, but if you follow the rules, you can have a vigorous religious, cultural, and intellectual life. The Jewish experience under the Nazis illustrates something different—the state exercised the firmest possible control over its subjects' lives, a control that included the ending of those lives by starvation and disease or deportation to concentration camps. If we define the ghetto in terms of unequal housing, as important as that is, we miss how segregation can be compatible with a range of outcomes, compatible, that is, with wide variations in both control and flourishing.

In this light, we can understand why Jewish ghettos are of continued relevance to understanding the trajectory of the black ghetto. In the early years of the ghetto, black men worked at servile jobs carrying luggage as Pullman porters and at backbreaking jobs in the stockyards and steel mills. But they went home to a ghetto in which there was semi-flourishing, just as they lived with less fear of being stopped or even shot by the police. Whereas cops policed the boundaries of black neighborhoods and would even violently repress those communities when they decided to do so, they were by today's standards unconcerned with safety and violence within black neighborhoods. Drake and Cayton barely make any references to the police as a presence.

Though blacks have made substantial progress in many realms, those still stuck in the ghetto experience less flourishing and more intrusive control than ever before. From the 1960s onward, more money flowed into urban police departments to support an ever-more-determined War on Drugs. The number of black men from the ghetto in jail and prison rose dramatically. Thus, in the United States today, nearly 20 percent of black men in their thirties have served time in prison, as have 60 percent of black male high school dropouts, most of whom come from and return to a small number of inner-city zip codes.

My argument is not that there is an analogy to be drawn between the Nazi ghetto and the black ghetto. There is not. While the American black ghetto today is subject to far more intrusive control than in earlier periods, the nature of that control can be contradictory. From its beginning, that control was partly countenanced in the name of producing safety and order in the ghetto itself. Black newspapers such as Harlem's *Amsterdam News* were among the first to support the War on Drugs, with editorials in support of mandatory minimum sentences for drug dealing, "an act of cold, calculated, premeditated, indiscriminate murder of our community."[4] The ghettos of many U.S. cities cannot be discussed simply in terms of external control by whites or invidious efforts to limit or contain human flourishing. Nor, as Issa Kohler-Hausmann and Alice Goffman have demonstrated, can we see the contemporary ghetto as exerting an overwhelming control over *all* aspects of life (as we would have seen in the Nazi ghettos).[5] What we have seen is a move toward a more exclusive use of penal control to deal with social ills. Authorities today have become increasingly concerned with crime alone.

Nor am I arguing that blacks must stand in awe of Jewish suffering or endurance before they can comprehend what a ghetto is. To the contrary, the black ghetto and the Jewish ghetto have never been comparable reference points for understanding the hardship of either group. The Jewish ghetto was a way station for the victims who died in concentration camps during the Holocaust, while the black ghetto became an intergenerational residence for freed slaves and their descendants. Slavery and the Holocaust each generated too much inhumanity and loss of life to become fodder for vulgar disputes about who endured more— debates that do not ennoble their participants.

What I *am* arguing is this: When postwar American social scientists fell for the Nazis' trick—amalgamating the ghettos of the Middle Ages with those imagined by Hitler—they missed the chance to highlight the variations in both control and human flourishing that can be found under conditions of forced segregation. When we compare, rather than conflate, the medieval ghetto and the Nazi ghetto, we can see that Venice and Warsaw are completely different. Recognizing this difference not only broadens our historical understanding of these cases, but also allows us to describe how black ghettos have changed over the past century—that they are now characterized by much more social control by outside forces than before, and much less cultural and human flourishing. So far, we are missing a systematic study of the variations in both flourishing and control that are found in ghettos around the world and across history.[6]

THE IDEA OF THE BLACK GHETTO

The legacy of the ideas discussed in these pages remains important if we are to summarize the significance of the idea of the ghetto for understanding the situation of poor blacks today.

First, the sine qua non of the black ghetto in America has always been restriction in residential space on the basis of race, income, and wealth. While blacks are increasingly less isolated than they were decades ago, Richard Alba has demonstrated that this is partly because poor Latinos have integrated some ghettos.[7] Though ghettos can also be found in suburbs (40 percent of the poor live in suburbs today, and they are mainly black and Latino),[8] the most notable black-white segregation continues within the major Midwestern and Northeastern metropolitan areas. John Logan has called these neighborhoods "America's Ghetto Belt." They house about one in six African Americans today, a condition exacerbated by ongoing black-white wealth differences and the disproportionate impact of the foreclosure crisis on black homeowners.[9] Douglas Massey and his collaborators have demonstrated that although overt discrimination has declined in the United States, segregation is maintained today by suburban zoning regulations that place restrictions on residential density.[10]

Second, the idea of a black ghetto offers a way to explain how prejudice on the part of public or private officials can be perpetuated against blacks without causing harm to the dominant population.[11] It is still simpler to allow hospitals, schools, and police protection to sink to the lowest level if those institutions are in segregated places with separate clienteles.[12] This notion of the ghetto, developed from the 1940s to the 1960s, came into being when it was necessary to explain how racial inequality would still be perpetuated in the absence of Jim Crow legislation. It remains relevant today, though, for space still has the effect of withholding resources and opportunities from poor blacks. The ghetto is an expression of societal power.[13]

Third, the black ghetto has been the site of a series of vicious cycles in which space plays a distinctive role. When schools or streets or hospitals are rendered unequal through societal power, they come to symbolize the black way of life. This way of life is made visible through the physical living space that becomes known as the ghetto.[14] Once the ghetto can be apprehended as a physical reality, subjective perception plays a major role in its perpetuation: the association between blacks and the observed physical conditions becomes a rationalization for further discrimination. Correlation is naturally mistaken for causation, and many white Americans therefore become convinced that the group should be blamed for the conditions at hand. Although the conditions observed generally lead reformers to call for amelioration, the countervailing tendency is for the physical reality of the ghetto to become the rationalization for further segregation.

In our own times, the vicious cycle can be seen at work in the realms of wealth and crime. Because African Americans were blocked from purchasing homes in the newly expanding suburbs, they could not partake in the generation of wealth that is now necessary to move into most better neighborhoods. Even where discriminatory practices no longer prevail, many middle-class blacks with good educations and jobs are unable to leapfrog into neighborhoods that would be accessible to similarly successful whites whose families benefited from the postwar housing market.[15] Likewise, crime—a social ill that the history of the ghetto helped create—has turned into a major justification for

practices that help maintain the ghetto. Whereas people were once excluded because they were black, now criminal behaviors, partly brought
about by the ghetto itself, lead to further exclusion—first in prisons and
jails and later in certain zip codes where large numbers of ex-felons tend
to live.

Fourth, the designation "ghetto" highlights how the variations in
disadvantage between black neighborhoods and other neighborhoods
throughout the city are differences of kind and not differences of degree. Thus, the ghetto is a concept that demands comparative thinking.
When Drake and Cayton linked the words "black" and "ghetto," they
were emphasizing that *unlike* other poor neighborhoods, the black communities of Chicago did not evolve through natural market forces. The
restrictive covenant was a unique condition that did not vary across
other neighborhoods. Likewise, when Kenneth Clark emphasized the
multiplicity of vicious cycles feeding upon one another, he was depicting an absolute level of degradation and powerlessness. These conditions were so extreme that, *taken together*, they could not be found
across the different neighborhoods of the city. The ghetto becomes a
less meaningful concept if it is watered down to simply designate a black
neighborhood that varies in degree (but not in kind) from white and
ethnic neighborhoods of the city.

Thus, the idea of the ghetto in U.S. social science has been most
useful when it provided a conceptual apparatus for distinguishing between black neighborhoods and those occupied by immigrants and
poor whites. Whether the differences at any particular historical moment between the residential communities of poor blacks and other
groups are indeed still meaningful is an empirical question. But as long
as poor black neighborhoods continue to differ in kind from other poor
communities, it is useful to have a concept that makes this point. Extending the definition to other minority groups or to the increasingly
unequal neighborhoods of rich and poor carries the cost of obscuring
the specific mechanisms by which the white majority has historically
used space to achieve power over blacks—from restrictive covenants to
public housing policies to place-based policing.

While much comparative work is still to be done along these lines,
the emphasis on the distinctiveness of different groups' historical experiences has been central to the use of the word "ghetto" for blacks in

particular. Chinatowns, which could have been considered ghettos, had taken on their own identities long before the word came into existence to speak about blacks, and the assumption has always been that the ghetto idea, which emerged from the experiences of Jews and then blacks, did not provide a model for understanding the residential situation of most Spanish-speaking peoples in the United States. This assumption was generally accepted by black and Latino intellectuals, even those who viewed blacks and many Hispanics as "people of color" who shared a common "third world" experience. Spanish-speaking migrants had long used the term "barrio" to name the neighborhoods where they lived, from the Northeast to the Southwest and West of the United States. Unlike "ghetto," which had a negative association, "barrio" often had a more positive cast. Residents used it with pride even as they were discriminated against due to their race, class, or country of birth. At the same time, some scholars have subsequently used the word "barrioization" to speak of the social processes that pushed most Mexican Americans or Puerto Ricans into well-defined areas.[16] These two different uses demonstrate how Latinos have both flourished and been restricted under conditions of segregation. They also show that vast intellectual work still remains for anyone who would use a concept that comes out of generations of the black experience to explain the spatial conditions of Spanish-speaking peoples today.

Fifth, the black ghetto is created and controlled by outside institutions, whether these be large national real estate organizations or federal, state, and local government. The black ghetto is therefore not a phenomenon that can be defined merely through demographic indices of dissimilarity or segregation; rather, it must be understood in dialogue with policies such as blockbusting and redlining. Nor is the ghetto simply a segregated place that was at one time created by racist forces. Rather, it is a phenomenon of ongoing external domination and neglect.

The experience of life in the black ghetto has been one of continuous control by external powers—though the amount and type of control varies in every era. The bureaucratic apparatus of the welfare system, public schools, and the housing authority is still experienced by ghetto dwellers as a demeaning and demoralizing system run by outsiders to the community, even though blacks sometimes staff these organizations, even at the top. Today, an increasingly visible role has been taken by the police and the criminal justice system, but the real estate industry and finance remain as significant as when Clark pointed out their importance at the end of his career.

Sixth, black ghetto residents have since the 1940s lived with a sense of continuous oppression. At the most basic level, then and now, the ghetto has been a social situation of continuous exploitation in which private landlords who own run-down buildings extract as much profit as possible on minimal investment. Alternatively, ghetto dwellers often live in state-run housing projects that are unsafe and poorly maintained. Residents of all these private and public housing entities suffer the additional insult of paying higher prices for substandard products, particularly food. All these buildings are situated in neighborhoods that were historically sites for the supply of unskilled labor to Northern industries. In more recent decades, poor blacks have increasingly lived with an even greater evil—nonexploitive economic oppression,[17] in which residents of the ghetto cannot access the means to apply their labor at all. Absent any opportunity to participate in productive activity, many poor blacks end up reduced to "penny capitalism" within or outside the ghetto, often exploiting one another through legal hustles and illegal schemes.

Seventh, it is often said that a ghetto dweller's relations with the outside world are cold and antagonistic, while in the ghetto he or she thrives on a rich inner life. This view of ghetto life, in which inhabitants are essentially held together by external prejudice, is consistent with a more general view of in-groups and out-groups since the turn of the century—namely, that "the exigencies of war with outsiders are what makes peace inside."[18] While the ghetto dweller's associations within the residential space can be warm, what is equally characteristic is that ghetto conditions do not naturally lead to an "inner solidarity." Instead, residents go to great lengths to differentiate among themselves in moral terms. Ghettos consist of "kinds of people" who would not ordinarily choose to live side by side or even coexist in the same community. Put loosely, ghettos are places where the typically dialectic relationship between in-groups and out-groups does not necessarily hold. Instead, a remarkably consistent fact of ghetto life seems to be that its inhabitants, who are despised by the larger society, expend as much energy drawing distinctions between one another as they do defending themselves against that external force. Even if in many instances the ghetto's inhabitants are bonded together by external prejudice, their internal differentiation is so strong that collective action is less likely—even under the greatest threat.

Eighth, while the ghetto tends to be characterized by outsiders in terms of its pathologies, most of its inhabitants are struggling to live in accordance with standards of moral worth and decency. If these attempts are often desperate and sometimes unsuccessful, it is because they occur against great odds. But the history of the U.S. black ghetto, like that of the Jewish ghettos before them, is not merely the history of those who have lived in that space for generations. It is also the history of all those who are no longer there to be seen, those who have flourished and even escaped into the ranks of the middle and upper classes.[19]

Ninth, the black ghetto is an intergenerational phenomenon.[20] One thing that makes the U.S. ghetto different in kind from other neighborhoods is that it is an *intergenerational* expression of *a series of* vicious cycles within the realms of education, work, family life, violence, and local politics; all are feeding on one another—in a spatial context.[21] The cumulative impact of such self-perpetuating vicious cycles makes the ghetto a place in which too many things have gone wrong for a simple fix—the kind of fix so often deemed possible by misguided reformers. This aspect of the post–World War II black ghetto has easily been obscured by approaches that have focused exclusively on fixing a single problem (the family, jobs, culture, or the school system, to name the most popular) at a time. A reversal of the vicious cycles of the ghetto by any single war on poverty within a single generation seems next to impossible; the dynamic that exists is by this point far too complicated.[22]

Only in recent years has the idea emerged that if poor blacks are moved out of ghettos, then measurable changes should somehow soon follow. When Drake and Cayton wrote in the 1940s, they saw the ghetto *and* the job ceiling working together. By their logic, even if blacks were moved out of the ghetto, their prospects would be dim unless they could also get a foothold in the economy. While Kenneth Clark believed that the physical characteristics of the ghetto—overcrowding, run-down buildings, and general filth—intensified feelings of inferiority, he did not claim or imply that the behaviors he had been witnessing would vanish if the physical structure of the community was improved. To make buildings safer or more attractive, or to move people out of the ghetto, without changing the other basic elements of their lives—low-status jobs, broken families, and deficient schools, for example—would not take them out of what he called "the tangle of community and personal pathology," which, to some extent, had a life of its own and by now existed independently of the ghetto.[23]

Today, the ghetto has increasingly become grist for the most advanced experimental and statistical methods bent on measuring change in the short to medium term. With the emergence of studies such as the Moving to Opportunity experiment as the gold standard for determining whether people benefit from moving out of ghettos, there has been a danger of concluding too much, too quickly. The impact of black ghettos on their inhabitants occurs over generations, not decades. The Jewish ghettos of early modern Europe provide a useful point of comparison. When Pope Paul IV enclosed the Jews of Rome in a ghetto in 1555, few Jews understood the extent of the division that was being created between them and their fellow Italians. For centuries, the Jews of Rome had lived with a strong sense of their membership in the city, sharing a way of life with its Gentile population that included food (despite Jewish dietary rules) and language.[24] At least a century passed before the Jews were deprived of their most important source of income, their loan banks. The ranks of poor Jews swelled and created much social discomfort, if not disturbance. It took many generations for their slow deterioration to be fully manifest, and no experiment with a window of a few years could have been able to document the shift.

In the case of Rome, ghettoization came to an immediate end with the founding of modern Italy and the dismantling of the Papal States in 1870. Had experiments been done to measure the effects of Jewish emancipation after seven years, or even one generation, their findings might have suggested that full integration did not occur overnight, even though Roman Jews had never stopped being Romans in so many ways. Those who wrote about Jews in the late nineteenth century issued reminders that not even half a century had gone by since their emancipation, and that "the habits formed during centuries cannot be expected to wear off in a few decades."[25] As Israel Zangwill wrote of Eastern European Jews, "People who have been living in a ghetto for a couple of centuries are not able to step outside merely because the gates are thrown down, nor to efface the brands on their souls by putting off the yellow badges. The isolation from without will have come to seem the law of their being."[26] Yet policymakers routinely focus on the short term when they try to decide whether it is worthwhile to improve ghetto neighborhoods or simply enable people to move away from them. These habits of mind show how much is lost when the larger history of ghettoization recedes.

To be sure, as Myrdal forcefully argued, we should also always be looking for ways to improve life in the short and medium term whenever possible.[27] Yet one of the differences between an everyday game of chance like a state lottery and a lottery like the MTO experiment is that in the former, the results are known immediately, while in the latter, the consequences unfold over time—in some cases over many years or generations—even if they appear to be known immediately.[28] If, as Patrick Sharkey argues in *Stuck in Place*, the concentration of blacks in the poorest ghettos is a continuation of decades of disadvantage that go back generations, why should it not also take several generations to demonstrate the kind of economic progress that, for some, constitutes convincing evidence of a policy's success? "To understand racial inequality today," Sharkey correctly argues, "it is crucial to approach [it] from a multigenerational perspective."[29] Taken together with the Jews' experience, this insight should inform any snap judgments of experimental results. When the poorest and most isolated blacks have been out of the ghetto for as long as the most isolated and destitute Jews, their situation could look very different from how it looks now.

So the ghetto is an idea that can be quite powerful. Properly understanding its history is essential to understanding the lives of poor blacks and the broader relations of race and poverty in America. Yet the idea also has its limitations.

First, as I've emphasized, it was developed largely by prominent male scholars in eras when women were excluded from academia; the key issues that have emerged from their analyses have centered on the lives of men. To be sure, the scholars discussed in this study vary in the extent to which they have recognized women as an integral part of their analyses. Drake and Cayton did focus on women's experiences throughout their massive account of Chicago's South Side, while Kenneth Clark, despite working closely with Mamie Phipps Clark (whose role was sometimes understated), ended up devoting little or no space to their concerns. William Julius Wilson, whose work dates to the era when black feminist scholars first began occupying a notable place at the table of social science, certainly focused on the influence of political economy on gender relations. Yet the spatial-mismatch hypothesis, which suggested that employment problems among blacks could be resolved through better transportation between the ghetto and distant suburbs, was not generally attentive to the limitations of this solution for women with major child-care responsibilities. The work of Geoffrey Canada's Harlem Children's Zone has tended to focus more attention on the experiences of women—from the early stages of motherhood to their lives as working or nonworking parents—than that of any of his predecessors. He focuses on women primarily because he sees their parenting as contributing to the future well-being of their children. However, no comprehensive conception of the ghetto has yet emerged that would, at a minimum, take into account the female experience of residential restriction imposed on blacks. This is more important than ever in a ghetto where women are so often the ones left behind to cope with the costs of black male incarceration.[30]

A second limitation is that in social science, explanations of the black ghetto have typically had a liberal bias. They have tended to exclude both conservative and radical possibilities. From a conservative's perspective, such explanations are unsatisfying because they leave little room for the black community to take responsibility for problems and pathologies and instead lay almost all blame on whites.[31] From a radical's point of view, the idea of the black ghetto tends to focus on conditions that are near at hand rather than on larger political or economic forces.[32] Even when scholars have tried to keep both levels of analysis at the forefront of their research, the larger policy establishment has seized upon those aspects of the analysis that focus on the neighborhood itself. Thus, while all of the figures surveyed here had some radical element in their work, each of them has been successful partly because certain aspects of their approach were palatable to the liberal political establishment of the time.

Third, the black ghetto is a concept that is difficult to generalize. The best-known studies have concentrated on just a few cities, most prominently Chicago and New York. By comparison, there is scant research about poor blacks in other U.S. cities, where the experiences of ghetto residents might be very different.[33] Likewise, slum dwellers outside the United States have experiences different from those of residents of U.S.

ghettos. Most importantly, not all slums owe their existence to involuntary residential segregation, as ghettos do by definition. The assumption that one can apply what has been learned from studies of the U.S. ghetto to social and historical contexts as different as the megaslums of Mumbai and Nairobi or the favelas of Rio has turned out to be fraught with unexamined complexities. As Loïc Wacquant concluded in *Urban Outcasts*, the surface commonalities between U.S. ghettos and the *banlieues* of Paris "conceal deep structural and functional differences. . . . We are in fact comparing sociospatial specimens of different species—urban 'apples and oranges,' as it were."[34] This is not to suggest that were a massive comparative study to be undertaken, important similarities would not be found. If we can make comparisons—in terms of flourishing and control—between early modern Venice, Nazi-era Warsaw, and twenty-first-century Chicago, then surely present-day Mumbai and Chicago can be compared as well. The American social scientists who developed the ghetto as an idea after World War II were often perfectly satisfied with explaining their own cities and their own societies. Those who would try to apply the concepts they developed to other kinds of U.S. ghettos (those in suburbs or small cities, for example), or to contexts beyond the United States, should at least be aware of the limitations of such an enterprise in the absence of systematic comparative studies that would allow them to situate their cases within the broader landscape.[35]

THE FORGOTTEN GHETTO

The appropriation of the term "ghetto" by certain black scholars and activists in the 1940s should be seen as an alternative to the portrait of the black situation in America that was painted by the Swedish economist and later Nobel laureate Gunnar Myrdal in *An American Dilemma* (1944). Myrdal argued that racial inequality was a moral problem rooted in the contradiction between the American Creed (the ideals embodied in the Constitution and by the Enlightenment) and the American way of life. He ended his book on an optimistic note, expressing confidence that Americans would ultimately come around on their own and live up to their ideals.

But in underplaying the urban North, Myrdal missed a chance to focus on the exclusively black neighborhoods that were forming at the time despite the absence of segregation laws. He thus also failed to deal with the racial attitudes of whites in the urban North. Myrdal's prediction that the United States would eventually resolve the tension between the American Creed and its racist practices by moving in the direction of the Creed seemed reasonable to those white liberals who turned the Myrdal book into a bestseller in 1945. As late as 1954, liberals could see the Supreme Court's decision in *Brown v. Board of Education* as a triumph of Myrdal's vision. The decision, after all, was made voluntarily by American elites without pressure from mass political protest. It had been influenced by social scientific evidence (including a reference to Myrdal's book) that segregation between blacks and whites led to inherently inferior black institutions. For another decade, Myrdal and his followers looked at *Brown* as they did at the Declaration of Independence or the first ten amendments to the U.S. Constitution—as a powerful set of ideas that the citizens of a democracy could continue to uphold in the fight for justice and equality.

The *Brown* momentum carried over into Martin Luther King's Montgomery bus boycott and into related sit-ins calling for the desegregation of public transportation and lunch counters, as well as voting rights across the South. Throughout this period, national attention remained fixed on de jure segregation, the legally mandated form that the Supreme Court had tried to tackle in *Brown*. But even prior to the passage of the Civil Rights Act of 1964, when the civil rights movement went north, solutions became more complicated. After the Watts riot in Los Angeles in 1965 and after Martin Luther King moved into an apartment in Chicago in 1966 to draw attention to racial discrimination, it was impossible to disentangle the "race issue" from the substance of economic, not just legal, deprivation.

Racial segregation in the North—the de facto ghetto—generated separate schools, parks, hospitals, police protection, and the like—even without Jim Crow or the "Southern mentality" to support it. The white conscience was not enough. Whites in big cities such as New York, Chicago, Boston, and Philadelphia, who had been gloating over their moral superiority to their counterparts in the South, were in fact living with an unresolved conflict between their stated ideals and behaviors. By the late 1960s, Myrdal's approach seemed increasingly naive and incapable of grasping the force of Northern prejudice.

Myrdal might, even at the time, have gone in other directions if he had taken advantage of alternative viewpoints near at hand—including the viewpoints of scholars who themselves had largely been kept at bay by systems of discrimination reaching into the academy itself. From my own archival research, I have argued that Myrdal might have dealt with race in America very differently had he struck a deal with Horace Cayton, a black graduate student at the University of Chicago, whom Myrdal tried to bring on board for his Carnegie-funded project. When Cayton joined forces with St. Clair Drake to coauthor the classic *Black Metropolis* (1945), their mission, and accomplishment, was to systematically explain the situation of blacks who had recently moved from the rural South to the urban North.

Their deliberate use of the word "ghetto" highlighted that nothing about the concentration of more than half the blacks of Chicago in the most "blighted" areas of the city was natural. *Black Metropolis* dealt with issues of race and poverty by emphasizing how the white majorities in Northern states were using their power to restrict blacks to certain spaces and thus exacerbating their disadvantages as a matter of expediency and not in pursuit of cultural or moral ideals. In failing to make a deal with Cayton, Myrdal never gained access to the research that might have led him to a different conclusion, one that placed less reliance on cognitive stress among the powerful to lead to changes on the ground, and more on the power of white racism.

The next great scholar of the ghetto was one of Myrdal's many assistants, Kenneth Clark—another rising but already important African American researcher. Like Drake and Cayton two decades earlier, his work left no doubt that ghettos were different in kind (rather than degree or "stage" of evolution) from other neighborhoods. Their problems were of epidemic proportions. Although today it is known mainly for its focus on pathology, *Dark Ghetto* in its time provided a new way of seeing that the problems of urban blacks were so complicated that they could not easily be changed by even the direct action of the civil rights movement, such as boycotts or sit-ins. Clark also argued that ghettos were powerless colonies of white society, in which blacks—and here his social psychology comes to the fore—felt routinely demeaned and humiliated.

In subsequent years, in interviews and conversations, Clark developed his own version of the Myrdal thesis about the United States: it was characterized by "the existence of the ideals in spite of the consistent violation of them."[36] Again in the language of his discipline, Clark translated this as "cognitive dissonance"—the mind's simultaneous grappling with conflicting ideas—in the realm of morality. Alas, with the election of Ronald Reagan in 1980, and a federal retreat from remedying racial injustice, Clark threw up his hands in despair.

This era saw the emergence of yet another key scholar, an African American again, but with a very different point of view from most of his scholarly forebears of any race. William Julius Wilson would challenge what had grown into an accepted canon of ideas among other ghetto scholars. Writing in 1978, he claimed that class factors were now overtaking race in determining the life chances of blacks in and out of the ghetto. In the past, blacks of all social classes had a shared fate; from the perspective of the larger society they were simply black. Now, Wilson argued, as more blacks obtained better-paying jobs, the new middle class escaped the ghetto, leaving behind a destitute, socially isolated population. That blacks of different social classes no longer occupied the same neighborhoods did not mean that they no longer identified as a people. However, it did mean that they no longer shared the common fate of the ghetto dweller. The price of escape for some was that those left behind were at further disadvantage.

As the social gap between the black poor and black middle class grew, these distinctive class divisions expressed themselves in physical space. Unlike in the ghetto described by Drake and Cayton in the forties, and even the one that Clark observed in the sixties, middle-class blacks in Wilson's day were no longer found in large numbers in the same communities with poor blacks, who were now socially isolated in "concentrated poverty." As many of the poor black neighborhoods Wilson described continued to lose population, a new form of the U.S. ghetto emerged, characterized by geographic, social, and economic isolation. Unlike in previous eras, middle-class and lower-class blacks were having very different life experiences in the 1980s.

Wilson's work marked the emergence of an idea of the ghetto as brought about by impersonal structural forces, as opposed to deliberate acts of race-based subjugation—hence the possibility for some blacks to rise even with the prevalence of ghetto life. Yet as he made his arguments, it became increasingly questionable to him whether anything could be gained by appealing to the ethical standards of whites to help the new ghetto poor. As an alternative strategy, Wilson proposed that progressives work from a "hidden agenda" by fighting for race-neutral public policies that would help all poor Americans.

Pulling back from race as a central problem had special appeal to the political right, which tried to appropriate both Wilson and his ideas. Wilson resisted rightists' invocation of his work by explicitly articulating a clearly liberal agenda. All the same, his proposals were not acceptable to many on the left, who argued that by de-emphasizing racial factors, Wilson was legitimating America's turn away from racial justice. Some of the same scholars who criticized Myrdal for his naive ideas on America's conscience were now criticizing Wilson for strategically trying to do an end run around the conscience of whites.[37]

Like Drake and Cayton before him, though, Wilson was actually acknowledging that nothing in the morality of whites would make them receptive to appeals to help poor blacks. The only way to interest whites in joblessness among black adults or even poverty among black children was to focus on programs that would also help whites. He was now advocating that those who cared about poor blacks should match the indirect, inexplicit racism of white people with an indirectness of their own.

Many valiant efforts have been made to understand the ghetto and bring it to public and scholarly attention, as documented in the works of the individuals discussed here. But with the exception of the War on Poverty, has the nation that consumed these great works in any way lived up to its own ideals? Given the lack of federal initiatives since the War on Poverty, one could reasonably conclude that America has simply proven itself unworthy of Myrdal's optimism. Yet a crucial characteristic of U.S. race relations in recent decades is the unevenness of progress and regression. The U.S. black ghettos today exist side by side with a significant black middle class. This class did not come into existence because, as Myrdal predicted, whites voluntarily lived up to their ideals, but rather, due to the demands of the civil rights movement. Nevertheless, the condition of the ghetto today must be seen in relation to those who are no longer there. The specter of the ghetto can blot out the success of the people who have exited, just as those successes can blot out the ghetto itself.

In his important book of the early nineties, *The Promised Land*, Nicholas Lemann offered detailed accounts of the singular significant effort to tackle the black ghetto between 1964 and 1972—an effort that failed in large part because the federal attempt to promote citizen participation in community poverty programs alienated local officials.[38] Another reason that the War on Poverty failed was because America had been trying to pursue a real war in Vietnam at exactly the same time.[39] As the country could not sustain the tax burden of both these initiatives, the government decided that the War on Poverty had to be limited in sweep. Yet by the 1990s, when the Clinton presidency came to an end, the United States was swimming in a budget surplus. If ever there was a moment to engage in a second War on Poverty, that was it.

Instead, the Republican Party came to power. While maintaining its position as a consistently low-tax country, the United States fought wars in Iraq and Afghanistan. While the federal government did little to improve poor urban areas, young whites moved back to cities such as New York and Chicago, including some of the very neighborhoods that Clark and Canada had focused upon. These people had grown up in the suburbs and attended good colleges. While they had been socialized to believe in "difference," diversity, and antiracism, many of them were largely oblivious to the systematic head start they had received in life. Writing in 1972, Robert Blauner had referred to this as white privilege, but now among them were large numbers of what Andrew Hacker would later call "honorary whites," including Asians and even successful blacks.[40] These populations made investments in real estate—frequently with the aid of down payments from their parents—and in some cases even began raising their children in the very neighborhoods that had once been known as ghettos. Living in these communities with poor blacks, other minorities, and even (in some cities) poor whites in their midst, these children could be raised with the expectation that the dirty work around them would always be done by these "others," and not by people like them. Some of these new urban residents had grown up in progressive homes and had supported progressive politics throughout their young lives. When it came time to place their own children in urban schools, they followed the traditions of affluent and even politically radical urban whites before them by separating their own kids in private, parochial, or, once they were available, charter schools.

By the time that Geoffrey Canada emerged on the scene, Wilson's view had become widely accepted: no program to help the ghetto could work if it asked the white masses to make sacrifices on behalf of blacks. This resignation assumed that whites were motivated by racism, though that might have been too simple. For whereas the black middle class has a sense of shared peoplehood with the black poor, middle-class whites may not identify closely enough with poor whites to support initiatives on their behalf either. Furthermore, middle-class whites were interested in protecting their own racial *and* class privileges. The disregard of middle-class whites for the white poor may need to be addressed on its own terms before any "hidden agenda" can succeed.

Like Myrdal's, Canada's appeal was a moral one. He focused on the importance of the total human being from cradle to adulthood, but his ultimate appeal lay in educating Harlem's poor without asking whites to make sacrifices on behalf of any children other than their own. Rather than wait for whites to overcome their cognitive dissonance, Canada appealed to deeply committed, generous white billionaires to fund his programs—an idea that was hardly replicable across the country, unless tax dollars were to be spent. Canada's approach was consistent with one of the important lessons that has become evident since Myrdal, namely, that the highest priority of most white people (and most Americans of any race) is to protect and advance the welfare of themselves and their families. Above and beyond racism, this ability of the American people to compartmentalize, to live with moral dissonance, is the crucial underlying foundation of the forgotten ghetto.

NOTES

PREFACE

1. Cora Daniels, *Ghettonation: A Journey into the Land of the Bling and the Home of the Shameless* (New York: Doubleday, 2007), 3.
2. Maria Baez and Larry B. Seabrook, Resolution Declaring a Symbolic Ban on the Negative Use of the Word "Ghetto" in New York City, Res 1723-2008, 2008.
3. Mario Luis Small, "Four Reasons to Abandon the Idea of 'The Ghetto,'" *City & Community* 7, no. 4 (December 2008): 389. Small's distinguished essay is complex, and his reason for abandoning the concept of the ghetto touches as much upon dilemmas surrounding how social science should form concepts as it does upon the ghetto's stigmatizing qualities, which are also discussed as reasons.
4. Some of this ground has been covered in the exemplary introductory essay to Ray Hutchison and Bruce D. Haynes, eds., *The Ghetto: Contemporary Global Issues and Controversies* (Boulder, Colo.: Westview Press, 2012), vii–1. The main difference in our approaches is that they do not discuss the Nazi era.
5. St. Clair Drake and Horace R. Cayton, *Black Metropolis: A Study of Negro Life in a Northern City* (Chicago: University of Chicago Press, 1993), xli.
6. For the definitive general history of the transformation in the study of U.S. poverty, see Alice O'Connor, *Poverty Knowledge* (Princeton, N.J.: Princeton University Press, 2001).

1. A NAZI DECEPTION

1. W.E.B. Du Bois, "The Negro and the Warsaw Ghetto," *Jewish Life* 6, no. 7 (May 1952): 14–15. All related information and quotations are from this source.
2. Aldon Morris, *The Scholar Denied: W.E.B. Du Bois and the Birth of Modern Sociology* (Berkeley: University of California Press, 2015), 57.
3. W.E.B. Du Bois, "Awake America," *Crisis*, September 1917, cited in David

Levering Lewis, *W.E.B. Du Bois: Biography of a Race, 1868–1919* (New York: Henry Holt, 1993), 539. See also Kwame Anthony Appiah, *Lines of Descent: W.E.B Du Bois and the Emergence of Identity* (Cambridge, Mass.: Harvard University Press, 2014).

4. Israel Abrahams, *Jewish Life in the Middle Ages* (Mineola, N.Y.: Dover Publications, 2004), 15. See generally Kenneth Stow, *Theatre of Acculturation: The Roman Ghetto in the Sixteenth Century* (Seattle: University of Washington Press, 2001); and Benjamin C. I. Ravid, *Studies on the Jews of Venice, 1382–1797* (Aldershot, Hampshire, Great Britain: Ashgate/Variorum, 2003).

5. Benjamin C. I. Ravid, "All Ghettos Were Jewish Quarters but Not All Jewish Quarters Were Ghettos," in *The Frankfurt Judengasse: Life in an Early Modern German City*, ed. Fritz Backhaus et al. (London and Portland, Ore.: Vallentine Mitchell, 2010), 5–22.

6. Benjamin C. I. Ravid, "The Venetian Government and the Jews," in *The Jews of Early Modern Venice*, ed. R. C. Davis and B. Ravid (Baltimore: Johns Hopkins University Press, 2001), 3–30. The information in the following paragraphs has largely been drawn from this and other previously listed sources.

7. Richard Sennett, *Flesh and Stone: The Body and the City in Western Civilization*, 245.

8. Ferdinand Gregorovius, *The Ghetto and the Jews of Rome*, trans. Moses Hadas (New York: Schocken Books, 1966), 44–45.

9. Ibid., 49–50.

10. Ibid., 55. According to the *Oxford Dictionary of Jewish Religion*, during the coronation ceremony, Jews would hand the new pope a Torah scroll, and he would acknowledge the link between Judaism and Christianity, which justified the existence of Jews within a Christian community.

11. Pope Paul IV, "Cum nimis absurdum," July 14, 1555. I thank Professor Kenneth Stow for providing me with his English translation of this document.

12. Kenneth Stow, *Theatre of Acculturation: The Roman Ghetto in the Sixteenth Century* (Seattle: University of Washington Press, 2001), 62.

13. Ibid., 36.

14. Irina Oryshkevich, "Accommodating Jews in the New Jerusalem" (lecture, Italian Academy for Advanced Studies at Columbia University, New York, February 12, 2010). On the architecture and physical setting of the Roman ghetto, see also Fabio Barry, "Roman Apartheid? The Counter-Reformation Ghettoes," *Daidalos* 59 (March 1996): 18–31.

15. Stow, *Theatre of Acculturation*, 64.

16. Ibid.

17. Ibid., 127.

18. Gregorovius, *Ghetto and the Jews of Rome*, 110.

19. Stow, *Theatre of Acculturation*, 126.

20. Michael Goldfarb, *Emancipation: How Liberating Europe's Jews from the Ghetto Led to Revolution and Renaissance* (New York: Simon and Schuster, 2009), 93. See also Jacob Katz, "Leaving the Ghetto," *Commentary*, February 1996; Paul Mendes-Flohr and Jehuda Reinharz, *The Jew in the Modern World: A Documentary History* (New York: Oxford University Press, 1980), 121–76; Arthur Hertzberg, *The French Enlightenment and the Jews: The Origins of Modern Anti-Semitism*

(New York: Columbia University Press, 1990); and David Jan Sorkin, *The Transformation of German Jewry, 1780–1840* (Detroit: Wayne State University Press, 1999).

21. Gregorovius, *Ghetto and the Jews of Rome*, 89–90.

22. Salo W. Baron, "Ghetto and Emancipation: Shall We Revise the Traditional View?" *Menorah Journal* 14, no. 6 (June 1928): 515–26.

23. Ibid., 523–24.

24. Michael Gold, *Jews Without Money*, 3rd ed. (New York: Carroll & Graf, 2004), 55.

25. Ibid., 8.

26. Dan Michman, *The Emergence of Jewish Ghettos During the Holocaust*, trans. Lenn J. Schramm (Cambridge and New York: Cambridge University Press, 2011).

27. Ibid., 3.

28. Saul Friedländer, *Nazi Germany and the Jews: Volume I: The Years of Persecution, 1933–1939* (New York: HarperCollins, 1997), 143.

29. "Unsigned Note," in *Documents on German Foreign Policy, 1918–1945: From the Archives of the German Foreign Ministry*, by Auswärtiges Amt. Germany, vol. I, U.S. Department of State Publication 3277, C (Washington, D.C.: USGPO, 1949), 347–48.

30. Friedländer, *Nazi Germany and the Jews*, 47.

31. Ibid.

32. "Nuremberg Document 1816-PS, 'Stenographic Report on the Meaning of the Jewish Question under the Chairmanship of Field Marshall Goering in the Reich's Air Force,' 12 November 1938, 11:00am," in *Nazi Conspiracy and Aggression*, by United States Department of State, vol. 4 (Washington, D.C.: USGPO, 1946), 425–54.

33. Ibid., 452.

34. Ibid., 454.

35. Ibid.

36. Topics of the Times, *New York Times*, July 9, 1938.

37. Jeremy Noakes and Geoffrey Pridham, eds., *Nazism, 1919–1945: A Documentary Reader* (Exeter, Great Britain: University of Exeter Press, 2001), 465.

38. Ronnie S. Landau, *The Nazi Holocaust: Its History and Meaning* (London: I.B. Tauris, 2006), 153.

39. Christopher R. Browning, *The Origins of the Final Solution: The Evolution of Nazi Jewish Policy, September 1939–March 1942* (Lincoln: University of Nebraska Press, 2004), 111.

40. See Reviel Netz, *Barbed Wire: An Ecology of Modernity* (Middletown, Conn.: Wesleyan University Press, 2004), 56–127; and Alan Krell, *Devil's Rope: A Cultural History of Barbed Wire* (London: Reaktion Books, 2002).

41. Noakes and Pridham, *Nazism*, 455.

42. See Raul Hilberg, *The Destruction of the European Jews* (Chicago: Quadrangle Books, 1961); and Zygmunt Bauman, *Modernity and the Holocaust* (Ithaca, N.Y.: Cornell University Press, 2000).

43. Noakes and Pridham, *Nazism*, 464.

44. Ibid., 464–65.

45. Ibid., 462.

46. Michael C. Thomsett, *The German Opposition to Hitler: The Resistance, the Underground, and Assassination Plots, 1938–1945* (Jefferson, N.C., and London: McFarland, 1997), 6.

47. Noakes and Pridham, *Nazism*, 539–40.

48. Katrin Steffan, "Connotations of Exclusion—'Ostjuden,' 'Ghettos' and Other Markings," in *Jahrbuch Des Simon-Dubnow-Instituts IV*, ed. Dan Diner (Göttingen, Germany: Vandenhoeck und Ruprecht, 2005), 459–79.

49. Michman, *Emergence of Jewish Ghettos*, 72.

50. Ibid.

51. Ibid., 73.

52. Christopher R. Browning, "Genocide and Public Health: German Doctors and Polish Jews," *Holocaust and Genocide Studies* 3, no. 1 (1988): 21–36; Paul Weindling, *Epidemics and Genocide in Eastern Europe, 1890–1945* (Oxford and New York: Oxford University Press, 2000); and Gordon J. Horowitz, *Ghettostadt: Łódź and the Making of a Nazi City* (Cambridge, Mass.: Belknap Press of Harvard University Press, 2008).

53. Emmanuel Ringelblum, *Notes from the Warsaw Ghetto: The Journal of Emmanuel Ringelblum*, trans. J. Sloan (New York: McGraw-Hill, 1958), 135.

54. Christopher R. Browning, "Nazi Ghettoization Policy in Poland: 1939–41," *Central European History* 19, no. 4 (December 1986): 345.

55. Christopher R. Browning, "Before the 'Final Solution': Nazi Ghettoization Policy in Poland (1940–1941)," in *Ghettos 1939–1945: New Research and Perspectives on Definition, Daily Life, and Survival* (Washington, D.C.: Center for Advanced Holocaust Studies, United States Holocaust Memorial Museum, 2001), 4.

56. Browning, "Nazi Ghettoization Policy in Poland," 345.

57. "Extremists Sway Nazis and Jews Are Menaced with More Drastic Rule," *New York Times*, November 14, 1938.

58. Max Weinreich, *Hitler's Professors: The Part of Scholarship in Germany's Crimes Against the Jewish People* (New Haven, Conn.: Yale University Press, 1999), 94.

59. Ibid., 91; Michman, *Emergence of Jewish Ghettos*, 9.

60. "No Regret Voiced: Goebbels Declares That the Nation Followed Its 'Healthy Instincts,'" *New York Times*, November 12, 1938.

61. Hilberg, *Destruction of the European Jews*, cited in Michman, *Emergence of Jewish Ghettos*, 11.

62. Martin Gilbert, *The Holocaust: The History of the Jews of Europe During the Second World War* (New York: Holt, Rinehart and Winston, 1986), 89.

63. Louis Wirth, "Ghetto," in *World Book Encyclopedia* (Chicago: Quarrie, 1947), 2986.

64. "The Trial of Adolf Eichmann, Session 12 (Part 7 of 7)," *The Nizkor Project*, n.d., http://www.nizkor.org/hweb/people/e/eichmann-adolf/transcripts/Sessions/Session-012-07.html.

65. Christopher Browning, "The Holocaust and History," in Peter Hayes, ed., *Lessons and Legacies: Memory, Memorialization, and Denial* (Evanston, Ill.: Northwestern University Press, 1999), 24–25, as cited in Eric J. Sundquist, *Strangers in the Land: Blacks, Jews, Post-Holocaust America* (Cambridge, Mass., and London: Belknap Press of Harvard University Press, 2005), 444.

66. Loïc Wacquant and Michelle Alexander, among others, have prominently drawn attention to the ghetto as a vehicle of control. See Wacquant, *Urban Outcasts: A*

Comparative Sociology of Advanced Marginality (Cambridge and Malden, Mass.: Polity Press, 2008); "Ghetto," in *International Encyclopedia of the Social Sciences*, ed. Neil M. Smelser and Paul B. Baltes (London: Pergamon Press, 2004); and Alexander, *The New Jim Crow: Mass Incarceration in the Age of Colorblindness* (New York: New Press, 2010).

67. Du Bois, "Negro and the Warsaw Ghetto," 15.

2. CHICAGO, 1944: HORACE CAYTON

1. Herman H. Long and Charles S. Johnson, *People vs. Property: Race Restrictive Covenants in Housing* (Nashville, Tenn.: Fisk University Press, 1947), 75–76.

2. Arnold R. Hirsch, *Making the Second Ghetto: Race and Housing in Chicago, 1940–1960* (Chicago: University of Chicago Press, 1998), 36. See also Leonard S. Rubinowitz and Imani Perry, "Crimes Without Punishment: White Neighbor's Resistance to Black Entry," *Journal of Criminal Law and Criminology* 92, no. 2 (2003): 335–428.

3. See Horace Cayton, *Long Old Road: An Autobiography* (New York: Trident Press, 1965).

4. Ibid., 250–51.

5. "An Address by Horace Cayton, Director of the Parkway Community House, Before the Committee of Racial Equality" (Woodlawn AME Church, East Sixty-Fifth and Evans Streets, Chicago, Illinois, November 17, 1944), Box 2, Folder 5, Louis Wirth Papers, Special Collections Research Center, University of Chicago Library.

6. Carey McWilliams, *Brothers Under the Skin* (Boston: Little, Brown, 1943), 42.

7. Cayton, *Long Old Road*, 229–30.

8. See, for example, "Cites Germany's Treatment of Jews Like Race in U.S.," *Chicago Defender*, December 31, 1938; and Trezzvant W. Anderson, "Hideous Housing Treatment Sickens Stoutest Stomachs," *Pittsburgh Courier*, April 16, 1949.

9. "Cites Germany's Treatment of Jews."

10. Kevin Boyle, *Arc of Justice: A Saga of Race, Civil Rights, and Murder in the Jazz Age* (New York: Henry Holt, 2004).

11. For an excellent study, see Kevin Fox Gotham, "Urban Space, Restrictive Covenants and the Origins of Racial Residential Segregation in a US City, 1900–50," *International Journal of Urban and Regional Research* 24, no. 3 (September 2000): 616–33.

12. Long and Johnson, *People vs. Property*, 17, 21.

13. Ibid., 23.

14. Ibid., 10.

15. Ibid., 11.

16. Ibid., 23.

17. Ibid., 82–83.

18. Ibid., 58; and "Realtor: Its Meaning and Use," Association of Real Estate Boards, Chicago.

19. Long and Johnson, 58.

20. Long and Johnson.

21. Ibid., 11–12.

22. The Cameraman, "Colorful News Movies," *Broad Ax*, November 13, 1926.

23. "Restrictive Covenants Illegal Rules Chicago Municipal Judge," *Los Angeles Tribune*, November 29, 1943.

24. Long and Johnson, *People vs. Property*, 100–101.

25. Drake and Cayton, *Black Metropolis*, 382.

26. Long and Johnson, *People vs. Property*, 21.

27. Ibid., 3; and Hirsch, *Making the Second Ghetto*, 32–33.

28. Hirsch, *Making the Second Ghetto*, 35.

29. Gilbert Osofsky, *Harlem: The Making of a Ghetto, Negro New York, 1890–1930*, 2nd ed. (New York: Harper and Row, 1971), 106.

30. Robert C. Weaver, *The Negro Ghetto* (New York: Russell and Russell, 1948), 120–24, 231–56.

31. Hortense Powdermaker, *After Freedom: A Cultural Study in the Deep South* (New York: Viking, 1939), cited in Karl E. Taeuber and Alma F. Taeuber, *Negroes in Cities* (Chicago: Aldine, 1965), 180–81.

32. Ibid., 7.

33. Inversely, "the proportion of all Negroes living in the North and West rose to 23.8% in 1940." See Gunnar Myrdal, *An American Dilemma: The Negro Problem and Modern Democracy* (New York and London: Harper and Brothers, 1944), 183.

34. See Charles S. Johnson, *Backgrounds to Patterns of Negro Segregation* (New York: Crowell, 1970), 8–13.

35. Taeuber and Taeuber, *Negroes in Cities*, 3.

36. Aldon Morris argues that "the Tuskegee experience proved critical in the development of Park's sociological imagination and his subsequent understandings of race." He shows that Tuskegee strengthened Park's dislike of social activism, and that Washington's dislike of Du Bois and his methods filtered into Park's own views: "Park transplanted Washington's doctrine into the Chicago school of sociology and continued to marginalize Du Bois's pioneering sociology" (*Scholar Denied*, 108).

37. Park's own position on naturally occurring ghettos is most clearly articulated in his foreword to Louis Wirth, *The Ghetto* (Chicago: University of Chicago Press, 1956), vii–ix.

38. The following description of the Chicago School draws primarily on John D. Kasarda, "Urbanization, Community, and the Metropolitan Problem," in *Handbook of Contemporary Urban Life*, ed. David Street (San Francisco: Jossey-Bass, 1979), 28–29.

39. As such, one of Park's key insights was that all entities are interrelated, regardless of species. See William Michelson, *Man and His Urban Environment: A Sociological Approach: With Revisions* (Reading, Mass.: Addison-Wesley, 1976). As Abbott formulates it: "In a single sentence, the Chicago school thought—and thinks—that one cannot understand social life without understanding the arrangements of particular social actors in particular social times and places." See Andrew Abbott, *Department and Discipline: Chicago Sociology at One Hundred* (Chicago and London: University of Chicago Press, 1999), 196.

40. See also Ernest W. Burgess, "Residential Segregation in American Cities," *Annals of the American Academy of Political and Social Science* 140 (November 1928): 122; and Martin Bulmer, *The Chicago School of Sociology: Institutionalization, Diversity, and the Rise of Sociological Research* (Chicago and London: University of Chicago Press, 1984), 75.

41. Clifford R. Shaw, *Delinquency Areas: A Study of the Geographic Distribution of School Truants, Juvenile Delinquents, and Adult Offenders in Chicago* (Chicago: University of Chicago Press, 1929), 205.

42. Ibid.

43. Ibid., 201.

44. Robert E. Park, "The Urban Community as a Spatial and a Moral Order," in *The Urban Community: Selected Papers from the Proceedings of the American Sociological Society,* ed. Ernest W. Burgess (Chicago: University of Chicago Press, 1926), 9.

45. Thus, "the movement of Negro population into new residential areas is often considered as different in kind from that of other racial, immigrant, or economic groups. When studied, however, from the standpoint of human ecology, it appears to vary little, if at all, from those of other groups," wrote Burgess, "Residential Segregation in American Cities," 110.

46. Horace R. Cayton, "A Great Man Died, but Leaves Keen Observation on Our Democracy," *Pittsburgh Courier,* February 26, 1944.

47. Edward Shils and Joseph Epstein, *Portraits: A Gallery of Intellectuals* (Chicago: University of Chicago Press, 1997), 386.

48. Ibid.

49. Ibid., 237.

50. St. Clair Drake, "*Black Metropolis* Revisited," n.d., Box 39, St. Clair Drake Papers, Schomburg Center for Research in Black Culture, New York Public Library. See also Henri Peretz, "The Making of *Black Metropolis,*" *Annals of the American Academy of Political and Social Science* 595 (September 2004): 171.

51. Drake, "Black Metropolis Revisited."

52. Ibid.

53. Ibid.

54. Wirth, *Ghetto,* 4–5.

55. Ibid., 36.

56. Ibid., 19.

57. Ibid., 27.

58. Ibid., 36.

59. David Philipson, *Old European Jewries* (Philadelphia: Jewish Publication Society of America, 1894), cited in Wirth, *Ghetto,* 280.

60. Wirth, *Ghetto,* 263.

61. Philipson, *Old European Jewries,* cited in Wirth, *Ghetto,* 280.

62. Wirth, *Ghetto,* 69.

63. Wirth was not alone. With but few exceptions, those blacks who proposed to use the idea of the ghetto to refer to black neighborhoods also believed the ghetto was shaped by market and voluntaristic forces. George Haynes, for example, claimed that black ghettos had been created when poor blacks were left behind by the voluntary outmigration of the black business and professional classes, an explanation that would be revived in later decades to explain the decline of black neighborhoods. Haynes wrote, "But the growing Negro business and professional classes and those engaged in other than domestic and personal service find separate sections in which to dwell. Thus the Negro ghetto is growing up." See George Edmund Haynes, "Conditions Among Negroes in the Cities," *Annals of the American Academy of Political and Social Science* 49 (1913): 105.

64. Wirth, *Ghetto*, 265.
65. Ibid., 279.
66. Baron, "Ghetto and Emancipation."
67. Ibid., 526.
68. Ibid., 520.
69. Harvey Zorbaugh, *Gold Coast and Slum: A Sociological Study of Chicago's Near North Side* (Chicago: University of Chicago Press, 1929), 198–99, cited in William Foote Whyte, "Social Organization in the Slums," *American Sociological Review* 8, no. 1 (February 1943): 35–36.
70. Wirth, *Ghetto*, 61–62.
71. Ibid., 283.
72. Ibid., 203.
73. Ibid., 41.
74. Ibid., 50–51.
75. "Decree on Jews and Neophytes: Session 19 of the Council of Basel, 1431–45 A.D.," September 7, 1434, http://www.papalencyclicals.net/Councils/ecum17.htm.
76. On the establishment and history of the ghetto in Frankfurt, see F. Backhaus, "The Jewish Ghetto in Frankfurt," in *The Life and Times of N. M. Rothschild, 1777–1826*, ed. V. Gray and M. Aspey (London: N. M. Rothschild & Sons, 1998), 22–33, and the collection of essays in F. Backhaus, ed., *The Frankfurt Judengasse: Jewish Life in an Early Modern German City* (London and Portland, Ore.: Vallentine Mitchell, 2010). Records related to the foundation of the Judengasse can be found in the Bürgermeisterbücher in the Institut für Stadtgeschichte (ISGF) in Frankfurt, and are published in full in Dietrich Andernacht, *Regesten zur Geschichte der Juden in der Reichsstadt Frankfurt am Main von 1401–1519* (Hannover: Hahnsche Buchhandlung, 1996), Volume 1/1.
77. Wirth, *Ghetto*, 50–51.
78. W. Lloyd Warner and Leo Srole, *The Social Systems of American Ethnic Groups* (New Haven, Conn.: Yale University Press, 1945), 45.
79. Gandolfo v. Hartman et al., 49 Fed. 181, 1892.
80. Victor G. Nee and Brett de Bary Nee, *Longtime Californ': A Documentary Study of an American Chinatown* (Stanford, Calif.: Stanford University Press, 1972), 60.
81. Ibid., 60–61.
82. Ibid., 155.
83. William Foote Whyte, *Street Corner Society: The Social Structure of an Italian Slum*, 4th ed. (Chicago: University of Chicago Press, 1993), 356.
84. Ibid., 276.
85. Ibid.
86. Stephen Steinberg takes this one step further, arguing, "We can say with only slight exaggeration that American sociology had its roots in an effort to provide erudite justification for racial hierarchy." See Stephen Steinberg, *Race Relations: A Critique* (Stanford, Calif.: Stanford University Press, 2007), 50.
87. See Louis Curtis Washington, "A Study of Restrictive Covenants in Chicago" (M.A. diss., University of Chicago, 1948), 19; and Long and Johnson, *People vs. Property*, 29.
88. Hirsch, *Making the Second Ghetto*, 145–70.
89. "Letter from the Big Brothers Association to the University of Chicago. In

Chicago Defender Files," January 1938, Box 2, Folder 5, Louis Wirth Papers, Special Collections Research Center, University of Chicago Library.

90. R. Fred Wacker, "The Sociology of Race and Ethnicity in the Second Chicago School," in *A Second Chicago School? The Development of a Postwar American Sociology*, ed. Gary Alan Fine (Chicago: University of Chicago Press, 1995), 141.

91. "Copy of Memorandum Regarding University Real Estate, from Louis Wirth to L. Steares," March 30, 1936, Box 54, Folder 2, Louis Wirth Papers, Special Collections Research Center, University of Chicago Library.

92. Abbott, *Department and Discipline*, 41; and Edward Shils, *A Fragment of a Sociological Autobiography: The History of My Pursuit of a Few Ideas*, ed. Steven Grosby (New Brunswick, N.J.: Transaction Books, 2006), 46.

93. W. H. McNeil, *Hutchins' University: A Memoir of the University of Chicago, 1929–1950* (Chicago: University of Chicago Press, 1991), 134–38. See also F. B. Lindstrom, "The Negro Invasion of the Washington Park Subdivision" (M.A. diss., University of Chicago, 1941).

94. Wendy Plotkin, *Deeds of Mistrust: Race, Housing, and Restrictive Covenants in Chicago, 1900–1953* (doctoral diss., University of Illinois–Chicago, 1999), 80–81, citing Long and Johnson, *People vs. Property*, 49.

95. Ibid.

96. "Letter from the Big Brothers Association to the W.P.A.," January 1938.

97. Ibid.

98. Letter from Horace Cayton to Fred Kramer (enclosed in a letter from Cayton to Louis Wirth), March 3, 1944, Box 2, Folder 5, Louis Wirth Papers, Special Collections Research Center, University of Chicago Library.

99. An interview with a knowledgeable Chicago attorney in 1945 revealed that some restrictive agreements existed against Jews, but that these "were either unchallenged or unenforced." See Washington, "Study of Restrictive Covenants in Chicago."

100. See John R. Logan and Harvey L. Molotch, *Urban Fortunes: The Political Economy of Place* (Berkeley and Los Angeles: University of California Press, 1987).

101. Long and Johnson, *People vs. Property*, 12; and Lindstrom, "Negro Invasion of the Washington Park Subdivision."

102. Drake, "*Black Metropolis* Revisited," 7.

103. Cayton, *Long Old Road*, 247–48.

104. "Record of Conversation with Horace Cayton," February 16, 1940, Sc Micro F-13242, Ser. 2, No. 15, Carnegie-Myrdal Study of the Negro in America research memoranda collection, Schomburg Center for Research in Black Culture, New York Public Library.

105. Walter A. Jackson, *Gunnar Myrdal and America's Conscience: Social Engineering and Racial Liberalism, 1938–1987* (Chapel Hill: University of North Carolina Press, 1990), xvii; and Stephen Steinberg, *Turning Back: The Retreat from Racial Justice in American Thought and Policy* (Boston: Beacon Press, 1995), 21.

106. Oliver Cox, *Race, Caste, and Class* (New York: Monthly Review Press, 1948), 509, cited in Steinberg, *Turning Back*, 45.

107. Robert K. Merton, "Insiders and Outsiders: A Chapter in the Sociology of Knowledge," *American Journal of Sociology* 78, no. 1 (July 1972): 33.

108. Myrdal, *American Dilemma*, xviii.

109. Ibid., xviii–xix.
110. Steinberg, *Turning Back*, 26–27.
111. Myrdal, *American Dilemma*, xviii.
112. Ibid.
113. Jackson, *Gunnar Myrdal*, 131.
114. Harvey Zorbaugh, "The Natural Areas of the City," in *Urban Community*, ed. Burgess, 217.
115. "Myrdal Correspondence," n.d., Sc Micro F-13242, Ser. 2, No. 15, Carnegie-Myrdal Study of the Negro in America research memoranda collection, Schomburg Center for Research in Black Culture, New York Public Library.
116. Bulmer, *Chicago School of Sociology*, 37.
117. Patrick J. Gilpin and Marybeth Gasman, *Charles S. Johnson: Leadership Beyond the Veil in the Age of Jim Crow* (Albany: State University of New York Press, 2003), 71.
118. "Myrdal Correspondence."
119. "Record of Interview: CD and Horace Cayton," July 24, 1940, Sc Micro F-13242, Set 2, No. 15, Carnegie-Myrdal Study of the Negro in America research memoranda collection, Schomburg Center for Research in Black Culture, New York Public Library.
120. Ibid.
121. "Myrdal Correspondence."
122. "Cayton to Myrdal," June 14, 1939, Sc Micro F-13242, Ser. 2, No. 15, Carnegie-Myrdal Study of the Negro in America research memoranda collection, Schomburg Center for Research in Black Culture, New York Public Library.
123. "Myrdal Correspondence," January 15, 1940.
124. "Record of Conversation with Horace Cayton."
125. "Myrdal to Cayton," February 27, 1940, Sc Micro F-13242, Ser. 2, No. 15, Carnegie-Myrdal Study of the Negro in America research memoranda collection, Schomburg Center for Research in Black Culture, New York Public Library.
126. "Cayton to Myrdal," March 2, 1940, Box 2, Folder 5, Louis Wirth Papers, Special Collections, Research Center, University of Chicago Library.
127. Jackson, *Gunnar Myrdal*, 163, 170.
128. Myrdal, *American Dilemma*, 1050.
129. Ibid., 929. For an incisive and original discussion that places Myrdal's argument in a different context, see Khalil Gibran Muhammad, *The Condemnation of Blackness* (Cambridge, Mass.: Harvard University Press), 276–77.
130. Ibid., 75–76.
131. Ibid., xlviii.
132. Ibid., 1003.
133. Ibid., 1024.
134. Ibid., 48.
135. Ibid., 1001.
136. Ibid., xix.
137. Ibid., 75.
138. Ibid., 76, 1067.
139. Ibid., 1066.
140. Ibid., 28.

141. Ibid., 624.
142. Ibid., 618.
143. Ibid., 623.
144. Ibid., 618.
145. Ibid.
146. Ibid., 1010.
147. Ibid., 568.
148. Ibid., 1011.
149. Ibid., 1004.
150. Ibid., 749; and Gunnar Myrdal, "The Black Revolt in the South" (unpublished manuscript, April 9, 1974), 30.
151. Jackson, *Gunnar Myrdal*, 275.
152. Ibid., 252.
153. Myrdal, *American Dilemma*, 1034.
154. Robert Washington, "Horace Cayton: Reflections on an Unfulfilled Sociological Career," *American Sociologist* 28, no. 1 (Spring 1997): 63.
155. W. Lloyd Warner, Horace R. Cayton, and St. Clair Drake, "Proposal for *Black Metropolis*: A Study of Negro Life in a Northern City," n.d., Box 38, St. Clair Drake Papers, Schomburg Center for Research in Black Culture, New York Public Library.
156. Ibid.
157. "Letter to Director," January 6, 1980, Box 38, Folder 14, St. Clair Drake Papers, Schomburg Center for Research in Black Culture, New York Public Library.
158. "Letter to Lloyd Warner," October 1, 1944, Box 38, St. Clair Drake Papers, Schomburg Center for Research in Black Culture, New York Public Library. See also Peretz, "Making of *Black Metropolis*," 173.
159. Orville Prescott, Books of the Times, *New York Times*, December 28, 1945.
160. Drake and Cayton, *Black Metropolis*, 101, 109.
161. Ibid., 284.
162. Ibid., 285, 296.
163. Ibid., 266.
164. Ibid., 240–41.
165. Ibid., 188.
166. Ibid., 385.
167. St. Clair Drake, "The Social and Economic Status of the Negro in the United States," *Daedalus* 94, no. 4 (Fall 1965): 811.
168. Drake and Cayton, *Black Metropolis*, 385.
169. Ibid., 121.
170. Ibid., 122.
171. Ibid., 120.
172. Ibid., 124.
173. Ibid., 12.
174. Ibid., 201.
175. Ibid., 79.
176. Ibid., 174, 201.
177. Ibid., 382.
178. The complexity of this relationship is described best in Sundquist, *Strangers in*

the Land. For a sense of the black identification with Jews, see James Baldwin, "The Harlem Ghetto," *Commentary,* February 1, 1948, 165–70.

179. Drake and Cayton, *Black Metropolis,* 432.

180. Louis Harap, "Anti-Negroism Among Jews," *Negro Quarterly* 1, no. 2, (1942): 105–11, cited in Maurianne Adams and John Bracey, eds., *Strangers and Neighbors: Relations Between Blacks and Jews in the United States* (Amherst: University of Massachusetts Press, 1999), 445.

181. Drake and Cayton, *Black Metropolis,* 263.

182. Ibid., 381.

183. Homer Hoyt, *One Hundred Years of Land Values in Chicago* (Chicago: University of Chicago Press, 1933), 317, cited in Drake and Cayton, *Black Metropolis,* 175.

184. Drake and Cayton, *Black Metropolis,* 174.

185. Ibid., 114–15.

186. Ibid., 198.

187. Ibid., 206.

188. While Drake and Cayton did not believe that the ghetto was a social context that *necessarily* brought about the problems of the people that lived there, they also did not believe that the outcomes in specific neighborhoods could best be understood by focusing on the preexisting cultural and economic characteristics of the people who had moved there.

189. Drake and Cayton, *Black Metropolis,* 204.

190. Ibid., 202.

191. Ibid., 600.

192. Ibid., 603.

193. Ibid., 174.

194. Ibid., 175.

195. Ibid., 211.

196. Ibid., 268.

197. Ibid., 619.

198. Ibid., 583–84.

199. Ibid., 584.

200. Ibid.

201. Ibid., 246.

202. Ibid.

203. Ibid.

204. Ibid., 543.

205. Ibid.

206. Abbott, *Department and Discipline,* 41.

207. Drake and Cayton, *Black Metropolis,* 270–94.

208. "Everett Hughes to St. Clair Drake," n.d., Box 38, St. Clair Drake Papers, Schomburg Center for Research in Black Culture, New York Public Library.

209. Washington, "Horace Cayton," 66.

210. Ibid.

211. Ibid.

212. Clement E. Vose, *Caucasians Only: The Supreme Court, the NAACP, and the Restrictive Covenant Cases* (Berkeley and Los Angeles: University of California Press, 1967), xii.

213. Google's Ngram dataset is built from books and metadata (such as bibliographic information) taken from university libraries, publishers, and private collectors. Each book's metadata describe the year the book was published. The American English collection contains 3,333,271 digitized books, predominantly in English and published in the United States. The dataset we consider contains books published between 1920 and 1975 and totals 799,251 volumes. Books were digitized using optical character recognition (OCR), and those with low OCR quality were removed. The data are represented here as three-year moving averages, so the value observed at, for example, 1960 is the average of the values at 1959, 1960, and 1961. The same substantive conclusions follow from the unsmoothed data. See Jean-Baptiste Michel et al., "Quantitative Analysis of Culture Using Millions of Digitized Books," *Science* 331, no. 6014 (January 2011): 176–82.

214. Because the overall numbers are so low, I do not seek to draw any inferences from the data other than that references to the word "ghetto" spiked after—and not prior to—the Nazi ghettos.

215. I looked carefully at the individual uses of the word "ghetto" from the early part of the century to the 1930s in books cataloged by Google and found that most uses described the Jewish neighborhoods of the early part of the century, as well as the medieval and early modern Jewish ghettos. Searching on the words "Jewish ghetto" also confirms the overall findings: usage peaks a bit earlier and "black ghetto" is a slightly delayed echo of it.

216. "Negroes and Jews," *New York Amsterdam Star-News*, August 22, 1942.

217. "Drive Opens Today to Better Harlem: City-Wide Citizens' Unit Plans a Week-Long Program Aimed at 4 Objectives," *New York Times*, May 24, 1942.

3. HARLEM, 1965: KENNETH CLARK

1. For an important social and intellectual history of the era leading up to these events, see Jonathan Scott Holloway, *Confronting the Veil* (Chapel Hill: University of North Carolina Press, 2002).

2. Unless otherwise noted, all details of this story and of Clark's years at Howard and Columbia in the subsequent five paragraphs are from "Reminiscences of Kenneth Bancroft Clark, as Interviewed by Ed Edwin," 1976, 75, Columbia Oral History Archives, Rare Book and Manuscript Library, Columbia University.

3. "Negro Students Rush Congress Restaurant in Vain Effort to Test the Rule Barring Race," *New York Times*, March 18, 1934.

4. See Gerald Markowitz and David Rosner, *Children, Race, and Power: Kenneth and Mamie Clark's Northside Center* (New York: Routledge, 2000). This wonderful monograph goes far beyond its subject to present a detailed portrait of Kenneth and Mamie Clark.

5. "Reminiscences of Kenneth Bancroft Clark," 136.

6. Brown v. Board of Education of Topeka, 347 U.S. 483, 1954, 495.

7. Jack M. Bloom, *Class, Race, and the Civil Rights Movement* (Bloomington: Indiana University Press, 1987), 210.

8. "Reminiscences of Kenneth Bancroft Clark," 134.

9. Ibid., 148.

10. Ibid., 156.
11. Kenneth Clark, *Youth in the Ghetto: A Study of the Consequences of Powerlessness and a Blueprint for Change* (New York: Harlem Youth Opportunities Unlimited, 1964), 79–80.
12. Ibid., 401.
13. Malcolm X Network, *Malcolm X Interviewed by Dr. Kenneth Clark*, YouTube video, 2011, https://www.youtube.com/watch?v=T9C_e0EUbas.
14. Bloom, *Class, Race, and the Civil Rights Movement*, 199.
15. Ibid.
16. Herbert J. Gans, *The Urban Villagers: Group and Class in the Life of Italian-Americans* (New York: Free Press, 1962), 4.
17. Ibid.
18. Nathan Glazer and Daniel Patrick Moynihan, *Beyond the Melting Pot: The Negroes, Puerto Ricans, Jews, Italians, and Irish of New York City* (Cambridge, Mass.: MIT Press, 1963), 52.
19. Ibid., 43–44.
20. Ibid., 65.
21. St. Clair Drake, *Race Relations in a Time of Rapid Social Change: Report of a Survey* (New York: National Federation of Settlements and Neighborhood Centers, 1966), 9.
22. Ideas in this and the subsequent two paragraphs are drawn from Taeuber and Taeuber, *Negroes in Cities*, 1–8.
23. Drake, "Social and Economic Status of the Negro," 776.
24. Ibid.
25. Clark, *Youth in the Ghetto*, 79.
26. Myrdal, *American Dilemma*, 1069.
27. John D. Kasarda, "Caught in the Web of Change," *Society* 21, no. 1 (December 1983): 45.
28. California Governor's Commission on the Los Angeles Riots, *Violence in the City: An End or a Beginning? A Report* (Los Angeles, 1965).
29. Drake and Cayton, *Black Metropolis*, 218.
30. Ibid., 220.
31. Later published as John F. Kain, *The Effects of the Ghetto on the Distribution and Level of Nonwhite Employment in Urban Areas* (Santa Monica, Calif.: Rand Corporation, 1965).
32. See John F. Kain, *Essays on Urban Spatial Structure* (Cambridge, Mass.: Ballinger, 1975), 87–97.
33. Ibid., 342.
34. Ibid., 345.
35. See Edward L. Glaeser, Eric A. Hanushek, and John M. Quigley, "Opportunities, Race, and Urban Location: The Influence of John Kain," *Journal of Urban Economics* 56 (2004): 70–79.
36. Kain, *Essays on Urban Spatial Structure*, 344–45.
37. Lyndon B. Johnson, "To Fulfill These Rights: Commencement Address at Howard University," June 4, 1965, http://www.whatsoproudlywehail.org/wp-content/uploads/2013/01/Johnson_To-Fulfill-These-Rights.pdf.
38. Steven R. Weisman, ed., *Daniel Patrick Moynihan: A Portrait in Letters of an American Visionary* (New York: Public Affairs, 2010), 75.

39. Peter-Christian Aigner, "What the Left and the Right Both Got Wrong About the Moynihan Report," *The Atlantic*, April 6, 2014.

40. Daniel Patrick Moynihan, *The Negro Family: The Case for National Action* (Washington, D.C.: U.S. Department of Labor, Office of Policy Planning and Research, 1965), 19.

41. Ibid., 29.

42. Ibid., 5, 29.

43. Ibid., 5.

44. Ibid., 12.

45. Ibid., 16.

46. Ibid.

47. Ibid., 25.

48. Ibid., 44.

49. Ibid.

50. Ibid., 30.

51. Daniel Patrick Moynihan, "Employment, Income, and the Ordeal of the Negro Family," *Daedalus* 94, no. 4 (Fall 1965): 766.

52. Christopher Jencks, "The Moynihan Report," *New York Review of Books*, October 14, 1965.

53. Martin Luther King, Jr., "Family Planning—A Special and Urgent Concern," May 5, 1966, http://www.plannedparenthood.org/planned-parenthood-gulf-coast /mlkacceptance-speech.

54. Ibid.

55. Peter Kihss, "'Benign Neglect' on Race Is Proposed by Moynihan," *New York Times*, March 1, 1970.

56. Weisman, *Daniel Patrick Moynihan*, 116.

57. Ibid.

58. Myrdal, *American Dilemma*, 1069.

59. Ibid., 1068.

60. "7 Win Awards for Books at Ceremony in New York," *Evening Bulletin* (Philadelphia), March 9, 1967.

61. Oscar Lewis, *La Vida: A Puerto Rican Family in the Culture of Poverty, San Juan and New York* (London: Panther Books, 1968), 48.

62. Ibid., 53.

63. Ibid., 51.

64. See Rodolfo Stavenhagen's critique in Oscar Lewis, "Review: The Children of Sánchez, Pedro Martínez and La Vida," *Current Anthropology* 8, no. 5 (December 1967): 490.

65. Lewis, *La Vida*, 50.

66. Ibid., 57.

67. Ibid., 24.

68. Ibid., 54.

69. Ibid., 24.

70. Edward C. Banfield, *The Unheavenly City: The Nature and the Future of Our Urban Crisis* (Boston: Little, Brown, 1968), 125.

71. Ibid., 126.

72. See, for example, Charles A. Valentine, *Culture and Poverty: Critique and Counter-Proposals* (Chicago and London: University of Chicago Press, 1968), 144.

73. Douglas Butterworth, "Oscar Lewis, 1914–1970," *American Anthropologist* 74, no. 3 (June 1972): 750; also Micaela di Leonardo, *Exotics at Home* (Chicago: University of Chicago Press, 1998) (see generally).

74. Oscar Lewis, "The Culture of Poverty," *Scientific American* 215, no. 4 (October 1966): 20.

75. Ibid., 25.

76. Ibid., 23.

77. Howard M. Bahr, Theodore T. Johnson, and M. Ray Seitz, "Influential Scholars and Works in the Sociology of Race and Minority Relations, 1944–1968," *American Sociologist* 6, no. 4 (November 1971): 297.

78. Charles E. Silberman, *Crisis in Black and White* (New York: Vintage Books, 1964), 10. See also Jackson, *Gunnar Myrdal*, 302; and Steinberg, *Turning Back*, 72.

79. Silberman, *Crisis in Black and White*, 10.

80. See Carl Degler's view to this effect in his famous article on Myrdal in *The New York Times*, as summarized in Steinberg, *Turning Back*, 65–67.

81. James Baldwin et al., "Liberalism and the Negro: A Round-Table Discussion," *Commentary*, March 1, 1964, 39.

82. Ibid., 41.

83. Carl N. Degler, "The Negro in America: Where Myrdal Went Wrong," *New York Times Magazine*, December 7, 1969.

84. Myrdal, *American Dilemma*, 1069.

85. Kenneth B. Clark, *Dark Ghetto: Dilemmas of Social Power* (New York: Harper and Row, 1965), xv.

86. Ibid., xvii.

87. Ibid., 79–80.

88. Ibid., 80.

89. Ibid., 63.

90. Ibid., 63–64.

91. Ibid., 11.

92. Ibid., 174.

93. Ibid., 10–11, 79–80.

94. Ibid., 156.

95. Ibid., 171.

96. Ibid., 156.

97. Ibid., 34.

98. Ibid., 107.

99. Ibid., 95.

100. Ibid., 109.

101. Ibid., 238.

102. Betty Friedan, *The Feminine Mystique* (New York: Norton, 2001), 15.

103. Clark, *Dark Ghetto*, 148.

104. Ibid., 115.

105. Ibid., 117–18.

106. Ibid., 204.

107. Ibid., book jacket.

108. "Kenneth Clark to Grayson Kirk," July 12, 1966, General Correspondence, Box 28, Kenneth Bancroft Clark Papers, Manuscript Division, Library of Congress, Washington, D.C.

109. Albert Murray, *The Omni-Americans: Black Experience and American Culture* (New York: Harper and Row, 1966), 75–76.
110. Ibid., 26.
111. Ibid.
112. In this section, I draw on my earlier article: Mitchell Duneier, "On the Legacy of Elliot Liebow and Carol Stack: Context-Driven Fieldwork and the Need for Continuous Ethnography," *Focus* 25, no. 1 (Spring–Summer 2007): 33–38.
113. Elliot Liebow, *Tally's Corner: A Study of Negro Streetcorner Men* (Boston: Little, Brown, 1967), 211.
114. Ibid., 212–13.
115. Ibid., 213.
116. Carol B. Stack, *All Our Kin: Strategies for Survival in a Black Community* (New York: Harper and Row, 1974), 57.
117. Ibid.
118. Ibid., 39.
119. Ibid., 127.
120. Kenneth B. Clark, "The Riots Within the Human Spirit" (unpublished manuscript, 1967), Kenneth Bancroft Clark Papers, Manuscript Division, Library of Congress, Washington, D.C. Clark's subjective response, as depicted in this section, draws on this memoir.
121. Ibid., 2–3.
122. Ibid., 3.
123. Ibid., 5.
124. Ibid., 8.
125. Ibid.
126. Steven V. Roberts, "Black Studies Aim to Change Things," *New York Times*, May 15, 1969, 49.
127. Ibid.
128. St. Clair Drake, "Exploratory Research on Types of Black Communities in the United States That Have Not Been Adequately Studied," n.d., Box 2, Folder 21, St. Clair Drake Papers, Schomburg Center for Research in Black Culture, New York Public Library.
129. St. Clair Drake, "Letter to the *Stanford Daily*," n.d., St. Clair Drake Papers, Schomburg Center for Research in Black Culture, New York Public Library.
130. Robert Blauner, *Racial Oppression in America* (New York: Harper and Row, 1972), 12.
131. Ibid., 21–22. Here Blauner relies on the work of Albert Memmi.
132. Ibid., 22.
133. Ibid.
134. Ibid., 28–29.
135. These sentences on connections between the gay civil rights programs and black organizations are drawn from Laud Humphreys, *Out of the Closets: The Sociology of Homosexual Liberation* (Englewood Cliffs, N.J.: Prentice-Hall, 1972), 61.
136. Carl Wittman, "A Gay Manifesto" (New York: Red Butterfly, 1970), 1.
137. Harvey L. Molotch, "Gay Ghetto" (unpublished lecture, Princeton University, July 20, 2013). For an exemplary updated study, see also Amin Ghaziani, *There Goes the Gayborhood?* (Princeton, N.J.: Princeton University Press, 2014).
138. John T. Metzger, "Rebuilding Harlem: Public Housing and Urban Renewal, 1920–1960," *Planning Perspectives* 9 (1994): 256.

139. Kenneth B. Clark, *The Negro Protest: James Baldwin, Malcolm X, and Martin Luther King Talk with Kenneth B. Clark* (Boston: Beacon Press, 1963), 9.

140. Kenneth B. Clark, "Beyond the Ghetto" (unpublished manuscript, August 6, 1979), 28–29, Kenneth Bancroft Clark Papers, Manuscript Division, Library of Congress, Washington, D.C.

141. Jonathan T. Rothwell and Douglas S. Massey, "The Effect of Density Zoning on Racial Segregation of Racial Minorities in the U.S Urban Areas," *Urban Affairs Review* 44: 799–806.

142. Nicholas Lemann, *The Promised Land: The Great Black Migration and How It Changed America* (New York: Vintage Books, 1992).

143. Hirsch, *Making the Second Ghetto*, xi.

144. Charles Abrams, *The City Is the Frontier* (New York: Harper and Row, 1967), 22.

145. Ibid.

146. Clark, "Beyond the Ghetto," 141–42.

147. Ibid., 161.

148. Ibid. For the Marxist school of urban sociology, see Logan and Molotch, *Urban Fortunes*; John Mollenkopf, *The Contested City* (Princeton, N. J.: Princeton University Press, 1983); and David Harvey, *Social Justice and the City* (Baltimore: Johns Hopkins University Press, 1973).

149. "The Sveriges Riksbank Prize in Economic Sciences in Memory of Alfred Nobel" (Nobel Media, 1974), http://www.nobelprize.org/nobel_prizes/economic-sciences/laureates/1974/.

150. "Reminiscenes of Kenneth Bancroft Clark."

4. CHICAGO, 1987: WILLIAM JULIUS WILSON

1. I first discovered the phrase "America's Jews" in Eric Sundquist's monumental *Strangers in the Land*. It is impossible to overstate the breadth, depth, and originality of this work for an understanding of relations between Jews and blacks.

2. William Julius Wilson, "Poor Blacks' Future," *New York Times*, February 28, 1978, 33.

3. Ibid.

4. Frank Harold Wilson, *Race, Class, and the Postindustrial City: William Julius Wilson and the Promise of Sociology* (Albany: State University of New York Press, 2004), 1–4. This book, based on a vast knowledge of social science and its history, is the most comprehensive treatment of Wilson's work to date.

5. Gordon D. Morgan, "The Training of Black Sociologists," *Teaching Sociology* 7, no. 2 (January 1980): 117.

6. Gretchen Reynolds, "The Rising Significance of Race," *Chicago*, December 1992, 84, cited in Wilson, *Race, Class, and the Postindustrial City*, 7.

7. William Julius Wilson, *Power, Racism, and Privilege: Race Relations in Theoretical and Sociohistorical Perspectives* (New York: Free Press, 1973).

8. Milton M. Gordon, *Assimilation in American Life: The Role of Race, Religion, and National Origins* (New York: Oxford University Press, 1964), 53.

9. Ibid., 264.

10. Thomas F. Pettigrew, "The Changing, but Not Declining, Significance of Race," *Michigan Law Review* 77, no. 3 (March 1979): 917–24.

11. The idea originated with a comment that Richard Alba made to me.

12. William Julius Wilson, *The Declining Significance of Race: Blacks and Changing American Institutions*, 3rd ed. (Chicago and London: University of Chicago Press, 2012), 136.

13. Kenneth B. Clark, "No. No. Race, Not Class, Is Still at the Wheel," *New York Times*, March 22, 1978.

14. Ibid.

15. Wilson, *Race, Class, and the Postindustrial City*, 19.

16. See Drake, "Social and Economic Status of the Negro in the United States."

17. "Gunnar Myrdal–Kenneth Clark Seminar: The American Dilemma Revisited," March 17, 1975, 7, Kenneth Bancroft Clark Papers, Manuscript Division, Library of Congress, Washington, D.C.

18. Charles Murray, *Losing Ground: American Social Policy, 1950–1980* (New York: Basic Books, 1984), 14.

19. Ibid., 24–25.

20. Ibid., 14.

21. See, for example, Paul Starr, "Not Simply Black and White: Race," *New York Times*, January 7, 1979.

22. Wilson, *Declining Significance of Race*, 1.

23. Herbert J. Gans, *The War Against the Poor: The Underclass and Antipoverty Policy* (New York: Basic Books, 1995), is partly a study of the history of the idea of the underclass. He presents this quote from the *Time* cover story, but does not mention Wilson's book of six months later. In Michael B. Katz, *The Undeserving Poor: America's Enduring Confrontation with Poverty* (New York: Oxford University Press, 2013), the other prominent history covering this subject, the author also makes no reference to *The Declining Significance of Race*.

24. Wilson, *Declining Significance of Race*, 120.

25. Ibid., 166.

26. Ibid., 134.

27. Ibid., 108.

28. Ibid., 108–9.

29. Ibid., 108.

30. Ibid.

31. Ken Auletta, *The Underclass* (New York: Random House, 1982).

32. Murray, *Losing Ground*, 24–25.

33. Eric Sorensen, "Race, Class, and William Julius Wilson's World of Opportunity," *Washington State Magazine*, Fall 2012.

34. Jason DeParle, "Daring Research or 'Social Science Pornography'?," *New York Times*, October 9, 1994.

35. Murray, *Losing Ground*, 220.

36. Ibid., 75.

37. Ibid., 184–85.

38. Ibid., 185.

39. Ibid., 188.

40. Ibid., 190.

41. Ibid., 226.

42. Paul Starr, "Losing More Ground," *New Republic*, December 5, 1988, 32–36.

43. Christopher Jencks, *Rethinking Social Policy: Race, Poverty, and the Underclass* (Cambridge, Mass.: Harvard University Press, 1992), 85.

44. Ibid., 87.
45. As noted in Steinberg, *Turning Back*, 267n45, at least one book published at the same time as *Truly Disadvantaged* refers to the book as forthcoming under the title *Hidden Agenda*. See, for example, Logan and Molotch, *Urban Fortunes*, 361.
46. Bill Moyers, *A World of Ideas: Conversations with Thoughtful Men and Women About American Life Today and the Ideas Shaping Our Future*, ed. Betty Sue Flowers (New York: Doubleday, 1989), 77.
47. Ibid.
48. William Julius Wilson, *The Truly Disadvantaged: The Inner City, the Underclass, and Public Policy* (Chicago: University of Chicago Press, 1987), 7.
49. Ibid., 8.
50. Ibid., 6.
51. Ibid., 137.
52. Ibid., 83.
53. Ibid., 101.
54. Ibid., 102.
55. Ibid., 46.
56. Ibid., 58.
57. Ibid., 138.
58. Ibid., 58–59.
59. Ibid., 56.
60. Ibid., 57.
61. Douglas S. Massey and Nancy A. Denton, *American Apartheid: Segregation and the Making of the Underclass* (Cambridge, Mass.: Harvard University Press, 1993), 9.
62. Ibid., 8.
63. Ibid., 162–65.
64. See the earlier studies referenced in William Labov, *Dialect Diversity in America: The Politics of Language Change* (Charlottesville and London: University of Virginia Press, 2012), 55.
65. William Labov and Wendell A. Harris, "De Facto Segregation of Black and White Vernaculars," in *Diversity and Diachrony*, ed. David Sankoff (Amsterdam and Philadelphia: John Benjamins, 1986), 20.
66. Massey and Denton, *American Apartheid*, 15.
67. Statistic collected using the interactive tool of the Philadelphia Police Department, available at "Homicides in Philadelphia," *Philly.com*, n.d., http://www .philly.com/philly/news/special_packages/inquirer/Philadelphia_Homicides _1988_2011.html.
68. Elijah Anderson, *Streetwise: Race, Class, and Change in an Urban Community* (Chicago: University of Chicago Press, 1990), 164.
69. Ibid., 167.
70. Ibid., 172.
71. Ibid., 182.
72. Ibid., 167.
73. See Roger Waldinger, *Still the Promised City? African-Americans and New Immigrants in Postindustrial New York* (Cambridge, Mass.: Harvard University Press, 1996).
74. Wilson, *Truly Disadvantaged*, 102.

75. Waldinger, *Still the Promised City?*, 172–73.
76. Ibid., 234.
77. Ibid., 172.
78. Ibid., 316.
79. bell hooks, *Feminist Theory: From Margin to Center* (Boston: South End Press, 1984), 98.
80. See Combahee River Collective, "The Combahee River Collective Statement," in *Home Girls: A Black Feminist Anthology*, ed. Barbara Smith (New Brunswick, N.J., and London: Rutgers University Press, 2000), 264–74.
81. Gordon, *Assimilation in American Life*, 264.
82. Patricia Hill Collins, *Black Feminist Thought: Knowledge, Consciousness, and the Politics of Empowerment*, 2nd ed. (New York and London: Routledge, 2000), 244.
83. John D. Kasarda and Kwok-fai Ting, "Joblessness and Poverty in America's Central Cities: Causes and Policy Prescriptions," *Housing Policy Debate* 7, no. 2 (1996): 412.
84. Xavier de Souza Briggs, Susan J. Popkin, and John M. Goering, *Moving to Opportunity: The Story of an American Experiment to Fight Ghetto Poverty* (New York: Oxford University Press, 2010), 41–42.
85. David Remnick, "Dr. Wilson's Neighborhood," *New Yorker*, April 29, 1996, 105.
86. William Julius Wilson, *When Work Disappears: The World of the New Urban Poor* (New York: Alfred A. Knopf, 1996), 12.
87. Paul A. Jargowsky and Mary Jo Bane, "Ghetto Poverty in the United States, 1970–1980," in *The Urban Underclass*, ed. Christopher Jencks and Paul E. Peterson (Washington, D.C.: Brookings Institution, 1991), 8–9, cited in William Julius Wilson, "The Underclass: Issues, Perspectives, and Public Policy," in *The Ghetto Underclass: Social Science Perspectives*, ed. William Julius Wilson (Newbury Park, Calif.: Sage Publications, 1993), 13.
88. Wilson, *When Work Disappears*, xxi.
89. Ibid., 16.
90. Ibid., 6, 46.
91. Ibid., 122.
92. Ibid., 127.
93. Ibid., 131.
94. Orlando Patterson, *The Ordeal of Integration: Progress and Resentment in America's "Racial" Crisis* (New York: Basic Civitas, 1997), 134.
95. Wilson's disciple and collaborator Loïc Wacquant critiqued this perspective, arguing that it left out what he saw as deliberate institutionalized structures that either held people down or placed them in prison.
96. Welfare Reform Working Group, "President Clinton, NBC News Interview 12/3/93: Response to Charles Murray," May 3, 1994, William J. Clinton Presidential Library, http://www.clintonlibrary.gov/assets/storage/Research-Digital-Library/dpc/reed-welfare/20/612964-meetings-2.pdf.
97. I thank Paul Starr for making this point to me, as well as for his ideas on the significant differences between Murray and the liberal social scientists who influenced welfare reform.
98. David Ellwood, *Poor Support: Poverty in the American Family* (New York: Basic Books, 1988), 180.

99. I thank Paul Starr for making this point to me.

100. Peter Edelman, "The Worst Thing Bill Clinton Has Done," *Atlantic Monthly*, March 1997, 44.

101. Ibid.

102. See Katherine S. Newman, *Chutes and Ladders: Navigating the Low-Wage Labor Market* (New York: Russell Sage Foundation, 2006). Edelman himself would spend many years trying to understand the impact of welfare reform, concluding, "The unavailability of welfare is a major contributor to deep poverty. The percentage of families in deep poverty rose by nearly half between 1994 and 2004, with the unavailability of welfare identified as a major cause of the increase.... One in five low-income single mothers neither worked nor received government cash assistance during the 2004–2008 period, as opposed to one in eight in 1996–1997." See Peter Edelman, *So Rich, So Poor: Why It's So Hard to End Poverty in America* (New York: New Press, 2012), 97. For the most up-to-date and devastating assessment, see Kathryn Edin and H. Luke Shaefer, *$2.00 a Day: Living on Almost Nothing* (New York: Houghton Mifflin Harcourt, 2015).

103. Leonard S. Rubinowitz and James Rosenbaum, *Crossing the Class and Color Lines: From Public Housing to White Suburbia* (Chicago: University of Chicago Press, 2000).

104. The scientific validity of studies such as those of Gautreaux and others that relied on observational data was compromised by the lack of a rigorous experimental design—namely, residents got to self-select where they moved, introducing uncertainties about whether better neighborhoods caused better outcomes or merely attracted go-getters who would have succeeded no matter where they ended up. In other words, neighborhoods can act as a filter, just as research shows that immigrant groups who face the hardest challenges getting to the United States tend to thrive the most—the harder the gradient they must swim against to get here, the more they are selected for the most entrepreneurial, savvy movers.

105. Susan E. Mayer and Christopher Jencks, "Growing Up in Poor Neighborhoods: How Much Does It Matter?," *Science* 243, no. 4897 (March 17, 1989): 1441–45.

106. Susan Clampet-Lundquist and Douglas S. Massey, "Neighborhood Effects on Economic Self-Sufficiency: A Reconsideration of the Moving to Opportunity Experiment," *American Journal of Sociology* 114, no. 1 (July 2008): 116.

107. Ibid., 113.

108. Jay Mathews, "Neighborhoods' Effect on Grades Challenged; Moving Students out of Poor Inner Cities Yields Little, Studies of HUD Vouchers Say," *Washington Post*, August 14, 2007.

109. Robert J. Sampson, "Moving to Inequality: Neighborhood Effects and Experiments Meet Social Structure," *American Journal of Sociology* 114, no. 1 (July 2008): 189–231.

110. Robert J. Sampson, *Great American City: Chicago and the Enduring Neighborhood Effect* (Chicago and London: University of Chicago Press, 2012), 285.

111. Clampet-Lundquist and Massey, "Neighborhood Effects on Economic Self-Sufficiency," 116.

112. Ibid.

113. Ibid., 139.

114. Jens Ludwig et al., "Neighborhoods, Obesity, and Diabetes: A Randomized Social Experiment," *New England Journal of Medicine* 365 (2011): 1509–19.

115. Ibid., as suggested.
116. Ronald C. Kessler et al., "Associations of Housing Mobility Interventions for Children in High-Poverty Neighborhoods with Subsequent Mental Disorders During Adolescence," *Journal of the American Medical Association* 311, no. 9 (2014): 937–47.
117. Briggs, Popkin, and Goering, *Moving to Opportunity*, v.
118. Raj Chetty, Nathaniel Hendren, and Lawrence F. Katz, "The Effects of Exposure to Better Neighborhoods on Children: New Evidence from the Moving to Opportunity Experiment" (working paper, Harvard University and NBER, May 2015).
119. However, since this was not a true experiment, supposed neighborhood effects could still reflect the impact of other "time-varying" factors. For instance, it could be that parents move to a higher-quality neighborhood when they get a good job or marry or merely attain a greater level of maturity—it could be these changes that drive the effects for their children. In that case, neighborhood conditions merely act as a proxy for the rising and falling fortunes of families (and the siblings within them). Of course, the economists can try to factor out conditions that vary over time along with neighborhoods—such as parental income or marital status—but they cannot eliminate all the possible other factors that could be driving their results. Such "unobserved" differences might range from parental depression to net-worth changes that are not reflected in IRS data. Further, differences between the children themselves might actually cause the parents to move. Think of a family with a precocious, gifted second-born child that moves to a high-quality neighborhood so that she can attend a great school. In this case, the child's ability causes the neighborhood change, rather than the neighborhood causing the child to thrive vis-à-vis her older sibling.

Chetty and Hendren estimate their effects based on families who moved. This raises three additional issues. First, as Robert Sampson pointed out with regard to the MTO experiment, the move itself could have a detrimental effect on the older child, which then presents in the data as an effect of neighborhood conditions when it is really the disruptive effect of moving during adolescence (bad) versus moving when in early childhood (not so bad). Second, the treatment of "good neighborhood" may have an effect only on the "movers"—that is, only on families who are mobile and not on all families. These may be families who are responsive to their local conditions, for example. Finally, as the sociologist Dalton Conley has argued in his book *The Pecking Order*, moving may accentuate differences between siblings, thus making them appear larger, in essence, than the true treatment effect of the neighborhood would be if we compared across families (without selection bias). This would occur if siblings used their different neighborhood exposures to define their respective niches in the family, for instance, one embracing a more "street" attitude in response to moving while the other defines himself against the identity of his elder sibling. For an appreciation of the complexity of within-family dynamics, see Dalton Conley, *The Pecking Order: A Bold New Look at How Family and Society Determine Who We Become* (New York: Vintage, 2005).
120. Peter Dreier, "Moving from the Hood: The Mixed Success of Integrating Suburbia," *American Prospect*, December 10, 2001, 11.
121. Brown v. Board of Education of Topeka, 495.
122. Steinberg, *Turning Back*, 267.

123. See, for example, Steinberg's analysis of both Myrdal and Wilson in *Turning Back*.
124. Steinberg, *Turning Back*, 126.

5. HARLEM, 2004: GEOFFREY CANADA

1. See Geoffrey Canada, *Fist Stick Knife Gun: A Personal History of Violence in America* (Boston: Beacon Press, 1995). Canada's book is the best source on his life. Though he bears no responsibility for the interpretation I have put to them, all of my descriptions of his life are derived from this source unless otherwise noted.
   On learning the code of the street, see pp. 13, 15–16, 21, 36–37, 60; on the hierarchy of street fights, see pp. 21, 30–32, 51, 59, 61; on the ghetto before guns, see pp. 53, 61, 69–71; on the K55 knife, see pp. 71, 73–74; on Canada's beginnings at Bowdoin, see pp. 24, 77–78; on Canada's first gun, see pp. 24, 100–3; on working at the Robert White School, see pp. 23–28; on the Rheedlen Center for Children and Families, see pp. 89, 107, 110–112; on the introduction of guns and crack to the ghetto, see pp. 78–81, 90; on shifting norms of interaction, see pp. 35–36, 84–86, 100; on responses to violence in the ghetto, see pp. 124–26, 130–33; on the development of the Beacon Model, see chapter 20 and pp. 135–37, 139–41, 144–45; on Canada's thoughts on funding for jails, see p. 133.
2. Paul Tough, *Whatever It Takes: Geoffrey Canada's Quest to Change Harlem and America* (Boston: Houghton Mifflin, 2008), 53–55. The material in this paragraph is derived from this source, an outstanding on-the-scene account of the Harlem Children's Zone. All of my descriptions of on-the-ground events in the Harlem Children's Zone came from this source, though Tough is not responsible for my interpretations.
   On Joyce Henderson and family, see pp. 53–55; on Canada's response to violence in the ghetto, see p. 30; on Canada's "tipping point" theory of positive contamination, see pp. 3–4, 123, 125; on Stanley Druckenmiller, see pp. 9–10; on Baby College, see pp. 4–5, 58, 66; on Promise Academy, see pp. 4–6, 8; on the Promise Academy lottery, see pp. 1, 8–9, 12, 15–16, 18; on test scores, see pp. 132–33, 153; on Canada and his funders, see pp. 156–65, 168, 250–51; on restructuring the Harlem Children's Zone, see pp. 135, 144–45, 167–68, 170–71, 175, 179, 182–83, 240; on the March 2007 letter, see p. 234; on Canada's forthrightness, see pp. 234–35, 284; on students' reactions to Canada's announcement, see p. 238; on Canada's address to the eighth-grade class, see pp. 239–40, 243–44; on the meeting with parents, see pp. 246–47; on dominant theories in 2007, see pp. 234–35; on the Harlem Gems, see pp. 195, 198, 205–8; on the importance of early childhood education, see chapter 9 and pp. 193–94 and 197; on Tough's vision for the Harlem Children's Zone, see pp. 281–83.
3. Ibid., 53–54.
4. David Garland, *The Culture of Control: Crime and Social Order in Contemporary Society* (Oxford: Oxford University Press, 2001), 132.
5. "A Look Inside: Countee Cullen Beacon Center" (Harlem Children's Zone, July 1, 2006), http://wac.adef.edgecastcdn.net/80ADEF/hcz.org/wp-content/uploads/2014/04/ALI-CounteeCullen.pdf.

6. Malcolm Gladwell, *The Tipping Point: How Little Things Can Make a Big Difference* (Boston: Little, Brown, 2000), 168.

7. Tough, *Whatever It Takes*, 4.

8. Bowdoin College, *Geoffrey Canada '74 and Stanley Druckenmiller '75: Generational Theft*, Vimeo video, 2013, at 26:30, https://vimeo.com/65731171.

9. Becky Pettit and Bruce Western, "Mass Imprisonment and the Life Course: Race and Class Inequality in U.S. Incarceration," *American Sociological Review* 69, no. 151 (April 2004): 161.

10. Diane Ravitch, "Charter School Leader Paid $553,000 Yearly," *Diane Ravitch's Blog: A Site to Discuss Education for All*, July 28, 2012, http://dianeravitch.net /2012/07/28/charter-school-leader-paid-553000-yearly/.

11. Harlem Children's Zone, *Barack Obama on the Harlem Children's Zone*, YouTube video, 2008, https://www.youtube.com/watch?v=Xh5QRMaa_KE. See also Tough, *Whatever It Takes*, 265–66.

12. Amanda Erickson, "Why Hasn't the Harlem Children's Zone Been Replicated Even Without Obama's Help?," *CityLab* from *The Atlantic*, August 16, 2012, http://www.citylab.com/politics/2012/08/why-hasnt-harlem-childrens-zone-been -replicated-even-without-obamas-help/2968/.

13. David Brooks, "The Harlem Miracle," *New York Times*, May 8, 2009.

14. Will Dobbie and Roland G. Fryer, Jr., "Are High-Quality Schools Enough to Increase Achievement Among the Poor? Evidence from the Harlem Children's Zone," *American Economic Journal: Applied Economics* 3, no. 3 (July 2011): 158.

15. Brooks, "Harlem Miracle."

16. Letter from Geoffrey Canada to Roland Fryer and Philip Kasinitz, December 8, 2010.

17. Tough, *Whatever It Takes*, 283.

18. Charles Murray, "On Being a Killjoy," *AEIdeas*, May 11, 2009, http://www.aei.org /publication/on-being-a-killjoy/.

19. James M. Quane and William Julius Wilson, "All Together Now, One by One: Building Capacity for Urban Education Reform in Promise Neighborhoods," *Pathways*, Summer 2011, 11.

20. Ibid.

21. Ibid., 12.

22. Ibid.

23. Clark, *Dark Ghetto*, 117–18.

24. "Can the Newly-Reelected Obama Save the American Public School? A Conversation Between William Julius Wilson and Sylvie Laurent," *Pathways*, Fall 2012, 29.

25. Cited in Peter Dreier, "Philanthropy's Misguided Ideas for Fixing Ghetto Poverty: The Limits of Free Markets and Place-Based Initiatives," *Non-Profit Quarterly*, March 19, 2015. https://nonprofitquarterly.org/2015/03/19/philan thropy-ideas-for-fixing-ghetto-poverty-the-limits-of-free-markets-and-place -based-initiatives.

6. THE FORGOTTEN GHETTO

1. Du Bois, "Negro and the Warsaw Ghetto," fn. 1.

2. See Loïc Wacquant, "Deadly Symbiosis: When Ghetto and Prison Meet and

Mesh," *Punishment and Society* 3, no. 1 (2001): 95–134; and Michelle Alexander, *New Jim Crow.*

3. My use of the word "semi-flourishing" (instead of "flourishing") is meant to high-light that there were still major gaps in such basic measures as life expectancy. Men born in the ghetto in the early fifties had a life expectancy of fifty-nine years, while white men could be expected to live to age sixty-six. These gaps would only increase over time. See Reeve Vanneman, "Life Expectancy by Race and Gender" [PowerPoint slide], www.vanneman.umd.edu/socy441/trends/liferace.html.

4. Vanessa Barker, *The Politics of Imprisonment: How the Democratic Process Shapes the Way America Punishes Offenders* (New York: Oxford University Press, 2009), 151, quoted in James Forman, Jr., "Racial Critiques of Mass Incarceration," *New York University Law Review* 87, no. 1 (2012): 115.

5. See Issa Kohler-Hausmann, "Misdemeanor Justice: Control Without Conviction," *American Journal of Sociology* 119, no. 2 (September 2013): 351–93; Issa Kohler-Hausmann, "Managerial Justice and Mass Misdemeanors," *Stanford Law Review* 66, no. 3 (March 2014): 611–94; and Alice Goffman, "On the Run: Wanted Men in a Philadelphia Ghetto," *American Sociological Review* 74, no.3 (June 2009): 355.

6. Loïc Wacquant's unparalleled body of work, including his contrast of the U.S. and French cases, is the closest contemporary example of such an effort within the social sciences. See *Urban Outcasts.* For an impressive recent effort by a historian, see Carl H. Nightingale, *Segregation: A Global History of Divided Cities* (Chicago: University of Chicago Press, 2012).

7. Richard Alba and Steven Romelewsky, "The End of Segregation? Hardly" (Center for Urban Research, March 2012).

8. Peter Dreier and Todd Swanstrom, "Suburban Ghettos Like Ferguson Are Ticking Time Bombs," *Washington Post*, August 21, 2014.

9. John R. Logan, "The Persistence of Segregation in the 21st Century Metropolis," *City & Community* 12, no. 2 (June 2013): 160–68, in the Supreme Court of the United States, Brief of Housing Scholars as Amici Curiae Supporting Respondent, Texas Department of Housing and Community Affairs et al. v. The Inclusive Communities Project, Inc.; Jacob S. Rugh and Douglas Massey, "Racial Segregation and the American Foreclosure Crisis," *American Sociological Review* 75, no. 5 (October 2010): 629–51; and Richard Rothstein, "A Comment on Bank of America/Countrywide's Discriminatory Mortgage Lending and Its Implications for Racial Segregation," EPI Briefing Paper #335 (Economic Policy Institute, January 23, 2012).

10. Douglas S. Massey et al., *Climbing Mount Laurel: The Struggle for Affordable Housing and Social Mobility in an American Suburb* (Princeton, N.J.: Princeton University Press, 2013), 19.

11. See Myrdal, *American Dilemma*; and Drake and Cayton, *Black Metropolis.*

12. Myrdal, *American Dilemma*, 618.

13. In his influential essay, Mario Small has argued that some definitions of the ghetto make no assumptions about power, while others do. He uses the term "strong conceptions" to characterize definitions such as this one, arguing that purely demographic conceptions are "benign" with regard to such assumptions. See Small, "Four Reasons to Abandon the Idea of 'The Ghetto.'"

14. Drake and Cayton, *Black Metropolis*, 174–213.

15. See Melvin Oliver and Thomas Shapiro, *Black Wealth/White Wealth: A New Perspective on Racial Inequality* (New York: Routledge, 1995); Dalton Conley, *Being Black, Living in the Red* (Berkeley: University of California Press, 1999); Ta-Nehisi Coates, "The Case for Reparations," *The Atlantic*, June 2014; and in the Supreme Court of the United States, Brief of Housing Scholars.

16. George J. Sánchez, *Becoming Mexican American: Ethnicity, Culture, and Identity in Chicano Los Angeles, 1900–1945* (New York: Oxford University Press, 1993), 77; Ricardo Romo, *East Los Angeles: History of a Barrio* (Austin: University of Texas Press, 1983); and Arlene Dávila, *Barrio Dreams* (Berkeley: University of California Press, 2004). See also Edward Telles and Vilma Ortiz, *Generations of Exclusion* (New York: Russell Sage Foundation, 2008); Tomás Jiménez, *Replenished Ethnicity: Mexican Americans, Immigration, and Identity* (Berkeley: University of California Press, 2009); and Mike Davis, *Magical Urbanism: Latinos Reinvent the U.S. City* (New York: Verso, 2000).

17. For the distinction between exploitation and nonexploitive economic oppression, see Erik Olin Wright, *Class Counts* (New York: Cambridge University Press, 1997).

18. William Graham Sumner, *Folkways: A Study of the Sociological Importance of Usages, Manners, Customs, Mores, and Morals* (Boston and New York: Ginn, 1940), 12. Or, as Dahrendorf expressed it a half century later, "It appears to be a general law that human groups react to external pressure by increased internal coherence." See Ralf Dahrendorf, *Class and Class Conflict in Industrial Society* (Stanford, Calif.: Stanford University Press, 1959), 58.

19. I thank Richard Alba for this important point.

20. For an important recent book on this theme, see Patrick Sharkey, *Stuck in Place: Urban Neighborhoods and the End of Progress Toward Racial Equality* (Chicago and London: University of Chicago Press, 2013).

21. See Clark, *Dark Ghetto.*

22. See Sharkey, *Stuck in Place.*

23. Clark, *Dark Ghetto*, 106.

24. See Stow, *Theatre of Acculturation.*

25. Philipson, *Old European Jewries*, 194.

26. Ibid., 199.

27. Thomas DiPrete has put the dilemma of choice between short- and long-term policies well: "I suspect that if someone gave me a large amount of money and freed me up to spend it to improve the quality of people's lives in the short to medium term, I would probably want to spend some of it by giving it to poor people, I would want to spend some of it on social services. I would want to spend some of it on neighborhood organizations, and I would want to spend some of it on the physical infrastructure and aesthetics. But I don't know much about what proportions to spend in each of these categories. In other words, I don't know how much to allocate to individuals vs. on the neighborhood, and I don't know how much of neighborhood improvement would come through improvement of individual lives . . . and how much would come through direct investment in the neighborhood environment." See Thomas A. DiPrete, "Comments on *Great American City: Chicago and the Enduring Neighborhood Effect* (University of Chicago Press, 2012) by Robert J. Sampson" (Author Meets Critics

Session, American Sociological Association 108th Annual Meeting, August 11, 2013).

28. Erving Goffman, *Interaction Ritual: Essays on Face-to-Face Behavior* (New York: Pantheon Books, 1982), 155.

29. Sharkey, *Stuck in Place*, 6.

30. See Megan Comfort, *Doing Time Together: Love and Family in the Shadow of the Prison* (Chicago: University of Chicago Press, 2008).

31. See, for example, John McWhorter, *Losing the Race: Self-Sabotage in Black America* (New York: Free Press, 2000).

32. See, for example, Steinberg, *Turning Back*.

33. Small, "Four Reasons to Abandon the Idea of 'The Ghetto.'"

34. Loïc Wacquant, *Urban Outcasts*, 150.

35. I thank Richard Alba for making this point to me.

36. "Gunnar Myrdal–Kenneth Clark Seminar." February 10, 1975, 31.

37. See Steinberg, *Turning Back*.

38. Lemann, *Promised Land*.

39. "Gunnar Myrdal–Kenneth Clark Seminar." April 14, 1975, 34 (Myrdal).

40. Andrew Hacker, *Two Nations: Black and White, Separate, Hostile, Unequal* (New York: Ballantine Books, 1995).

BIBLIOGRAPHY

Abbott, Andrew. *Department and Discipline: Chicago Sociology at One Hundred.* Chicago and London: University of Chicago Press, 1999.

Abrahams, Israel. *Jewish Life in the Middle Ages.* Mineola, N.Y.: Dover Publications, 2004.

Abrams, Charles. *The City Is the Frontier.* New York: Harper and Row, 1967.

Adams, Maurianne, and John Bracey, eds. *Strangers and Neighbors: Relations Between Blacks and Jews in the United States.* Amherst: University of Massachusetts Press, 1999.

"An Address by Horace Cayton, Director of the Parkway Community House, Before the Committee of Racial Equality." Woodlawn AME Church, East Sixty-Fifth and Evans Streets, Chicago, Illinois, November 17, 1944. Box 2, Folder 5. Louis Wirth Papers, Special Collections Research Center, University of Chicago Library.

Aigner, Peter-Christian. "What the Left and the Right Both Got Wrong About the Moynihan Report." *Atlantic,* April 6, 2014.

Alba, Richard, and Steven Romelewsky. "The End of Segregation? Hardly." Center for Urban Research, March 2012.

Alexander, Michelle. *The New Jim Crow: Mass Incarceration in the Age of Colorblindness.* New York: New Press, 2010.

Andernacht, Dietrich. *Regesten zur Geschichte der Juden in der Reichsstadt Frankfurt am Main von 1401–1519.* Hannover: Hahnsche Buchhandlung, 1996, Volume 1/1.

Anderson, Elijah. *Streetwise: Race, Class, and Change in an Urban Community.* Chicago: University of Chicago Press, 1990.

Anderson, Trezzvant W. "Hideous Housing Treatment Sickens Stoutest Stomachs." *Pittsburgh Courier,* April 16, 1949.

Auletta, Ken. *The Underclass.* New York: Random House, 1982.

Backhaus, Fritz. "The Jewish Ghetto in Frankfurt." In *The Life and Times of N. M. Rothschild, 1777–1826,* ed. Victor Gray and Melanie Aspey. London: N. M. Rothschild & Sons, 1998.

————, ed. *The Frankfurt Judengasse: Jewish Life in an Early Modern German City*. London and Portland, Ore.: Vallentine Mitchell, 2010.

Baez, Maria, and Larry B. Seabrook. Resolution Declaring a Symbolic Ban on the Negative Use of the Word "Ghetto" in New York City. Res 1723-2008. 2008.

Bahr, Howard M., Theodore T. Johnson, and M. Ray Seitz. "Influential Scholars and Works in the Sociology of Race and Minority Relations, 1944–1968." *American Sociologist* 6, no. 4 (November 1971): 296–98.

Baldwin, James. "The Harlem Ghetto." *Commentary*, February 1, 1948.

Baldwin, James, Nathan Glazer, Sidney Hook, and Gunnar Myrdal. "Liberalism and the Negro: A Round-Table Discussion." *Commentary*, March 1, 1964.

Banfield, Edward C. *The Unheavenly City: The Nature and the Future of Our Urban Crisis*. Boston: Little, Brown, 1968.

Baron, Salo W. "Ghetto and Emancipation: Shall We Revise the Traditional View?" *Menorah Journal* 14, no. 6 (June 1928): 515–26.

Barry, Fabio. "Roman Apartheid? The Counter-Reformation Ghettoes." *Daidalos* 59 (March 1996): 18–31.

Bauman, Zygmunt. *Modernity and the Holocaust*. Ithaca, N.Y.: Cornell University Press, 2000.

Blauner, Robert. *Racial Oppression in America*. New York: Harper and Row, 1972.

Bloom, Jack M. *Class, Race, and the Civil Rights Movement*. Bloomington: Indiana University Press, 1987.

Bowdoin College. *Geoffrey Canada '74 and Stanley Druckenmiller '75: Generational Theft*. Vimeo video, 2013. https://vimeo.com/65731171.

Boyle, Kevin. *Arc of Justice: A Saga of Race, Civil Rights, and Murder in the Jazz Age*. New York: Henry Holt, 2004.

Briggs, Xavier de Souza, Susan J. Popkin, and John M. Goering. *Moving to Opportunity: The Story of an American Experiment to Fight Ghetto Poverty*. New York: Oxford University Press, 2010.

Brooks, David. "The Harlem Miracle." *New York Times*, May 8, 2009.

Browning, Christopher R. "Before the 'Final Solution': Nazi Ghettoization Policy in Poland (1940–1941)." In *Ghettos 1939–1945: New Research and Perspectives on Definition, Daily Life, and Survival*, 1–15. Washington, D.C.: Center for Advanced Holocaust Studies, United States Holocaust Memorial Museum, 2001.

————. "Genocide and Public Health: German Doctors and Polish Jews." *Holocaust and Genocide Studies* 3, no. 1 (1988): 21–36.

————. "Nazi Ghettoization Policy in Poland: 1939–41." *Central European History* 19, no. 4 (December 1986): 343–68.

————. *The Origins of the Final Solution: The Evolution of Nazi Jewish Policy, September 1939–March 1942*. Lincoln: University of Nebraska Press, 2004.

Brown v. Board of Education of Topeka. 347 U.S. 483. 1954.

Buhle, Paul, and Robin D. G. Kelley. "Allies of a Different Sort: Jews and Blacks in the American Left." In *Struggles in the Promised Land: Toward a History of Black-Jewish Relations in the United States*, edited by Jack Salzman and Cornel West, 197–231. New York and Oxford: Oxford University Press, 1997.

Bulmer, Martin. *The Chicago School of Sociology: Institutionalization, Diversity, and the Rise of Sociological Research*. Chicago and London: University of Chicago Press, 1984.

Burgess, Ernest W. "Residential Segregation in American Cities." *Annals of the American Academy of Political and Social Science* 140 (November 1928): 105–15.

Butterworth, Douglas. "Oscar Lewis, 1914–1970." *American Anthropologist* 74, no. 3 (June 1972): 747–57.

California Governor's Commission on the Los Angeles Riots. *Violence in the City: An End or a Beginning? A Report.* Los Angeles, 1965.

The Cameraman. "Colorful News Movies." *Broad Ax*, November 13, 1926.

Canada, Geoffrey. *Fist Stick Knife Gun: A Personal History of Violence in America.* Boston: Beacon Press, 1995.

"Can the Newly-Reelected Obama Save the American Public School? A Conversation between William Julius Wilson and Sylvie Laurent." *Pathways*, Fall 2012.

Cayton, Horace. *Long Old Road: An Autobiography.* New York: Trident Press, 1965.

Cayton, Horace R. "A Great Man Died, but Leaves Keen Observation on Our Democracy." *Pittsburgh Courier*, February 26, 1944.

"Cayton to Myrdal," June 14, 1939. Sc Micro F-13242, Ser. 2, No. 15. Carnegie-Myrdal Study of the Negro in America research memoranda collection, Schomburg Center for Research in Black Culture, New York Public Library.

"Cayton to Myrdal," February 29, 1940. Sc Micro F-13242, Ser. 2, No. 15. Carnegie-Myrdal Study of the Negro in America research memoranda collection, Schomburg Center for Research in Black Culture, New York Public Library.

Chetty, Raj, Nathaniel Hendren, and Lawrence F. Katz. "The Effects of Exposure to Better Neighborhoods on Children: New Evidence from the Moving to Opportunity Experiment." Working paper. Harvard University and NBER, May 2015.

"Cites Germany's Treatment of Jews Like Race in U.S." *Chicago Defender*, December 31, 1938.

Clampet-Lundquist, Susan, and Douglas S. Massey. "Neighborhood Effects on Economic Self-Sufficiency: A Reconsideration of the Moving to Opportunity Experiment." *American Journal of Sociology* 114, no. 1 (July 2008): 107–43.

Clark, Kenneth B. "Beyond the Ghetto." Unpublished manuscript, August 6, 1979.

——. *Dark Ghetto: Dilemmas of Social Power.* New York: Harper and Row, 1965.

——. *The Negro Protest: James Baldwin, Malcolm X, and Martin Luther King Talk with Kenneth B. Clark.* Boston: Beacon Press, 1963.

——. "No. No. Race, Not Class, Is Still at the Wheel." *New York Times*, March 22, 1978.

——. "The Riots Within the Human Spirit." Unpublished manuscript, 1967. Kenneth Bancroft Clark Papers, Manuscript Division, Library of Congress, Washington, D.C.

——. *Youth in the Ghetto: A Study of the Consequences of Powerlessness and a Blueprint for Change.* New York: Harlem Youth Opportunities Unlimited, 1964.

Coates, Ta-Nehisi. "The Case for Reparations," *Atlantic*, June 2014.

Collins, Patricia Hill. *Black Feminist Thought: Knowledge, Consciousness, and the Politics of Empowerment.* 2nd ed. New York and London: Routledge, 2000.

Combahee River Collective. "The Combahee River Collective Statement." In *Home Girls: A Black Feminist Anthology*, edited by Barbara Smith, 264–74. New Brunswick, N.J., and London: Rutgers University Press, 2000.

Comfort, Megan. *Doing Time Together: Love and Family in the Shadow of the Prison.* Chicago: University of Chicago Press, 2008.

Conley, Dalton. *Being Black, Living in the Red*. Berkeley: University of California Press, 1999.

———. *The Pecking Order: Which Siblings Succeed and Why*. New York: Pantheon Books, 2004.

"Copy of Memorandum Regarding University Real Estate, from Louis Wirth to L. Steares," March 20, 1936. Box 54, Folder 2. Louis Wirth Papers, Special Collections Research Center, University of Chicago Library.

Dahrendorf, Ralf. *Class and Class Conflict in Industrial Society*. Stanford, Calif.: Stanford University Press, 1959.

Daniels, Cora. *Ghettonation: A Journey into the Land of the Bling and the Home of the Shameless*. New York: Doubleday, 2007.

Dávila, Arlene. *Barrio Dreams: Puerto Ricans, Latinos, and the Neoliberal City*. Berkeley: University of California Press, 2004.

"Decree on Jews and Neophytes: Session 19 of the Council of Basel, 1431–45 A.D." September 7, 1434. http://www.papalencyclicals.net/Councils/ecum17.htm.

Degler, Carl N. "The Negro in America: Where Myrdal Went Wrong." *New York Times Magazine*, December 7, 1969.

"Demand Legislature Pass Bill Outlawing Restrictive Housing Covenants." *New York Amsterdam Star-News*, March 15, 1941.

DeParle, Jason. "Daring Research or 'Social Science Pornography'?" *New York Times*, October 9, 1994.

DiPrete, Thomas A. "Comments on *Great American City: Chicago and the Enduring Neighborhood Effect* (University of Chicago Press, 2012) by Robert J. Sampson." Author Meets Critics Session presented at the American Sociological Association 108th Annual Meeting, August 11, 2013.

Dobbie, Will, and Roland G. Fryer, Jr. "Are High-Quality Schools Enough to Increase Achievement Among the Poor? Evidence from the Harlem Children's Zone." *American Economic Journal: Applied Economics* 3, no. 3 (July 2011): 158–87.

Drake, St. Clair. "*Black Metropolis* Revisited," n.d. Box 39. St. Clair Drake Papers, Schomburg Center for Research in Black Culture, New York Public Library.

———. "Exploratory Research on Types of Black Communities in the United States That Have Not Been Adequately Studied," n.d. Box 2, Folder 21. St. Clair Drake Papers, Schomburg Center for Research in Black Culture, New York Public Library.

———. "Letter to the *Stanford Daily*," n.d. St. Clair Drake Papers, Schomburg Center for Research in Black Culture, New York Public Library.

———. *Race Relations in a Time of Rapid Social Change: Report of a Survey*. New York: National Federation of Settlements and Neighborhood Centers, 1966.

———. "The Social and Economic Status of the Negro in the United States." *Daedalus* 94, no. 4 (Fall 1965): 771–814.

Drake, St. Clair, and Horace R. Cayton. *Black Metropolis: A Study of Negro Life in a Northern City*. Chicago: University of Chicago Press, 1993.

Dreier, Peter, and Todd Swanstrom. "Suburban Ghettos Like Ferguson Are Ticking Time Bombs." *Washington Post*, August 21, 2014.

"Drive Opens Today to Better Harlem: City-Wide Citizens' Unit Plans a Week-Long Program Aimed at 4 Objectives." *New York Times*, May 24, 1942.

Du Bois, W.E.B. "The Negro and the Warsaw Ghetto." *Jewish Life* 6, no. 7 (May 1952): 14–15.

Duneier, Mitchell. "On the Legacy of Elliot Liebow and Carol Stack: Context-Driven

Fieldwork and the Need for Continuous Ethnography." *Focus* 25, no. 1 (Spring–Summer 2007).

Dweck, Yaacob. *The Scandal of Kabbalah: Leon Modena, Jewish Mysticism, Early Modern Venice.* Princeton, N.J.; Princeton University Press, 2013.

Edelman, Peter. *So Rich, So Poor: Why It's So Hard to End Poverty in America.* New York: New Press, 2012.

——. "The Worst Thing Bill Clinton Has Done." *Atlantic Monthly*, March 1997.

Ellwood, David. *Poor Support: Poverty in the American Family.* New York: Basic Books, 1988.

Erickson, Amanda. "Why Hasn't the Harlem Children's Zone Been Replicated Even Without Obama's Help?" *CityLab* from *The Atlantic*, August 16, 2012. http://www.citylab.com/politics/2012/08/why-hasnt-harlem-childrens-zone-been-replicated-even-without-obamas-help/2968/.

"Everett Hughes to St. Clair Drake," n.d. Box 38. St. Clair Drake Papers, Schomburg Center for Research in Black Culture, New York Public Library.

"Extremists Sway Nazis and Jews Are Menaced with More Drastic Rule." *New York Times*, November 14, 1938.

Forman, James, Jr. "Racial Critiques of Mass Incarceration: Beyond the New Jim Crow." *New York University Law Review* 87, no. 1 (February 2012): 101–46.

Frazier, E. Franklin. *The Negro Family in the United States.* Chicago: University of Chicago Press, 1939.

Friedan, Betty. *The Feminine Mystique.* New York: Norton, 2001.

Friedländer, Saul. *Nazi Germany and the Jews: Volume I: The Years of Persecution, 1933–1939.* New York: HarperCollins, 1997.

Gandolfo v. Hartman et al. 49 Fed. 181. 1892.

Gans, Herbert J. *The Urban Villagers: Group and Class in the Life of Italian-Americans.* New York: Free Press, 1962.

——. *The War Against the Poor: The Underclass and Antipoverty Policy.* New York: Basic Books, 1995.

Garfield, Eugene. *Citation Indexing: Its Theory and Application in Science, Technology, and Humanities.* Philadelphia: ISI Press, 1983.

Garland, David. *The Culture of Control: Crime and Social Order in Contemporary Society.* Oxford: Oxford University Press, 2001.

Ghaziani, Amin. *There Goes the Gayborhood?* Princeton, N.J.: Princeton University Press, 2014.

Gilbert, Martin. *The Holocaust: The History of the Jews of Europe During the Second World War.* New York: Holt, Rinehart and Winston, 1986.

Gilpin, Patrick J., and Marybeth Gasman. *Charles S. Johnson: Leadership Beyond the Veil in the Age of Jim Crow.* Albany: State University of New York Press, 2003.

Gladwell, Malcolm. *The Tipping Point: How Little Things Can Make a Big Difference.* Boston: Little, Brown, 2000.

Glaeser, Edward L., Eric A. Hanushek, and John M. Quigley. "Opportunities, Race, and Urban Location: The Influence of John Kain." *Journal of Urban Economics* 56 (2004): 70–79.

Glazer, Nathan, and Daniel Patrick Moynihan. *Beyond the Melting Pot: The Negroes, Puerto Ricans, Jews, Italians, and Irish of New York City.* Cambridge, Mass.: MIT Press, 1963.

Goffman, Alice. "On the Run: Wanted Men in a Philadelphia Ghetto." *American Sociological Review* 74, no. 3 (June 2009): 339–57.

Goffman, Erving. *Interaction Ritual: Essays on Face-to-Face Behavior.* New York: Pantheon Books, 1982.

Gold, Michael. *Jews Without Money.* 3rd ed. New York: Carroll & Graf, 2004.

Goldfarb, Michael. *Emancipation: How Liberating Europe's Jews from the Ghetto Led to Revolution and Renaissance.* New York: Simon and Schuster, 2009.

Gordon, Milton M. *Assimilation in American Life: The Role of Race, Religion, and National Origins.* New York: Oxford University Press, 1964.

Gregorovius, Ferdinand. *The Ghetto and the Jews of Rome.* Translated by Moses Hadas. New York: Schocken Books, 1966.

"Gunnar Myrdal–Kenneth Clark Seminar: The American Dilemma Revisited," March 17, 1975. Kenneth Bancroft Clark Papers, Manuscript Division, Library of Congress, Washington, D.C.

Hacker, Andrew. "Jewish Racism, Black Anti-Semitism." In *Strangers and Neighbors: Relations Between Blacks and Jews in the United States,* edited by Maurianne Adams and John Bracey, 18–23. Amherst: University of Massachusetts Press, 1999.

———. *Two Nations: Black and White, Separate, Hostile, Unequal.* New York: Ballantine Books, 1995.

Harlem Children's Zone. *Barack Obama on the Harlem Children's Zone.* YouTube video, 2008. https://www.youtube.com/watch?v=Xh5QRMaa_KE.

Harvey, David. *Social Justice and the City.* Baltimore: Johns Hopkins University Press, 1973.

Haynes, George Edmund. "Conditions Among Negroes in the Cities." *Annals of the American Academy of Political and Social Science* 49 (1913): 105–19.

Hertzberg, Arthur. *The French Enlightenment and the Jews: The Origins of Modern Anti-Semitism.* New York: Columbia University Press, 1990.

Hilberg, Raul. *The Destruction of the European Jews.* Chicago: Quadrangle Books, 1961.

Hirsch, Arnold R. *Making the Second Ghetto: Race and Housing in Chicago, 1940–1960.* Chicago: University of Chicago Press, 1998.

"Homicides in Philadelphia." *Philly.com,* n.d. http://www.philly.com/philly/news /special_packages/inquirer/Philadelphia_Homicides_1988_2011.html.

hooks, bell. *Feminist Theory: From Margin to Center.* Boston: South End Press, 1984.

Horowitz, Gordon J. *Ghettostadt: Łódź and the Making of a Nazi City.* Cambridge, Mass.: Belknap Press of Harvard University Press, 2008.

Humphreys, Laud. *Out of the Closets: The Sociology of Homosexual Liberation.* Englewood Cliffs, N.J.: Prentice Hall, 1972.

Hutchison, Ray, and Bruce D. Haynes, eds. *The Ghetto: Contemporary Global Issues and Controversies.* Boulder, Colo.: Westview Press, 2012.

Jackson, Walter A. *Gunnar Myrdal and America's Conscience: Social Engineering and Racial Liberalism, 1938–1987.* Chapel Hill: University of North Carolina Press, 1990.

Jargowsky, Paul A., and Mary Jo Bane. "Ghetto Poverty in the United States, 1970–1980." In *The Urban Underclass,* edited by Christopher Jencks and Paul E. Peterson, 342–56. Washington, D.C.: Brookings Institution, 1991.

Jencks, Christopher. "The Moynihan Report." *New York Review of Books,* October 14, 1965.

———. *Rethinking Social Policy: Race, Poverty, and the Underclass.* Cambridge, Mass.: Harvard University Press, 1992.

Johnson, Charles S. *Backgrounds to Patterns of Negro Segregation.* New York: Crowell, 1970.

Johnson, Lyndon B. "To Fulfill These Rights: Commencement Address at Howard University," 1966. http://www.whatsoproudlywehail.org/wp-content/uploads/2013/01/Johnson_To-Fulfill-These-Rights.pdf.

Kain, John F. *The Effects of the Ghetto on the Distribution and Level of Nonwhite Employment in Urban Areas.* Santa Monica, Calif.: Rand Corporation, 1965.

———. *Essays on Urban Spatial Structure.* Cambridge, Mass.: Ballinger, 1975.

Kasarda, John D. "Caught in the Web of Change." *Society* 21, no. 1 (December 1983): 41–47.

———. "Urbanization, Community, and the Metropolitan Problem." In *Handbook of Contemporary Urban Life*, edited by David Street, 27–57. San Francisco: Jossey-Bass, 1979.

Kasarda, John D., and Kwok-fai Ting. "Joblessness and Poverty in America's Central Cities: Causes and Policy Prescriptions." *Housing Policy Debate* 7, no. 2 (1996): 387–419.

Katz, Jacob. "Leaving the Ghetto." *Commentary*, February 1996.

Katz, Michael B. *The Undeserving Poor: America's Enduring Confrontation with Poverty.* New York: Oxford University Press, 2013.

"Kenneth Clark to Grayson Kirk," July 12, 1966. General Correspondence, Box 28. Kenneth Bancroft Clark Papers, Manuscript Division, Library of Congress, Washington, D.C.

Kessler, Ronald C., Greg J. Duncan, Lisa Gennetian, et al. "Associations of Housing Mobility Interventions for Children in High-Poverty Neighborhoods with Subsequent Mental Disorders During Adolescence." *Journal of the American Medical Association* 311, no. 9 (2014): 937–47.

Kihss, Peter. "'Benign Neglect' on Race Is Proposed by Moynihan." *New York Times*, March 1, 1970.

King, Martin Luther, Jr. "Family Planning: A Special and Urgent Concern," May 5, 1966. http://www.plannedparenthood.org/planned-parenthood-gulf-coast/mlk-acceptance-speech.

Kohler-Hausmann, Issa. "Managerial Justice and Mass Misdemeanors." *Stanford Law Review* 66, no. 3 (March 2014): 611–94.

———. "Misdemeanor Justice: Control Without Conviction." *American Journal of Sociology* 119, no. 2 (September 2013): 351–93.

Krell, Alan. *Devil's Rope: A Cultural History of Barbed Wire.* London: Reaktion Books, 2002.

Labov, William. *Dialect Diversity in America: The Politics of Language Change.* Charlottesville and London: University of Virginia Press, 2012.

Labov, William, and Wendell A. Harris. "De Facto Segregation of Black and White Vernaculars." In *Diversity and Diachrony*, edited by David Sankoff, 1–24. Amsterdam and Philadelphia: John Benjamins, 1986.

Landau, Ronnie S. *The Nazi Holocaust: Its History and Meaning.* London: I.B. Tauris, 2006.

Lemann, Nicholas. *The Promised Land: The Great Black Migration and How It Changed America.* New York: Vintage Books, 1992.

"Letter from the Big Brothers Association to the University of Chicago. In Chicago Defender Files," January 1938. Box 20, Folder 7. Louis Wirth Papers, Special Collections Research Center, University of Chicago Library.

"Letter from the Big Brothers Association to the W.P.A.," January 1938. Box 2, Folder 5. Louis Wirth Papers, Special Collections Research Center, University of Chicago Library.

"Letter to Director," January 6, 1980. Box 38, Folder 14. St. Clair Drake Papers, Schomburg Center for Research in Black Culture, New York Public Library.

"Letter to Lloyd Warner," October 1, 1944. Box 38. St. Clair Drake Papers, Schomburg Center for Research in Black Culture, New York Public Library.

Lewis, David Levering. W.E.B. Du Bois: Biography of a Race, 1868–1919. New York: Henry Holt, 1993.

Lewis, Oscar. "The Culture of Poverty." Scientific American 215, no. 4 (October 1966): 19–25.

———. La Vida: A Puerto Rican Family in the Culture of Poverty, San Juan and New York. London: Panther Books, 1968.

———. "Review: The Children of Sánchez, Pedro Martínez and La Vida." Current Anthropology 8, no. 5 (December 1967): 480–500.

Liebow, Elliot. Tally's Corner: A Study of Negro Streetcorner Men. Boston: Little, Brown, 1967.

Lindstrom, F. B. "The Negro Invasion of the Washington Park Subdivision." M.A. diss., University of Chicago, 1941.

Logan, John R. "The Persistence of Segregation in the 21st Century Metropolis." City & Community 12, no. 2 (June 2013): 160–68.

Logan, John R., and Harvey L. Molotch. Urban Fortunes: The Political Economy of Place. Berkeley and Los Angeles: University of California Press, 1987.

Long, Herman H., and Charles S. Johnson. People vs. Property: Race Restrictive Covenants in Housing. Nashville, Tenn.: Fisk University Press, 1947.

"A Look Inside: Countee Cullen Beacon Center." Harlem Children's Zone, July 1, 2006. http://wac.adef.edgecastcdn.net/80ADEF/hcz.org/wp-content/uploads/2014/04/ALI-CounteeCullen.pdf.

Ludwig, Jens, Lisa Sanbonmatsu, Lisa Gennetian, et al. "Neighborhoods, Obesity, and Diabetes: A Randomized Social Experiment." New England Journal of Medicine 365 (2011): 1509–19.

Malcolm X Network. Malcolm X Interviewed by Dr. Kenneth Clark. YouTube video, 2011. https://www.youtube.com/watch?v=T9C_e0EUbas.

Markowitz, Gerald, and David Rosner. Children, Race, and Power: Kenneth and Mamie Clark's Northside Center. New York: Routledge, 2000.

Massey, Douglas S., and Nancy A. Denton. American Apartheid: Segregation and the Making of the Underclass. Cambridge, Mass.: Harvard University Press, 1993.

Massey, Douglas S., et al. Climbing Mount Laurel: The Struggle for Affordable Housing and Social Mobility in an American Suburb. Princeton, N.J.: Princeton University Press, 2013.

Mathews, Jay. "Neighborhoods' Effect on Grades Challenged; Moving Students out of Poor Inner Cities Yields Little, Studies of HUD Vouchers Say." Washington Post, August 14, 2007.

Mayer, Susan E., and Christopher Jencks. "Growing Up in Poor Neighborhoods: How Much Does It Matter?" *Science* 243, no. 4897 (March 17, 1989): 1441–45.

McNeil, W. H. *Hutchins' University: A Memoir of the University of Chicago, 1929–1950.* Chicago: University of Chicago Press, 1991.

McWilliams, Carey. *Brothers Under the Skin.* Boston: Little, Brown, 1943.

Mendes-Flohr, Paul, and Jehuda Reinharz. *The Jew in the Modern World: A Documentary History.* New York: Oxford University Press, 1980.

Merton, Robert K. "Insiders and Outsiders: A Chapter in the Sociology of Knowledge." *American Journal of Sociology* 78, no. 1 (July 1972): 9–47.

Metzger, John T. "Rebuilding Harlem: Public Housing and Urban Renewal, 1920–1960." *Planning Perspectives* 9 (1994): 255–96.

Michel, Jean-Baptiste, Yuan Kui Shen, Aviva Presser Aiden, and Adrian Veres. "Quantitative Analysis of Culture Using Millions of Digitized Books." *Science* 331, no. 6014 (January 2011): 176–82.

Michelson, William. *Man and His Urban Environment: A Sociological Approach: With Revisions.* Reading, Mass.: Addison-Wesley, 1976.

Michman, Dan. *The Emergence of Jewish Ghettos During the Holocaust.* Translated by Lenn J. Schramm. Cambridge and New York: Cambridge University Press, 2011.

Mollenkopf, John. *The Contested City.* Princeton, N.J.: Princeton University Press, 1983.

Molotch, Harvey L. "Gay Ghetto." Unpublished lecture, Princeton University, July 20, 2013.

Morgan, Gordon D. "The Training of Black Sociologists." *Teaching Sociology* 7, no. 2 (January 1980): 115–25.

Morris, Aldon. *The Scholar Denied: W.E.B. Du Bois and the Birth of Modern Sociology.* Berkeley: University of California Press, 2015.

Moyers, Bill. *A World of Ideas: Conversations with Thoughtful Men and Women About American Life Today and the Ideas Shaping Our Future,* edited by Betty Sue Flowers. New York: Doubleday, 1989.

Moynihan, Daniel Patrick. "Employment, Income, and the Ordeal of the Negro Family." *Daedalus* 94, no. 4 (Fall 1965): 745–70.

———. *The Negro Family: The Case for National Action.* Washington, D.C.: U.S. Department of Labor, Office of Policy Planning and Research, 1965.

Murray, Albert. *The Omni-Americans: Black Experience and American Culture.* New York: Harper and Row, 1966.

Murray, Charles. *Losing Ground: American Social Policy, 1950–1980.* New York: Basic Books, 1984.

———. "On Being a Killjoy." *AEIdeas,* May 11, 2009. http://www.aei.org/publication/on-being-a-killjoy/.

Myrdal, Gunnar. *An American Dilemma: The Negro Problem and Modern Democracy.* New York and London: Harper and Brothers, 1944.

———. "The Black Revolt in the South." Unpublished manuscript, April 9, 1974.

"Myrdal Correspondence," n.d. Sc Micro F-13242, Ser. 2, No. 15. Carnegie-Myrdal Study of the Negro in America research memoranda collection, Schomburg Center for Research in Black Culture, New York Public Library.

"Myrdal to Cayton," February 27, 1940. Sc Micro F-13242, Ser. 2, No. 15. Carnegie-Myrdal Study of the Negro in America research memoranda collection, Schomburg Center for Research in Black Culture, New York Public Library.

Nee, Victor G., and Brett de Bary Nee. *Longtime Californ': A Documentary Study of an American Chinatown.* Stanford, Calif.: Stanford University Press, 1972.

"Negroes and Jews." *New York Amsterdam Star-News,* August 22, 1942.

"Negro Students Rush Congress Restaurant in Vain Effort to Test the Rule Barring Race." *New York Times,* March 18, 1934.

Netz, Reviel. *Barbed Wire: An Ecology of Modernity.* Middletown, Conn.: Wesleyan University Press, 2004.

Newman, Katherine S. *Chutes and Ladders: Navigating the Low-Wage Labor Market.* New York: Russell Sage Foundation, 2006.

Nightingale, Carl H. *Segregation: A Global History of Divided Cities.* Chicago: University of Chicago Press, 2012.

Noakes, Jeremy, and Geoffrey Pridham, eds. *Nazism, 1919–1945: A Documentary Reader.* Exeter, Great Britain: University of Exeter Press, 2001.

"No Regret Voiced: Goebbels Declares That the Nation Followed Its 'Healthy Instincts.'" *New York Times,* November 12, 1938.

"Nuremberg Document 1816-PS, 'Stenographic Report on the Meaning of the Jewish Question Under the Chairmanship of Field Marshall Goering in the Reich's Air Force,' 12 November 1938, 11:00am." In *Nazi Conspiracy and Aggression,* 4:425–54. Washington, D.C.: USGPO, 1946.

O'Connor, Alice. *Poverty Knowledge.* Princeton, N.J.: Princeton University Press, 2001.

Oliver, Melvin, and Thomas Shapiro. *Black Wealth/White Wealth: A New Perspective on Racial Equality.* New York: Routledge, 1995.

Oryshkevich, Irina. "Accommodating Jews in the New Jerusalem." Lecture presented at the Italian Academy for Advanced Studies at Columbia University, New York, February 12, 2010.

Osofsky, Gilbert. *Harlem: The Making of a Ghetto, Negro New York, 1890–1930.* 2nd ed. New York: Harper and Row, 1971.

Park, Robert E. "The Urban Community as a Spatial and a Moral Order." In *The Urban Community: Selected Papers from the Proceedings of the American Sociological Society,* edited by Ernest W. Burgess, 3–21. Chicago: University of Chicago Press, 1926.

Patterson, Orlando. *The Ordeal of Integration: Progress and Resentment in America's "Racial" Crisis.* New York: Basic Civitas, 1997.

Peretz, Henri. "The Making of *Black Metropolis.*" *Annals of the American Academy of Political and Social Science* 595 (September 2004): 168–75.

Pettigrew, Thomas F. "The Changing, but Not Declining, Significance of Race." *Michigan Law Review* 77, no. 3 (March 1979): 917–24.

Pettit, Becky, and Bruce Western. "Mass Imprisonment and the Life Course: Race and Class Inequality in U.S. Incarceration." *American Sociological Review* 69, no. 151 (April 2004): 151–69.

Philipson, David. *Old European Jewries.* Philadelphia: Jewish Publication Society of America, 1894.

Piven, Frances Fox, and Richard A. Cloward. *Regulating the Poor: The Functions of Public Welfare.* 2nd ed. New York: Vintage Books, 1993.

Plotkin, Wendy. "Deeds of Mistrust: Race, Housing, and Restrictive Covenants in Chicago, 1900–1953," doctoral diss., University of Illinois–Chicago, 1999.

Pope Paul IV. "Cum nimis absurdum," July 14, 1555.

Porter, Russell B. "Harlem Unrest Traced to Long-Standing Ills: Basic Racial Problem Seen Sharpened by New Complaints Born of War." *New York Times*, August 8, 1943.

Prescott, Orville. Books of the Times. *New York Times*, December 28, 1945.

Quane, James M., and William Julius Wilson. "All Together Now, One by One: Building Capacity for Urban Education Reform in Promise Neighborhoods." *Pathways*, Summer 2011.

Ravid, Benjamin C. I. "All Ghettos Were Jewish Quarters but Not All Jewish Quarters Were Ghettos." In *The Frankfurt Judengasse: Life in an Early Modern German City*, edited by Fritz Backhaus, Gisela Engel, Robert Liberlis, and Margarete Schlüter, 5–22. London and Portland, Ore.: Vallentine Mitchell, 2010.

———. *Studies on the Jews of Venice, 1382–1797*. Aldershot, Hampshire, Great Britain: Ashgate/Variorum, 2003.

———. "The Venetian Government and the Jews." In *The Jews of Early Modern Venice*, edited by R. C. Davis and B. Ravid, 3–30. Baltimore: Johns Hopkins University Press, 2001.

Ravitch, Diane. "Charter School Leader Paid $553,000 Yearly." *Diane Ravitch's Blog: A Site to Discuss Education for All*, July 28, 2012. http://dianeravitch.net/2012/07/28/charter-school-leader-paid-553000-yearly/.

"Record of Conversation with Horace Cayton," February 16, 1940. Sc Micro F-13242, Ser. 2, No. 15. Carnegie-Myrdal Study of the Negro in America research memoranda collection, Schomburg Center for Research in Black Culture, New York Public Library.

"Record of Interview: CD and Horace Cayton," July 24, 1940. Carnegie-Myrdal Study of the Negro in America research memoranda collection, Schomburg Center for Research in Black Culture, New York Public Library.

"Reminiscences of Kenneth Bancroft Clark, as Interviewed by Ed Edwin," 1976. Columbia Oral History Archives, Rare Book and Manuscript Library, Columbia University, New York.

Remnick, David. "Dr. Wilson's Neighborhood." *New Yorker*, April 29, 1996.

"Restrictive Covenants Illegal Rules Chicago Municipal Judge." *Los Angeles Tribune*, November 29, 1943.

Ringelblum, Emmanuel. *Notes from the Warsaw Ghetto: The Journal of Emmanuel Ringelblum*. Translated by J. Sloan. New York: McGraw Hill, 1958.

Roberts, Steven V. "Black Studies Aim to Change Things." *New York Times*, May 15, 1969.

Rothstein, Richard. "A Comment on Bank of America/Countrywide's Discriminatory Mortgage Lending and Its Implications for Racial Segregation." EPI Briefing Paper #335 (Economic Policy Institute, January 23, 2012).

Rugh, Jacob S., and Douglas Massey. "Racial Segregation and the American Foreclosure Crisis. *American Sociological Review* 75, no. 5 (October 2010): 629–51.

Salzman, Jack, and Cornel West, eds. *Struggles in the Promised Land: Toward a History of Black-Jewish Relations in the United States*. New York and Oxford: Oxford University Press, 1997.

Sampson, Robert J. *Great American City: Chicago and the Enduring Neighborhood Effect*. Chicago and London: University of Chicago Press, 2012.

———. "Moving to Inequality: Neighborhood Effects and Experiments Meet Social Structure." *American Journal of Sociology* 114, no. 1 (July 2008): 189–231.

Sánchez, George J. *Becoming Mexican American: Ethnicity, Culture, and Identity in Chicano Los Angeles, 1900–1945*. New York: Oxford University Press, 1993.

"7 Win Awards for Books at Ceremony in New York." *Evening Bulletin*, March 9, 1967.

Sharkey, Patrick. *Stuck in Place: Urban Neighborhoods and the End of Progress Toward Racial Equality*. Chicago and London: University of Chicago Press, 2013.

Shaw, Clifford R. *Delinquency Areas: A Study of the Geographic Distribution of School Truants, Juvenile Delinquents, and Adult Offenders in Chicago*. Chicago: University of Chicago Press, 1929.

Shils, Edward. *A Fragment of a Sociological Autobiography: The History of My Pursuit of a Few Ideas*, edited by Steven Grosby. New Brunswick, N.J.: Transaction Books, 2006.

Shils, Edward, and Joseph Epstein. *Portraits: A Gallery of Intellectuals*. Chicago: University of Chicago Press, 1997.

Silberman, Charles E. *Crisis in Black and White*. New York: Vintage Books, 1964.

Small, Mario Luis. "Four Reasons to Abandon the Idea of 'The Ghetto.'" *City & Community* 7, no. 4 (December 2008): 389–98.

Sorensen, Eric. "Race, Class, and William Julius Wilson's World of Opportunity." *Washington State Magazine*, Fall 2012.

Sorkin, David Jan. *The Transformation of German Jewry, 1780–1840*. Detroit: Wayne State University Press, 1999.

Stack, Carol B. *All Our Kin: Strategies for Survival in a Black Community*. New York: Harper and Row, 1974.

Starr, Paul. "Losing More Ground." *New Republic*, December 5, 1988.

——. "Not Simply Black and White: Race." *New York Times*, January 7, 1979.

Steffan, Katrin. "Connotations of Exclusion—'Ostjuden,' 'Ghettos' and Other Markings." In *Jahrbuch Des Simon-Dubnow-Instituts IV*, edited by Dan Diner, 459–79. Göttingen, Germany: Vandenhoeck & Ruprecht, 2005.

Steinberg, Stephen. *Race Relations: A Critique*. Stanford, Calif.: Stanford University Press, 2007.

——. *Turning Back: The Retreat from Racial Justice in American Thought and Policy*. Boston: Beacon Press, 1995.

Stow, Kenneth. *Theatre of Acculturation: The Roman Ghetto in the Sixteenth Century*. Seattle: University of Washington Press, 2001.

Sumner, William Graham. *Folkways: A Study of the Sociological Importance of Usages, Manners, Customs, Mores, and Morals*. Boston and New York: Ginn, 1940.

Sundquist, Eric J. *Strangers in the Land: Blacks, Jews, Post-Holocaust America*. Cambridge, Mass., and London: Belknap Press of Harvard University Press, 2005.

Supreme Court of the United States. Brief of Housing Scholars as Amici Curiae Supporting Respondent. Texas Department of Housing and Community Affairs et al. v. The Inclusive Communities Project, Inc.

"The Sveriges Riksbank Prize in Economic Sciences in Memory of Alfred Nobel." Nobel Media, 1974. http://www.nobelprize.org/nobel_prizes/economic-sciences/laureates/1974/.

Taeuber, Karl E., and Alma F. Taeuber. *Negroes in Cities*. Chicago: Aldine, 1965.

Thomsett, Michael C. *The German Opposition to Hitler: The Resistance, the Underground, and Assassination Plots, 1938–1945*. Jefferson, N.C., and London: McFarland, 1997.

Topics of the Times. *New York Times*, July 9, 1938.

Tough, Paul. *Whatever It Takes: Geoffrey Canada's Quest to Change Harlem and America*. Boston: Houghton Mifflin, 2008.

"The Trial of Adolf Eichmann, Session 12 (Part 7 of 7)." *The Nizkor Project*, n.d. www.nizkor.org/hweb/people/e/eichmann-adolf/transcripts/Sessions/Session -012-07.html.

United States Department of Justice, Civil Rights Division. "Investigation of the Ferguson Police Department," March 4, 2015.

"Unsigned Note." In *Documents on German Foreign Policy, 1918–1945: From the Archives of the German Foreign Ministry*, 1:347–48. U.S. Department of State Publication 3277, C. Washington, D.C.: USGPO, 1949.

Valentine, Charles A. *Culture and Poverty: Critique and Counter-Proposals*. Chicago and London: University of Chicago Press, 1968.

Vanneman, Reeve. "Life Expectancy by Race and Gender" [PowerPoint Slide]. www .vanneman.umd.edu/socy 441/trends/liferace.html.

Vose, Clement E. *Caucasians Only: The Supreme Court, the NAACP, and the Restrictive Covenant Cases*. Berkeley and Los Angeles: University of California Press, 1967.

Wacker, R. Fred. "The Sociology of Race and Ethnicity in the Second Chicago School." In *A Second Chicago School? The Development of a Postwar American Sociology*, edited by Gary Alan Fine, 136–63. Chicago: University of Chicago Press, 1995.

Wacquant, Loïc. "Deadly Symbiosis: When Ghetto and Prison Meet and Mesh." *Punishment and Society* 3, no. 1 (2001): 95–134.

——. "Ghetto." In *International Encyclopedia of the Social and Behavioral Sciences*, edited by Neil M. Smelser and Paul B. Baltes. London: Pergamon Press, 2004.

——. *Urban Outcasts: A Comparative Sociology of Advanced Marginality*. Cambridge and Malden, Mass.: Polity Press, 2008.

Waldinger, Roger. *Still the Promised City? African-Americans and New Immigrants in Postindustrial New York*. Cambridge, Mass.: Harvard University Press, 1996.

Warner, W. Lloyd, Horace R. Cayton, and St. Clair Drake. "Proposal for *Black Metropolis*: A Study of Negro Life in a Northern City," n.d. Box 38. St. Clair Drake Papers, Schomburg Center for Research in Black Culture, New York Public Library.

Warner, W. Lloyd, and Leo Srole. *The Social Systems of American Ethnic Groups*. New Haven, Conn.: Yale University Press, 1945.

Washington, Louis Curtis. "A Study of Restrictive Covenants in Chicago." M.A. diss., University of Chicago, 1948.

Washington, Robert. "Horace Cayton: Reflections on an Unfulfilled Sociological Career." *American Sociologist* 28, no. 1 (Spring 1997): 55–74.

Weaver, Robert C. *The Negro Ghetto*. New York: Russell and Russell, 1948.

Weindling, Paul. *Epidemics and Genocide in Eastern Europe, 1890–1945*. Oxford and New York: Oxford University Press, 2000.

Weinreich, Max. *Hitler's Professors: The Part of Scholarship in Germany's Crimes Against the Jewish People*. New Haven, Conn.: Yale University Press, 1999.

Weisman, Steven R., ed. *Daniel Patrick Moynihan: A Portrait in Letters of an American Visionary*. New York: Public Affairs, 2010.

Welfare Reform Working Group. "President Clinton, NBC News Interview 12/3/93: Response to Charles Murray," May 3, 1994. William J. Clinton Presidential

Library. http://www.clintonlibrary.gov/assets/storage/Research-Digital-Library/dpc/reed-welfare/20/612964-meetings-2.pdf.

Whyte, William Foote. "Social Organization in the Slums." *American Sociological Review* 8, no. 1 (February 1943): 34–39.

——. *Street Corner Society: The Social Structure of an Italian Slum.* 4th ed. Chicago: University of Chicago Press, 1993.

Wilson, Frank Harold. *Race, Class, and the Postindustrial City: William Julius Wilson and the Promise of Sociology.* Albany: State University of New York Press, 2004.

Wilson, William Julius. *The Declining Significance of Race: Blacks and Changing American Institutions.* 3rd ed. Chicago and London: University of Chicago Press, 2012.

——. "Poor Blacks' Future." *New York Times,* February 28, 1978.

——. *Power, Racism, and Privilege: Race Relations in Theoretical and Sociohistorical Perspectives.* New York: Free Press, 1973.

——. *The Truly Disadvantaged: The Inner City, the Underclass, and Public Policy.* Chicago: University of Chicago Press, 1987.

——. "The Underclass: Issues, Perspectives, and Public Policy." In *The Ghetto Underclass: Social Science Perspectives,* edited by William Julius Wilson, 1–25. Newbury Park, Calif.: Sage Publications, 1993.

——. *When Work Disappears: The World of the New Urban Poor.* New York: Alfred A. Knopf, 1996.

Wirth, Louis. "Ghetto." In *World Book Encyclopedia.* Chicago: Quarrie, 1947.

——. *The Ghetto.* Chicago: University of Chicago Press, 1956.

Wittman, Carl. "A Gay Manifesto." New York: Red Butterfly, 1970.

Wright, Erik Olin. *Class Counts.* New York: Cambridge University Press, 1997.

Zorbaugh, Harvey. *Gold Coast and Slum: A Sociological Study of Chicago's Near North Side.* Chicago: University of Chicago Press, 1929.

——. "The Natural Areas of the City." In *The Urban Community: Selected Papers from the Proceedings of the American Sociological Society,* edited by Ernest W. Burgess, 217–29. Chicago: University of Chicago Press, 1926.

ACKNOWLEDGMENTS

This book was deepened and transformed by a three-year ongoing dialogue with Alex Star, senior editor at Farrar, Straus and Giroux. Alex is one of the great intellectuals of contemporary publishing, and he brought the text out with consummate skill and élan. I also thank the publisher of FSG, Jonathan Galassi, for his encouragement of my work over many years, and Paul Elie for valuable earlier conversations. Laird Gallagher and Scott Borchert provided indispensable assistance.

Along the way, I received significant help from Harvey Molotch and Kenneth Stow, as well as Paul Starr, Irina Oryshkevich, Hakim Hasan, Charles Payne, Benjamin Ravid, Jeffrey Cohen, and Andreas Wimmer, all of whom provided comments on full drafts of the book. Others who made indispensable contributions include Elijah Anderson, Fritz Backhaus, Shaul Bassi, Christopher Browning, Miguel Centeno, Dalton Conley, Yaacob Dweck, Roger Friedland, Ana Maria Goldani, Alison Isenberg, Jerry Jacobs, Philip Kasinitz, William Kornblum, Peter Lubell-Doughtie, John Mollenkopf, Devah Pager, Brandon Stewart, Ivan Szelenyi, Edward Telles, Julia Goldani Telles, Robert Washington, Matt Weiner, Terry Williams, Paul Willis, and Julia Wrigley. Peter Bearman and his Columbia students provided comments on the first draft that helped me think more clearly about some difficult problems. I thank Mario Small for many memorable conversations while he was at Princeton. He is a consummate theorist and methodologist, and his creative ideas remain a source of inspiration.

Princeton University—its sociology department, its college, and the larger intellectual milieu—has been a special place to write this book. I owe special thanks to the PIIRS Global Seminar Program and its director and associate director, Mark Beissinger and Susan Bindig; as well as the Freshman Seminar Program and its director, Clayton Marsh. To all of my students in these and other seminars, and to my colleagues in the sociology department, I am very appreciative. The Princeton administration—Christopher Eisgruber, Shirley Tilghman, David Dobkin, David Lee, and Deborah Prentice—also deserve great thanks for fostering this intellectual atmosphere. I thank Peter Dougherty, Brigitta van Rheinberg, and my faculty and editorial colleagues on the editorial board of the Princeton University Press for many years of stimulating conversations about books.

Three Princeton graduate students—Alice Goffman, Kalyani Jayasankar, and Alexandra Murphy—deserve special thanks for coteaching with me undergraduate courses on the ghetto. Alice's participation in the initial stages of this project helped me a great deal. A number of students blessed me with their enthusiasm and intelligence as research assistants: Ulrike Bialas, Garreth Chan, Dixon Li, Estela Diaz, Naela El-Hinnawy, Rachael Ferguson, Liora Goldensher, Kristen Houston, Samantha Jaroszewski, Annalisa Galgano, Hannah Katz, Nathalie Levine, Bina Peltz, Leah Reisman, Ellen Shakespear, Vanessa Paul, Robert Bell, Charlotte Wang, and Alexander Wang. Hakim Hasan accompanied me to the Library of Congress and made separate trips there on my behalf. His insights and encouragement over many years have been indispensable.

Kenneth Stow, Richard Alba, Alice Goffman, and Terry Williams contributed greatly to my thinking when they cotaught seminars on the ghetto that met in Rome and New York. I also thank my colleagues and presidents William Kelly and Chase Robinson at City University of New York Graduate Center, where I have had the honor of teaching as a visiting professor. Shorter stints at NYU Abu Dhabi and NYU Shanghai were invaluable; thanks especially to Hilary Ballon, Carol Brandt, Hannah Brückner, Hervé Crès, Ron Robin, and Ivan Szelenyi.

For the hospitality extended to me on multiple visits, I thank the archivists at the Kenneth Clark papers of the Library of Congress, the Gunnar Myrdal papers and St. Clair Drake papers at the Schomburg Center, and the Vatican archives in Rome. For the hospitality extended to my research assistants, I thank the archivists of the Louis Wirth papers at the University of Chicago, the Oscar Lewis papers at the University of Illinois, and the Jüdisches Museum Frankfurt am Main. I also thank the Herculean office staff of the Princeton sociology department: Donna DeFrancisco, Cindy Gibson, and Amanda Rowe. I owe a special debt to my literary agent, Cullen Stanley—an unwavering source of encouragement, friendship, and wisdom over the past quarter century.

Kathleen Nolan's intellectual and emotional support made the research all the more fulfilling. That she and our son, Liam, could join me for the research in Italy and Poland made the writing of this book feel all the more part of a fully rounded life.

INDEX